Music and the
Personal Computer

Music and the Personal Computer

An Annotated Bibliography

Compiled by
William J. Waters

Music Reference Collection, Number 22

GREENWOOD PRESS
New York • Westport, Connecticut • London

Library of Congress Cataloging-in-Publication Data

Waters, William J.
  Music and the personal computer : an annotated bibliography /
compiled by William J. Waters.
    p. cm. — (Music reference collection, ISSN 0736-7740 ; no.
22)
  ISBN 0-313-26790-1 (lib. bdg. : alk. paper)
  1. Music—Data processing—Bibliography. 2. Microcomputers—
Bibliography. I. Title. II. Series.
ML128.C62W37 1989
016.78′0285—dc20   89-23287

British Library Cataloguing in Publication Data is available.

Library of Congress Catalog Card Number: 89-23287
ISBN: 0-313-26790-1
ISSN: 0736-7740

First published in 1989

Greenwood Press, Inc.
88 Post Road West, Westport, Connecticut 06881

Printed in the United States of America

The paper used in this book complies with the
Permanent Paper Standard issued by the National
Information Standards Organization (Z39.48-1984).

10 9 8 7 6 5 4 3 2 1

For my parents

Contents

Introduction

[Note: Numbers in parenthesis refer to bibliographic entries.]

Over the past six years personal computers have carved a niche in the music world so deep that it is hard to imagine any musician oblivious to their presence. This widespread popularity is largely due to the establishment of the MIDI (Musical Instrument Digital Interface) standard in 1983, a communications protocol that allows computers to send, receive, and store digital information generated by various electronic music instruments. Used in conjunction with a digital synthesizer, sampler, or drum machine, the personal computer is capable of an array of musical applications in a variety of settings.

Although personal computers are now regarded as useful tools for music educators, they are destined to become indispensible. The high degree of user control offered by CD + MIDI (975), the organizational abilities of hypertext applications such as *HyperCard* (595), the increased storage capacity of optical disks (862), and computers with built-in digital signal processors (1013), form the basic components of future musical workstations that will undoubtedly enhance instructional methods in all areas of music education. In addition to numerous writings exploring the possibilities of present and future technology, this collection offers educators many introductory sources (1138), articles on how to evaluate and purchase equipment (1178, 1251), and directories of available software (1298). Educational publications covered include the *Music Educators Journal*, *The Instrumentalist*, and the *Jazz Educators Journal*.

The art of music composition is also being affected by the ubiquitous microchip. Composers are using personal computers for high-quality score preparation, extracting parts from scores, and more recently, notating music in real time (as it is being played). It is significant that in 1987 Christopher Yavelow premiered *Countdown*, possibly the first opera composed and published with a personal computer (911). Since the timing aspects of composing for video involve numerous calculations, personal computers are becoming increasingly useful in television and motion picture production. Film composers are taking advantage of programs such as *Cue* and *Q-Sheet* that assist in synchronizing recorded music to film and controlling sounds and sound effects at precise moments. In other areas of music composition, microcomputers are being used as more than mechanical factotums. Some composers are incorporating elements of artificial intelligence in the creative process (824), and developers are designing new and exciting applications described as "intelligent software." Even the long standing argument that music created by a computer sounds cold and void of nuance is being attacked head-on as composers experiment with perhaps the ultimate challenge, programmed "feeling" (1028).

For good reason, professional performers regard the personal computer as friend or foe. On one hand, a microcomputer, appropriate software, and electronic instruments can offer a talented musician the opportunity to work alone with varying configurations of techno-accompaniment. On the other hand, article 659 describes how a complete orchestra for an opera company in Boston was replaced one evening by a computer and digital synthesizer. It seems performers may one day be faced with the decision to enhance their skills with new technology or be replaced by it.

Recent literature indicates that personal computers are also becoming standard equipment in recording studios and music publishing companies. A variety of sequencing software (digital recording software) is available for most popular microcomputers with levels of sophistication and price ranging from those suitable for beginners to professional products. Three very popular sequencers are *Performer*, *Master Tracks Pro*, and *Personal Composer*. In addition, new notation programs such as *Music Publisher*, *HB Music Engraver*, *Score*, and *Finale* are reducing the time and expense of music publishing while retaining a high degree of quality. A recent article indicative of this trend (721) describes how a prominent music engraver in New York City plans to integrate a computer-based system into his company.

In addition to the more conventional uses of personal computers in music, many new and interesting applications are being developed. Recently, a device known as "MIDIDancer" was designed using position sensors attached to a dancer's arm and leg joints, radio transmitters, a radio receiver, and a personal computer. As its title implies, this unique device turns dance into music (623). "DataGlove" is another example. Worn as a traditional glove, it senses the movement, position, and orientation of the user's hand in real time allowing the manipulation of objects in three dimensions on a computer screen. Presently, the DataGlove is being applied to the art of pantomime, turning hand movement into sound (811). Personal computers are also making their debut in the realm of art with music. Article 898 describes an unusual piece of interactive sculpture that allows participants to activate music and various other special effects. Other areas receiving much attention include computer viruses (999), how computers are helping disabled musicians (1291), and online services dedicated to music (985).

As the preceding paragraphs suggest, *Music and the Personal Computer* covers a variety of topics intended for practicing musicians, music educators, and computer enthusiasts with interests in music. Its specific purpose is fourfold: (1) to provide a collection of source material, (2) to offer an overview of significant publications in the field, (3) to serve as a point of departure for further inquiry, and (4) to supplement two related works, i.e., *Computer Applications in Music: A Bibliography*, by Deta Davis (1316) and *The Musical Microcomputer: A Resource Guide* by Craig Lister (1337). In a more general sense, it is hoped this collection will begin to reveal the extent to which personal computers have become involved in all areas of music production.

Whether approached from the perspective of music or of personal computers, it is not difficult to find a source in which both topics meet in an occasional article. However, four publications merit special attention as their coverage focuses consistently on significant developments in the field: *Electronic Musician*; *Keyboard Magazine*; *Music, Computers & Software* (formerly *Keyboards, Computers & Software*); and *Music Technology*. The reader can be sure that any recent issue will contain interesting information on some aspect of the musical applications of microcomputers. *Music and the Personal Computer* contains 1,294 citations from these and other popular music and computer periodicals in addition to 71 book citations and an appendix consisting of a short list of related associations and online services. By and large, only articles and books with relatively recent publication dates are included -- i.e., since the establishment of the MIDI standard in 1983. Most citations are briefly annotated and references to software and hardware reviews are included. Annotations to books include price, publisher's address, and toll-free phone numbers if available. Since many entries focus on MIDI technology, the reader will find a working knowledge of MIDI terminology helpful but not required. One of the most informative introductions to MIDI is *Music Through MIDI: Using MIDI to Create Your Own Electronic Music System*, by Michael Boom (1305).

Part I of the bibliography is subdivided into seven sections each devoted to information regarding a specific computer. Although the Amiga and Macintosh are manufactured by Commodore and Apple respectively, they warrant individual treatment as their popularity has established them as models each in its own right. The section on

Apple computers refers to the Apple II series (i.e., IIe, IIc, II+, and IIGS). Likewise, IBM covers a large family of machines, including the XT, AT, PS/2 Model 30, and compatibles with the exception of Tandy. Part II, entitled "Nonspecific and Other Computers," contains articles written about two or more popular computers or models not covered elsewhere. Music education is the focus of Part III. Part IV consists of books only. The reader should bear in mind this arrangement is largely a matter of convenience. Whether a citation has been placed in "Music Education" or "Macintosh" its usefulness may extend beyond that area exclusively. The appendix contains information on associations involved with the musical applications of personal computers and brief descriptions of several popular online services. Author and subject indexes referring to citation number are also included.

A note of thanks is due to several individuals for their help in the preparation of this work. First and foremost, I would like to thank my loving wife, Donna, for her patience and support. Dale Hudson of the Warren D. Allen Music Library, The Florida State University, was helpful on more than one occasion, and the expertise of Dan Hayden of Desktop Specialties was invaluable. Last, but surely not least, I would like to thank Marilyn Brownstein of Greenwood Press for her suggestions and guidance.

Part I
Specific Computers

Amiga

1. "Amiga Audio Products." *Amazing Computing* 3.4 (1988): 71. Comprehensive list of music hardware and software for the Amiga e.g., sequencers, editor/librarians, MIDI interfaces, etc. Includes addresses for manufacturers.

2. Bassen, Howard. "Upgrade Your A 1000 to 500/2000 Audio Power." *Amazing Computing* 3.4 (1988): 58+ Description of how one can augment the sampling capabilities of the Amiga 1000. Explains how to improve the high frequency response and includes a detailed schematic.

3. Battle, Ron. "The *PerfectSound* Digitizer." Rev of *PerfectSound*, from SunRize Industries. *Amazing Computing* 2.5 (1987): 17-18. Digitizer for the Amiga that allows one to record in stereo. Includes a sound editor (software) that graphs waveforms and monitors sounds.

4. Blank, David N. "Playing *Dynamic Drums* on the Amiga." Rev. of *Dynamic Drums*, from New Wave Software. *Amazing Computing* 2.12 (1987): 47-49. Drum machine software.

5. Block, Warren. "The *FutureSound* Sound Digitizer." Rev. of *FutureSound*, from Applied Visions. *Amazing Computing* 2.5 (1987): 19-20. Features include stereo recording and a software package that displays a peak-holding recording level meter. The option to mix and copy sounds between tracks is also available.

6. Braunstein, Mark D. "Amiga 1000 MIDI Interface." *Electronic Musician* Feb. 1988: 90+ In-depth description of how to build a MIDI interface for the Amiga 1000. Includes parts list and schematic.

7. Brown, Michael, and Gary Ludwick. Rev. of *Music Mouse*, from Opcode. *Amiga World* Mar. 1988: 74+ Interactive software that translates mouse movement into music.

8.   Burger,   Jeff.   "Mimetic's *SoundScape Pro MIDI Studio*." *Computer Shopper* Mar. 1988: 161+ *PMS* is described as a software version of a complete recording studio. Features include a tape deck, console keyboard, and sound sampler. Different modules can run simultaneously with Amiga's multitasking operating system.

9.   Ellis,   Robert.   "Digital Signal Processing in AmigaBASIC." *Amazing   Computing* 3.10 (1988): 65-73.   Discussion of how the transformation from numbers to sound is accomplished. Includes program listings that allow the user to experiment with digital signal processing using Fast Fourier Transform.

10. Eshleman, Jim. "Sound Design." *Music, Computers & Software* Aug. 1988: 74+ Brief discussion of *PerfectSound*. Consists of an outboard analog-to-digital converter and Amiga software. The author mentions it is used to produce the voice in the Hartsfield-Atlanta International Airport that warns passengers about subway doors opening and closing.

11. Fay, Todor. "Funky *SoundScape* Programming: Intercepting MIDI Events." *Amazing Computing* 2.11 (1987): 75+ Description of how to write a module for a VU meter.

12. ---. "Programming with MIDI, the Amiga, and *SoundScape*: Writing a *SoundScape* Module in C." *Amazing Computing* 2.5 (1987): 27+ Discussion of MIDI and *SoundScape* including two example programs that manipulate music from within the *SoundScape* environment.

13. ---. "Programming with *SoundScape*: Manipulating Samples in the Sampler Module." *Amazing Computing* 2.9 (1987): 81-87.

14. ---. "Writing a *SoundScape* Patch Librarian: Working Within the System Exclusive." *Amazing   Computing* 3.4 (1988): 38+ Patch librarian module that can load and save patch information from Yamaha synthesizers using System-Exclusive dumps.

15. Fisher, Chuck. "Amiga Music: *SoundScape* in a Multitasking Environment... A Current Look." *Music, Computers & Software* Nov. 1988: 56-57. With the Amiga's multitasking operating system and *SoundScape's* (Mimetics) modular design, one can run several programs from different manufacturers at the same time e.g., *Deluxe Music Construction Set*, *Music Mouse*, and *FastTracker*.

16. ---. "Amiga Music: Very Vivid *Mandala*." *Music, Computers & Software* June 1988: 58-59. Discussion of *Mandala* from Very Vivid (Canada) a MIDI sequencer that allows the user to create an interactive environment with real time control of all parameters of sound, graphic art, and video simultaneously.

17. ---. "Commodore Amiga: The Avant-Garde in Home Computer Animation Becomes the Musician's Choice Through Splitting Screens, Multitasking and Stretching the Imagination." *Keyboards, Computers & Software* Feb. 1987: 44+ In-depth discussion and evaluation of the Amiga. Includes a list of available music software and hardware.

18. ---. Rev. of *MIDISynergy 1*, from Geodesic Publications. *Music, Computers & Software* Oct. 1988: 66-67. A unique MIDI sequencer for the Amiga that includes the source code enabling users to modify the program to suit their specific needs.

19. ---. "ShorTakes." Rev. of *Deluxe Music Construction Set*, from Electronic Arts. *Music, Computers & Software* Feb.-Mar.1988: 76. Music composition and notation software. MIDI compatible.

20. ---. "ShorTakes." Rev. of *Sonix*, from Aegis. *Music, Computers & Software* June 1987: 68. Notation-based sequencer and scoring program for the Amiga. Features MIDI implementation for playing back scores.

21. Freff. "*Sound Oasis* Mirage Sample Disk Reader for the Amiga. *Keyboard Magazine* Nov. 1988: 155-56. Allows the user to load Mirage samples into the Amiga where they can be played, edited, and used with programs such as *Deluxe Music Construction Set*. From New Wave Software.

22. Friedman, Dean. Rev. of *DXII Master Editor/Librarian*, from Sound Quest. *Electronic Musician* Mar. 1988: 102+ Features include the ability to edit all DX7II system exclusive parameters, a random voice generator, envelope design, and excellent use of color display.

23. ---. "Music on the Amiga." *Electronic Musician* Apr. 1988: 34+ General discussion of the music capabilities of the Amiga 500. Includes an overview of sequencers, voice editor/librarians, etc., and a list of manufacturers of music products for the Amiga.

24. Greenwald, T. "Keyboard Report: *SoundScape* Sequencer/Sampler & MIDI Operating System." *Keyboard Magazine* Jan. 1988: 126+ General discussion of *SoundScape* from Mimetics.

25. Herrington, Peggy. "Amiga Jamboree: A Buyer's Guide to Music Products." *Amiga World* June 1988: 44+ Extensive list of music software and hardware for the Amiga. Informative annotations accompany each entry and the article concludes with a list of manufacturers.

26. ---. "*Deluxe Music Construction Set*: Professional Music Composition and Scoring with Amiga." *Commodore: The*

Microcomputer Magazine Sep.-Oct. 1986: 72-75. Features include multiple time and key signatures within a song, up to eight staves, two tracks per staff, and four-voice playback.

27. ---. "Musical Accessories: What Do a Box of Chocolates and the Amiga Have in Common?" *Amiga World* July-Aug. 1987: 74+ Brief descriptions of six disks of sampled sounds: *Dynamics, E.C.T. SampleWare, I.M. Instruments, Sound Advice Music Software, Sound Effects,* and *Symphony Library*.

28. ---. "Suzanne Ciani: Making Music That Sells." *Amiga World* July-Aug. 1987: 53. Suzanne Ciani describes how she uses the Amiga to compose and perform.

29. Jones, Tim. "An Exclusive Preview: *Music Mouse.*" *Commodore Magazine* Sep. 1987: 54+ Intelligent software that interprets how one moves the mouse, translating the movement into harmony or melody. Requires no keyboard or notation skills.

30. King, Steve. "MIDI Sequencers for the Amiga." *Commodore Magazine* Mar. 1989: 50+ Products discussed include *Keyboard Controlled Sequencer* from Dr. T., *Quest I: Texture* from Sound Quest, *SoundScape Pro* from Mimetics, *MIDI Magic* from Brown-Wagh Publishing, and *Dynamic Studio* from New Wave Software. The author includes some general information about MIDI technology and a sidebar containing a comparative list of features, prices, and publication information.

31. Kottler, John J. Rev. of *AudioMaster*, from Aegis. *Commodore Magazine* Apr. 1988: 46-47. Sampling program to be used with any digitizer. Sounds may be played through the Amiga's audio jacks.

32. ---. Rev. of *Sonix*, from Aegis Development. *Commodore Magazine* Sep. 1987: 114-15. Music composition software. Features include sound design, editing, and MIDI capabilities.

33. Larson, Brendan. Rev. of *AudioMaster*, from Aegis. *Amazing Computing* 3.4 (1988): 27-28. Sampling program to be used with any digitizer. Offers the ability to sample sound in real time and "pass" the sample to the Amiga's audio jacks.

34. Leeds, Matthew. "The *Music Studio*: Music Composition for the Amiga." Rev. of *Music Studio*, from Activision. *Commodore: The Microcomputer Magazine* July-Aug. 1986: 69-71.

35. Lindstrom, Bob. *MIDI Magic*: Saw Measures in Half and Make Notes Disappear. Rev. of *MIDI Magic*, from Circum Design Inc. *Amiga World* Mar. 1989: 14+ MIDI sequencer for the Commodore Amiga. Features include 16 tracks, quantization range from 1/2

notes to 1/32 note triplets, and the ability to open multiple windows simultaneously e.g., track-, song-, and sequencer-editing modes. Distributed by Brown-Wagh Publishing.

36. ---. Rev. of *D-50 Parameter Editor*, from Go Software; *D-50 Master Editor/Librarian*, from Sound Quest; and *Caged Artist's D-50 Editor/Librarian*, from Dr. T. *Amiga World* Sep. 1988: 66+ For the Roland D-50 FM synthesizer and the Amiga.

37. Lipson, Stefan B. "Commodore Amiga, the Alternative Micro." *Music Technology* Nov. 1987: 64-65. General overview of the Amiga. Special features include multitasking, IBM emulation, four-voice polyphonic sound, and stereo output.

38. ---. Rev. of *Dynamic Music Studio*, from Dynamic Drums. *Music Technology* Nov. 1988: 79-82. A sequencer that allows one to use the Amiga as a drum machine. Compatible with *Deluxe Music Construction Set* but does not support MIDI at the present time.

39. ---. Rev. of *MIDISynergy* 1.0, from Geodesic Publications. *Music Technology* Aug. 1988: 68-69. *MIDISynergy* is unique in that it provides the source code allowing users to alter the existing program to suit specific needs.

40. ---. Rev. of *MT32 Editor/Librarian*, from SoundQuest. *Music Technology* June 1988: 66-67. Editor/librarian for the Roland MT32 and the Amiga. Features include built-in reverb, rhythm editor, and *Quicksend*, a utility that allows the user to load MIDI files directly to the MT32 without bringing up the software.

41. ---. Rev. of *Synthia*, from the Other Guys Software Co. *Music Technology* Feb. 1988: 66-67. Digital synthesis software. Includes additive, subtractive, plucked string, and interpolative synthesis.

42. Loffink, John. Rev. of *Synthia*, from The Other Guys Software Co. *Electronic Musician* Dec. 1988: 120+ A program that allows the Amiga to emulate a digital synthesizer via software algorithms that calculate playback data for the Amiga's four-voice audio channels.

43. ---. "*Synthia*: High Performance Digital Synthesizer." *Computer Shopper* Mar. 1988: 162+ Description of *Synthia*, a sample editor from The Other Guys Software Company. Features include advanced sound generating capabilities.

44. Lowengard, J. Henry. Rev. of *Music Mouse*, from Opcode. *Amazing Computing* 3.4 (1988): 29-30. Software package that turns the Amiga into a musical instrument played in real time with the mouse. Requires no knowledge of music notation.

45. Massoni, Barry. "Barry Massoni's MIDI Interface Adapter for the Amiga 500 and 2000." *Amazing Computing* 2.12 (1987): 109-10. Presents a method for converting an Amiga 1000-type MIDI interface for use with an Amiga 500 or 2000.

46. McConkey, Jim. "Program Your Amiga for Music." *Electronic Musician* Dec. 1988: 61+ In-depth discussion of music programming for the Amiga. Includes libraries of routines, a patch librarian for the Casio CZ-101 synthesizer, and a schematic and parts list for an Amiga 500/2000 MIDI interface.

47. Meadows, Jim. "Real Stereo Sound Effects: Using *FutureSound* with AmigaBASIC." *Amazing Computing* 2.5 (1987): 21+ Includes a routine that allows one to add sounds to BASIC programs.

48. Means, Ben, and Jean Means. "76 Trombones, 110 Cornets, a Thousand Reeds..." *Amiga World* June 1988: 30+ Assuming the reader has an Amiga, the authors describe the equipment needed to implement a MIDI music system. Topics include equipment arrangement (with illustrations), sampling the rhythm section, and sequencing. Includes descriptive product information.

49. ---. "Amiga Music: Dr. T's *KCS* 1.6." *Music, Computers & Software* Aug. 1988: 52-53. Overview of *Keyboard Controlled Sequencer*, version 1.6. States that the features are basically the same as in the Atari version with a few small exceptions due to the different operating system.

50. ---. "MCScope: System." *Music, Computers & Software* Feb.-Mar.1988: 62+ In-depth discussion of the Amiga 500, 1000, and 2000. Topics include multitasking capabilities, graphics and animation, expandability, available sequencers and music software, and future predictions.

51. ---. "A Musical Environment: The *SoundScape Pro MIDI Studio*." *Amiga World* July-Aug. 1987: 35-40. Overview of *SoundScape*, a sequencer, sampler, and MIDI interface. Compatible with Electronic Arts' *Deluxe Music Construction Set* for printing scores. *Pro MIDI Studio* functions like a home recording studio with a sequencer and 16-channel MIDI mixer.

52. ---. "*Sonix*: Once Upon a Time There Was *Musicraft*." *Amiga World* July-Aug. 1987: 54-58. Discussion of *Sonix*, a notation-based sequencer and scoring program.

53. ---. Rev. of *Texture*, from Magnetic Music. *Amiga World* July-Aug. 1987: 70+ MIDI sequencer for the Amiga. Features include punch-in/out, tape sync, note-by-note editing, and global

creation of diminuendos, crescendos, accelerandos, etc. All program commands can be executed while the music plays.

54. Milano, D. "Keyboard Report: Commodore Amiga Computer." *Keyboard Magazine* Feb. 1986: 112+ General overview of the music capabilities of the Commodore Amiga. Features include multitasking and stereo sound.

55. Mohansingh, Tim. "*E.C.T. SampleWare*: Incredible Multisampled Sounds in *SoundScape* and IFF Formats." Rev. of *E.C.T. SampleWare*. *Amazing Computing* 3.12 (1988): 38-39. Collection of 88 sampled sounds on 4 disks i.e., "Rock," "Orchestral," "Grab Bag," and "Digital Synthesis." Sounds were sampled at 14 KHz with the Mimetics *SoundScape* sampler using *SoundScape Pro MIDI Studio*.

56. "Music Sequencer Released for the Amiga." *Computer Shopper* Jan. 1989: 112. Brief description of *MIDI Magic*, a MIDI sequencer from Brown-Wagh Publishing. Features include simultaneous multichannel recording, 480 ppqn resolution, and multiple time signatures. Compatible with all Amigas.

57. Peck, Rob. "Reaching the Notes: Easy Access to Amiga Audio: Simple and Straight Forward C Routines for Getting at the Power of the Amiga's Audio Device." *Amiga World* July-Aug. 1987: 18+ Presents a library of routines in C for sound production.

58. Proffitt, K. K. "Amiga Music: Dr. T's *MIDI Recording Studio*." *Music, Computers & Software* Jan. 1989: 52-53. Introductory-level, eight-track sequencing program for the Amiga. Includes an excellent manual and is compatible with *Keyboard Controlled Sequencer* 1.6 from Dr. T.

59. ---. "Amiga Music: The *Quest I: Texture*." *Music, Computers & Software* Dec. 1988: 52-53. Professional-level sequencer for the Amiga from Sound Quest. The author states that *Quest I* can be used with MusicSoft's version of *Texture* to form a 48-track sequencer.

60. Quinzi, S. Rev. of *AudioMaster*, from Aegis Development Inc. *Amiga World* Feb. 1988: 67-68. Sampling/sound editing software.

61. ---. Rev. of *Sound Lab*, from Blank Software. *Amiga World* Mar.1988: 68+ Interface software that transfers control of the Ensoniq Mirage to the Amiga.

62. Rae, Richard. "Amiga Notes: Mimetics *SoundScape Sound Sampler*." *Amazing Computing* 2.5 (1987): 51+ Features include stereo or mono sound, variable sampling rates, and editing capabilities.

63. ---. "More Amiga Notes: SunRize Industries' *PerfectSound* Audio Digitizer." *Amazing Computing* 2.5 (1987): 57-60. In-depth discussion of the sound editor software included with *PerfectSound*.

64. ---. "Amiga Notes: Music on the New Amigas." *Amazing Computing* 2.12 (1987): 85-87. General overview of the music capabilities of the Amiga 500 and 2000.

65. Randall, Neil. Rev. of *Instant Music*, from Electronic Arts. *Compute!* Apr. 1987: 67-68. Music composition software for the Amiga. Compatible with *Deluxe Music Construction Set* for printing compositions in standard notation.

66. Ritter, Lynn, and Gary Rentz. "Amiga 1000 Serial Port and MIDI Compatibility for Your Amiga 2000." *Amazing Computing* 3.3 (1988): 68-69. Describes how to add a serial port to an Amiga 2000 like the one found on the Amiga 1000.

67. Shields, James. "*Waveform Workshop* in AmigaBASIC." *Amazing Computing* 2.5 (1987): 41+ A utility program for any AmigaBASIC programmer who wishes to design, test, and save different waveforms for use in other AmigaBASIC programs.

68. "Short Takes: *Sound Lab* Amiga Software." *Keyboard Magazine* Jan. 1988: 140. Brief discussion of *Sound Lab* 1.1 sample editor for the Ensoniq Mirage and Amiga from Blank Software.

69. "Short Takes: Sound Quest *D-50 Master Editor/Librarian* for the Amiga." *Keyboard Magazine* Apr. 1988: 160+ Editor/librarian for the Roland D-50 and Amiga. All functions are menu-driven and in the patch edit mode all patch parameters of the D-50 can be edited on screen.

70. Sullivan, Jeffrey. "*SoundScape Pro MIDI Studio*: A Powerful Music Editor/Player." Rev. of *SoundScape Pro MIDI Studio*, from Mimetics. *Amazing Computing* 2.5 (1987): 11-16. Features include record, edit, transpose, and playback. Can record from the Amiga's QWERTY keyboard or from any external MIDI-equipped instrument.

71. Summers, Tan. Rev. of *Instant Music*, from Electronic Arts. *Family Computing* Apr. 1987: 78-79. Music composition software for the Amiga. Described as a "musical word processor" that is easy to use. Features include 4 voices, 19 instruments, 40 tunes, and 22 rock and jazz chord progressions.

72. Thiel, D. D. "Sound and the Amiga." *Byte* Oct. 1986: 139-42. In-depth discussion of the sound capabilities of the Amiga. States that the Amiga uses four variable-period DMA channels, each composed of an eight-bit DAC with five bits of amplitude control.

73. Tully, Tim. Rev. of *4-Op Deluxe Editor/Librarian*, from Dr. T. *Electronic Musician* Nov. 1988: 92-93. For the Amiga and the Yamaha TX81Z, FB-01, DX100/27/21. Allows the user to save, load, and edit MIDI instruments without quitting his or her sequencing program. This is possible with the Amiga's multitasking operating system.

74. ---. Rev. of *Dynamic Studio*, from New Wave Software. *Amiga World* Jan. 1989: 20+ Software package that utilizes the Amiga's sound chip as a sequencer and digital drum machine. Includes 16 sets of sampled drum sounds and features many advanced editing functions.

75. Vail, Mark. Rev. of *Sonix*, from Aegis Development. *Keyboard Magazine* Jan. 1988: 160+ Eight-track notation/sequencing software. Features include a voice editor for the Amiga's internal sonic hardware, sound design, and user-definable LFO waveforms. Has play-only MIDI implementation.

76. Webster, Bruce. "Season's Greetings." Rev. of *Instant Music*, from Electronic Arts. *Byte* Dec. 1986: 305-16. Intelligent music composition software. Compatible with *Deluxe Music Construction Set* for printing compositions in standard notation. Voted product of the month.

77. Williams, Gregg. "*Deluxe Music Construction Set* 1.1: A Music-Composition Program That Is Feature-Laden But not Flawless." *Byte* July 1987: 249-50. Evaluation of *DMCS* 1.1 for the Amiga from Electronic Arts. The author states that several serious problems of version 1.0 have been corrected. Problems that remain, however, involve the print, scroll, and score layout features.

Apple

78. Anderson, John. Rev. of the Roland Compu-Music 800. *Creative Computing* May 1984: 68+ Six-voice, nine octave synthesizer for the Apple II.

79. Apfelstadt, Marc. "Demystifying MIDI." *Call A.P.P.L.E.* June 1988: 12-17. Reviews 11 music programs for the Apple IIGS e.g., sequencers, transcription programs, and additional hardware.

80. ---. "You II Can Be Musical!" *Call A.P.P.L.E.* May 1987: 10-14. A look at music typesetting and programming utilities. Includes a list of six software packages.

81. Bender, Jack. "*Metronome.*" *Call A.P.P.L.E.* June 1984: 13. Applesoft BASIC program that lets the Apple II simulate a metronome.

82. "Breaking the Sound Barrier: The AlphaSyntauri Digital Sound Synthesizer Can Expand Your Musical Horizons." *A+* Feb. 1984: 62+

83. "Buyer's Guide to Apple II Music Software." *A+* Feb. 1986: 50-51. List of popular music software for the Apple II series. Includes brief descriptions, manufacturers, and prices.

84. Chien, Phil. "The Synthetic Sound of Music." *The Apple II Review* Spring-Summer 1987: 54+ Discussion of the Apple IIGS and its potential music applications.

85. Chin, Kathy. "AlphaSyntauri Music System." *InfoWorld* 30 Apr. 1984: 57-58. A look at the AlphaSyntauri series of three music programs i.e., *Simply Music*, *AlphaPlus*, and *Metatrak* for the Apple II series.

86.   Cohen, Jonathan.   "Happy Birthday: Let Your Apple Lead a Chorus of Happy Birthday, Playing the Tune and Displaying the Words on the Screen." *Nibble* Dec. 1985: 124-26. Applesoft BASIC program.

87.   Coker, Frank.   "Random Music: Generate Music with a Special Twist -- Just Type in These Four Little Listings." *inCider* Dec. 1984: 93-96.

88.   Cowart, R., and S. Cummings.   "A New Musical Revolution: What Is MIDI and How Does Your Apple II Fit In?" *A+* Feb. 1986: 26+ States that the Apple II is perfect for musical uses because of its open design and the variety of software and hardware available. Specific applications are discussed.

89.   Cummings, S.   "Keyboard Report: *Synthestra* MIDI Performance Software for the Apple II+/e." *Keyboard Magazine* Aug. 1986: 124+ MIDI sequencer and master control keyboard system software. Features include simultaneous playback of up to 16 sequences, rotating voice assignment to successive channels, and the ability to assign each key on the master keyboard its own channel. Requires a MIDI interface and a minimum of 48K of memory. For the Apple II+ or IIe.

90.   Dempsey, Dan.   "*The Notable Phantom*." Rev. of *The Notable Phantom*. *inCider* Jan. 1986: 81-82.   Musical games for children ages 5-10 that make it fun to learn how to play a keyboard instrument.

91.   Doherty, Charles W.   Rev. of *Music Construction Set*, from Electronic Arts. *inCider* Dec. 1984: 138-39.   Music composition software. Features include notation, playback, score editing, and transposition.

92.   Dolen, William.   "Eighteenth Century Dice Music Games." *Call A.P.P.L.E.* June 1984: 10-12.   Description of a method of composing music with a program that randomly selects measures of music from a table of options.

93.   ---.   Rev. of the *Soundchaser* System, from Passport Designs. *Call A.P.P.L.E.* June 1984: 27-30.   Music synthesizer for the Apple II to be used in conjunction with Mountain Computer's Music System.

94.   Dunn, Greg.   Rev. of Mountain Music System, from Mountain Computer, Inc.   *Call A.P.P.L.E.* June 1984: 23-26.   Music synthesizer for the Apple II series.

95.   Dwyer, William.   "I Sing the Apple Electric." *Call A.P.P.L.E.* June 1983: 61-62.   Evaluation and discussion of a program for the Apple II that produces music.

96. Field, Cynthia E. "Apple Serenade." *inCider* May 1988: 70+
Overview of music software for the Apple II series. Products
described include *The Notable Phantom, Music Theory* (MECC),
Stickybear Music, and *Bank Street Music Writer.*

97. Fink, Michael. "The Well-Tempered Apple." *Creative
Computing* July 1983: 196-98. Routines for better tuning and
expanded range for the Apple II.

98. Fischer, Michael. "Telecommunications: Modems, Music, and
Your Apple II." *A+* June 1988: 81-83. Overview of online services
that offer musical files and information for Apple II users. Services
mentioned include MAUG, GEnie, and Applesig. Includes a list of
MIDI-Net Member Boards.

99. Fisher, Chuck. "Apple Music: The *Music Studio* 2.0 for the
Apple IIGS from Activision Software." *Music, Computers &
Software* Dec. 1988: 54-55. The author states that at the present time
this is the only program that integrates MIDI sequencing, notation,
and scoring with the Ensoniq sound chip in the IIGS.

100. Freff. "MIDI Gear Galore: An Endless Array of Instruments
and Accessories Awaits You." *A+* Feb. 1986: 34+ Overview and
descriptions of MIDI equipment for the Apple II series. Includes a
list of sources for information on MIDI.

101. Fudge, Don. "Fudge It!: Tuning up Your Apple: Add Melody
and a Little Charm to Your Programs with Apple Music." *inCider*
June 1985: 53-60.

102. Gotcher, Peter. "Computers for Keyboardists: Preview of the
Apple IIGS." *Keyboard Magazine* Jan. 1987: 112+ General overview
of the IIGS and its potential music applications.

103. Greenwald, T. "Keyboard Report: *Master Tracks,* from Passport
Designs." *Keyboard Magazine* May 1986: 112+ MIDI sequencing
software that can record an unlimited number of tracks assignable to
16 MIDI channels. Features include conversion of real time
sequences to and from step time files, playback, and transposition.

104. Gustafsson, Roland. "Ensoniq Sounds." *A+* Jan. 1987: 52.
Discussion of the Ensoniq sound chip in the Apple IIGS. Includes a
program that allows the user to produce simple melodies in BASIC.

105. ---. "*IIGS Sound Oscilloscope*: A Wealth of Waveforms Awaits
You with This BASIC Program." *A+* Sep. 1987: 83-84. General
overview of a program that enables one to view sound waveforms
from a CD player, cassette player, stereo, or musical keyboard.

106. ---. "*Sound Sampler*: A Program That Lets You Play with Pitch Changes." *A+* Apr. 1987: 93. A program for the IIGS that allows one to alter the pitch of an audio signal by playing it back through the Ensoniq sound chip.

107. Hanson, Bob. "Making It Last." *Call A.P.P.L.E.* Mar. 1983: 99-102. Presents a routine in assembly language that allows the Apple II to play sustained tones.

108. "*Instant Music*: Be-Bop-A-Lula." Rev. of *Instant Music*, from Electronic Arts. *inCider* Oct. 1987: 144. Intelligent music composition software that allows the user to play an instrument while the computer provides background harmonies.

109. Jainschigg, John. "Apple Harmony." *Family Computing* Aug. 1986: 62-64. Presents a program that generates musical tones.

110. Jefferys, Douglass W. "Nibble Duet: Tired of Your Apple's Sound?" *Nibble* Dec. 1985: 137-41. Presents a program that synthesizes two-voice sound.

111. Kelly, Dave. "ALF Music Card MC1." Rev. of MC1, from ALF Products. *Call A.P.P.L.E.* June 1984: 17+ A nine-voice synthesizer board for the Apple II.

112. ---. "A Shortcut to Music Programming in Applesoft." *Call A.P.P.L.E.* June 1984: 9+

113. Kruger, Gary. Rev. of *Drum-Key*, from PVI. *Call A.P.P.L.E.* June 1984: 31. Percussion synthesizer for the Apple II series.

114. Kuzmich, J. "Upgrading Your Apple." *The Instrumentalist* Mar.1985: 60-65. Overview and descriptions of the D.A.C. (digital-to-analog converter) and synthesizer boards available for the Apple II. Includes a selective list of music software and manufacturers.

115. Latimer, Joey. Rev. of the Apple MIDI Interface. *Family & Home Office Computing* June 1988: 58. Considers the Apple MIDI interface an excellent tool for MIDI beginners. However, it may be limiting for professionals as it contains only one MIDI input and one MIDI output. It does not have a MIDI thru-port.

116. ---. Rev. of *Music Studio* 2.0, from Activision. *Compute!* Oct. 1988: 80+ Software for the Apple IIGS for composing, editing, arranging, recording, and playing music. Features pull-down menus, MIDI compatibility, and the ability to playback up to four instruments simultaneously.

117. Lehrman, Paul D. "The Alpha and the Apple, a Musical Team: AlphaSyntauri Computer Music System." *High Fidelity/Musical America* Sep. 1983: 51-54.

118. ---. "Sample and Hold: Recording and Playback for the Apple II." *High Fidelity/Musical America* Oct. 1984: 56-57.

119. Leonard, S. "Computers for Keyboardists: Computerus Interruptus; Or, Why That Software May not Run on an Enhanced Apple IIe." *Keyboard Magazine* July 1985: 82-83.

120. ---. "Computers for Keyboardists: Computer Peripheral Enhancements, Or Getting More Bytes from Your Apple." *Keyboard Magazine* Dec. 1985: 98.

121. Lindstrom, Bob. "The Dream Machine: Music." *A+* July 1988: 42+ Descriptions of computer music systems based on the Apple II series. The configurations include synthesizers, MIDI interface cards, memory expansion kits, and music software. Prices range from $8,756.00 -- $11,018.00.

122. ---. "Maximum MIDI: Serious Music-Making Comes to the IIGS." *A+* Feb. 1989: 56+ General overview of two MIDI sequencers for the Apple IIGS i.e., *Diversi-Tune* from Diversified Software Research, Inc. and *Master Tracks Jr.* from Passport Designs. Unique features of *Diversi-Tune* include the ability to record without a dictated tempo and a "sing-along" mode in which lyrics appear on-screen.

123. ---. "Product Spotlight: A Synthesizer, Sound Generator, Sampler, and Speakers, Plus a Book for MIDI Musicians." *A+* June 1988: 48-49. Brief descriptions of several music products that can be used with the Apple II. Products include the Yamaha DM-01 dual powered speaker set, the Casio HT-700 synthesizer, and *MIDI for Musicians* by Craig Anderton.

124. Longeneker, Patric, and Chuck Fisher. "The Apple IIGS." *Keyboards, Computers & Software* Dec. 1986: 33+ Description and evaluation of the Apple IIGS. Includes an in-depth discussion of its music capabilities.

125. Mann, Steve. Rev. of *Music Construction Set*, from Electronic Arts. *A+* July 1987: 60+ Music composition software for the Apple IIGS.

126. ---. "S Is for Sound; A Sonic Preview for Apple's Newest Computer." *A+* Jan. 1987: 49+ Preview of the Apple IIGS and a discussion of its potential music applications.

127. Mathieu, Blaine. "Apple Sounds--From Beeps to Music, Pt. I." *Compute!* Oct. 1983: 258-60. Description of ways to produce sound on the Apple II.

128. ---. "Apple Sounds--From Beeps to Music, Pt. II." *Compute!* Nov. 1983: 201-06. Presents *Apple Music Writer*, a program for composing or reproducing songs.

129. McCarthy, James. "The Pitch Test." *Creative Computing* Mar. 1984: 211+ Presents a program for the Apple II that tests the user's ability to discriminate between two tones.

130. McClain, Larry. "A+ All-Stars: Music, the Best Tuneful Software for the Apple II." *A+* Dec. 1987: 82+ Includes brief descriptions of *Music Studio, Instant Music, Kids Time II, Music Construction Set* (IIGS), *The Music Class, MIDI Music Tutor, Guitar Wizard, Stickybear Music, Peter & the Wolf Music*, and *Foundations of Music*.

131. ---. "A Crescendo of Products: Apple II MIDI Software." *A+* Feb. 1986: 44+ Includes a buyer's guide to Apple II music software.

132. ---. "Making Music: Serious Software for Music Mavens." *A+* June 1988: 36+ Overview of music software available for the Apple II series. Products mentioned include sequencers, note editing programs, and software for music education. Includes a glossary of terms and a list of manufacturers.

133. Meizel, Janet. Rev. of *Notewriter*. *inCider* Oct. 1983: 224-25. Real time, monophonic music transcriber when added to the *Soundchaser* music system.

134. ---. Rev. of *Polywriter*, from Passport Designs. *inCider* Mar. 1985: 85-86. Music printing program for the Apple II Plus or IIe. Requires a MIDI compatible instrument and a MIDI interface.

135. ---. Rev. of *Songwriter*, from Scarborough Systems. *inCider* Nov. 1984: 122-23. Music composition software for the Apple II series.

136. Milano, D. "Mind over MIDI: Note Numbers, Delay, and Apple IIc Interfaces." *Keyboard Magazine* Nov. 1985: 87.

137. Moore, Billy. "Piano Plinkin." *inCider* Jan. 1983: 148-49. Includes a program that turns an Apple III keyboard into a one-octave piano-type keyboard.

138. Morabito, Margaret. "Making Music." *inCider* Aug. 1987: 38+ Description and evaluation of music software available for the Apple II series.

139. ---. "A MIDI Musical Package: *MIDI Users Sequencer-Editor.*" *inCider* Nov. 1986: 42+ Evaluation of the MPU-401 MIDI interface unit, the MIF-APL interface card, and the *MIDI Users Sequencer-Editor* from Roland.

140. ---. "Name That Tune." Rev. of *Personal Musician*, from Sonus. *inCider* Feb. 1988: 97-98. Entry-level MIDI interface and sequencing software for the Apple IIe/GS. Features include four-track recording and seven demo songs.

141. O'Brien, Bill. Rev. of Cricket, from Street Electronics. *inCider* Dec. 1984: 154-56. Combined speech synthesizer, music synthesizer, and clock for the Apple IIc or IIe with expanded memory.

142. O'Donnell, Bob. Rev. of *Sound, Song & Vision*, from Advanced Software. *Music Technology* May 1988: 71. A pitch-to-MIDI conversion program for the Apple II+ or IIe. Graphically displays the pitch of the note on the screen as one sings it. Signals are directed to the Apple via the cassette input. MIDI interface required.

143. Oakey, John. "Grab the Music and Run." *Call A.P.P.L.E.* June 1984: 6-8. Description of how to add music to existing programs.

144. Parfitt, Rick. "Making IIGS Music." *Compute!'s Apple Applications* Dec. 1987: 12+ Basic description of the Apple IIGS and its music capabilities. Includes a list of music software and hardware and a mini-review of *Instant Music* from Electronic Arts.

145. Petersen, Marty. Rev. of AlphaSyntauri Computer Music System. *InfoWorld* 10 Oct. 1983: 78-81. Music system for the Apple II series.

146. ---. "*Soundchaser* Digital, Music Synthesizer for Apple." Rev. of *Soundchaser Digital*, from Passport Designs. *InfoWorld* 3 Jan. 1983: 58-64. To be used in conjunction with Mountain Computer's Music System.

147. ---. "*Turbo-Traks*, a 16-Channel Music Synthesizer." Rev. of *Turbo-Traks. InfoWorld* 12 Sep. 1983: 61-63. For the Apple II series.

148. Salamone, Ted. Rev. of Personal Speech System, from Votrax. *inCider* Feb. 1985: 112-13. Speech and music synthesizer.

149. Sandys, Jeff. "The Sound of Logo." *Call A.P.P.L.E.* June 1984: 32-33. Description of methods of creating music with Logo.

150. Schwartz, Steven. "Music Makers." Rev. of *Music Construction Set* and *Bank Street Music Writer* for the Apple II Series, and *Music Construction Set* and *Music Studio* for the Apple IIGS. *Nibble* July 1987: 40+

151. Smith, David L. "*Nibble Maestro*." *Nibble* July 1985: 52+ An Applesoft program that turns the Apple keyboard into an organ keyboard. Notes are displayed as the music plays.

152. Steere, Leslie. "One-Man Band." *A+* Dec. 1988: 37. Description of how conductor Jeff Whitmill uses an Apple IIe, a Roland D-50, two Yamaha TX81Zs, and a Kurzweil 1000PX to form an electronic orchestra. The orchestra is part of the theater in Saginaw, Michigan.

153. Steere, Leslie, Mary Bohannon, and Shannon Cullen. "Product Roundup: Have a Blast." *A+* Mar. 1989: 101. Brief overview of the Sonic Blaster stereo digitizer for the Apple IIGS from Applied Engineering. Records sounds from stereo receivers, CD players, or television. Additional features include edit, playback, fade in and out, echo recorded sounds, and a built-in amplifier. Includes illustrations.

154. Stockford, James. "*DX-Heaven*." Rev. of *DX-Heaven*, from Dr. T. *Whole Earth Review* Winter 1985: 111. Patch editor/librarian for the Yamaha DX7 synthesizer and Apple II.

155. Swigart, Rob. "Making Music: MIDI Makes Music." *A+* June 1988: 32-35. Overview of MIDI interfaces available for the Apple II series. Apple's new interface is mentioned and several music software packages are discussed. Includes addresses for manufacturers of MIDI products.

156. Swigart, Rob, and Steve Mann. "Super Sounds." Rev. of SuperSonic Cards, from MDIdeas; *Music Construction Set*, from Electronic Arts; and *Music Studio*, from Activision. *A+* July 1987: 60-68. For the Apple IIGS.

157. Thornburg, David D. "Learning Curve: A Homebrew Music Connection." *A+* June 1988: 85+ Discussion of how one can connect an Apple II to a CD player. Includes a schematic of the interface between the Apple II speaker connections and the CD infrared remote control.

158. Walker, R. "*FM Drawing Board*, a Comprehensive DX-7 Editor-Librarian for the Apple II." *Canadian Musician* 8.5 (1986): 32.

159. Wood, Roger, and Wayne Koberstein. "Listen to the Mockingboard: The Apple II Family's Weakness Is Its Lack of a

Built-In Sound Chip."   Rev. of Mockingboard, from Sweet Micro Systems. *Home Computer Magazine* Aug. 1985: 34-36. Speech and music board.

160. Youngblood, J. *"Little Organ Apple."* *Nibble* June 1984: 69-75. Applesoft BASIC program that turns the Apple keyboard into a two-octave electric organ.

161. Zimmerman, Scott. "Counting on Sixteen Fingers, Pt. II." *Nibble* July 1985: 75-84. Contains a machine language program for the Apple II that allows the user to produce music from the keyboard.

162. ---. "Nibbling at Assembly Language, Pt. XII: A Matter of Timing." *Nibble* Mar. 1987: 70+ Tutorial on counting clock cycles in an assembly language program and applying the information to music production.

163. ---. *"T.U.N.E.S. (Tone Utility and Note Encoding System)."* *Nibble* Nov. 1983: 21-38. A routine for entering any tune into an Applesoft program.

Atari

164. Aikin, Jim. "Keyboard Report: C-Lab *Creator* Sequencer Software for the Atari ST." *Keyboard Magazine* Apr. 1988: 142+ MIDI sequencer from Digidesign. Features include 192 ppqn clock resolution, multiple quantization modes, controller editing and translation, and remote start/stop from MIDI keyboard. Compatible with GEM desktop accessories.

165. ---. "Keyboard Report: C-Lab *Notator* Sequencing/Notation for Atari ST." *Keyboard Magazine* Feb. 1989: 132+ In-depth discussion and evaluation. Includes an excellent illustration of a score created with *Notator* and a nine-pin dot-matrix printer.

166. ---. "Keyboard Report: *CZ-Droid* Editing and Librarian Software for the Atari ST." *Keyboard Magazine* Nov. 1986: 136-38. Patch editor/librarian for Casio CZ synthesizers. Features include graphic envelope display and editing, mouse-oriented operation, and CZ-1 velocity and line level support. From Hybrid Arts.

167. ---. "Keyboard Report: *Fingers* & *Tunesmith* Interactive MIDI Music Generators for the Atari ST." *Keyboard Magazine* Oct. 1988: 144-47. Features include real time user control over pitch, rhythm, channel and phrase structure (*Fingers*), and five-voice accompaniment with rhythm and harmony algorithms (*Tunesmith*). Both programs are from Dr. T.

168. ---. "Keyboard Report: *KCS* and *MIDISoft Studio* Sequencer Software for the Atari ST." *Keyboard Magazine* Feb. 1987: 130+ *Keyboard Controlled Sequencer* is from Dr. T. Features include 48-track recording, 128 simultaneous independent sequences, auto-punch, and programmable tempo changes. *MIDISoft Studio* is from MIDISoft. Features include 32 channel-assignable tracks, real time and step data entry, and cut-and-paste editing.

169. ---. "Keyboard Report: *MIDITrack ST*, Hybrid Arts Sequencer Software." *Keyboard Magazine* Aug. 1987: 136+ MIDI sequencer for the 520 or 1040 ST. Features include real and step time recording, track mute and solo, 60 tracks, and 63,000 note capacity (1040 ST).

170. ---. "Keyboard Report: *MT-32 Capture!* & *SynthWorks MT-32*, Editor/Librarians for the Atari ST." *Keyboard Magazine* Sep. 1988: 141-43. *MT-32 Capture!* is from MIDIMouse Music, *SynthWorks MT-32* is from Steinberg/Jones. Described as having similar features, they are designed to work with the Roland MT-32 tone generator. Features common to both programs include a patch change table (allows any timbre to be assigned to any patch), the ability to edit the patch change table, and editing of system and individual sounds.

171. ---. "Keyboard Report: *Sonus SST* Sequencer Software for the Atari ST." *Keyboard Magazine* Feb. 1988: 152+ Sequencer and sequence editor from Sonus. Features include 24 tracks, 18 sequences, 192 ppqn clock resolution, auto punch-in/out, and point and click user interface.

172. ---. "Keyboard Report: *Soundfiler ST*, S900 Sample Editor." *Keyboard Magazine* May 1988: 136+ Sound and parameter editing software for the Atari ST and the Akai S900 sampler. Features include zoom in/out waveform display, undo buffers, and five-octave keyboard mapping.

173. ---. "Keyboard Report: Steinberg *Pro-24 Sequencer* for the Atari ST." *Keyboard Magazine* Dec. 1986: 122+ Features include 24 tracks, master track for tempo and meter changes, selectable input data filtering, and auto-locating and auto-punch.

174. ---. "Keyboard Report: Steinberg *SynthWorks DX/TX* 2.0 Editor/Librarian." *Keyboard Magazine* Apr. 1988: 155-57. Features include multiple edit buffers with two channel simultaneous editing, graphic envelope editing, 3-D harmonic analysis display with rotating views, 2-D waveform display, and a random patch generator.

175. ---. "Keyboard Report: Steinberg *SynthWorks D-50* Editor/Librarian for the Atari ST." *Keyboard Magazine* Jan. 1989: 135-36. Editor/librarian for the Roland D-50 and D-550 synthesizers. Features include sound cataloging and search, graphic envelope editing, and a patch generator. Requires 1 MB of RAM.

176. ---. "Keyboard Report: Sys-Ex Potpourri -- Editor/Librarians and Miscellany for the Atari ST." *Keyboard Magazine* May 1987: 126+ Discussion of *DX-Heaven*, *4-Op Deluxe*, *Perfect Patch*, *CZ-Patch*, and *Data Dumpstor ST*.

177. ---. "Keyboard Report: Updates: E-MU SP-1200 & Dr. T's *KCS-ST* 1.5." *Keyboard Magazine* Oct. 1987: 158. *KCS-ST* now includes live editing in track mode, quantization during recording, and full mouse operation.

178. ---. "Keyboard Report: Updates: Steinberg *Pro-24 Sequencer* 2.1, EMAX HD, and TX802." *Keyboard Magazine* Nov. 1987: 148+ Discussion of Steinberg *Pro-24 Sequencer*. The author states that version 2.1 still has some bugs but the power has increased dramatically. Requires an ST with at least 1 Meg of RAM.

179. ---. "Short Takes: *K1 Ed-Lib* for the Atari ST." *Keyboard Magazine* Nov. 1988: 155. Brief overview of *K1 Ed-Lib*, an editor/librarian from Drumware Software for the Kawai K1 synthesizer and the Atari St.

180. ---. "Keyboard Report: Hybrid Arts' *MIDITrack II* Sequencer for Atari Computers." *Keyboard Magazine* Dec. 1985: 112-13. For Atari 8-bit computers.

181. Alberts, Randy. Rev. of *Synthdroid+*, from Compu-Mates. *Electronic Musician* Dec. 1987: 85. Voice editor/random patch generator/librarian software for the Korg DW-8000/Atari ST.

182. Anderson, J. J. "Outpost: Atari." *Creative Computing* Mar. 1985: 152-53. Description of how to make a modern-day Theremin. Includes a schematic and program listing.

183. ---. "Sound Advice: The State of the Art in Audio Digitization." *Atari Explorer: The Official Atari Journal* May-June 1988: 39-42. Overview of digitizers available for Atari computers. Products described include the ST Sound Digitizer from Navarone Industries, Parrot II from Alpha Systems (Atari 8-bit), and ST Replay from MichTron.

184. Anderton, Craig. Rev. of *DX-Android*, from Hybrid Arts. *Electronic Musician* June 1986: 72+ Editor/librarian for the Atari ST and Yamaha DX7 synthesizer. Features include a patch librarian, numeric librarian, automated patch loader, and a graphic editor.

185. Arnell, Billy. "Atari Music: Drumware *Soundfiler ST*." *Music, Computers & Software* Aug. 1988: 56-57. Visual sample editing software for the Atari ST. Capable of holding up to six separate samples at once in a one Meg ST.

186. ---. "Atari Music: *MIDISoft Studio* Advanced Edition." *Music, Computers & Software* Nov. 1988: 60-61. MIDI sequencer for the Atari ST. Features include control over MIDI volume, transposition, program change, and MIDI channel settings while in playback

mode. The author states that it is easy to use and includes an excellent manual.

187. ---. "Atari Music: *Sonic Flight* from MIDImouse Music." *Music, Computers & Software* Dec. 1988: 56-57. Series of editor/librarians for various synthesizers and the Atari ST. Versions discussed are for the Roland D-10/110/20, MT-32, D-50/550, Ensoniq ESQ-1/M, ESQ-80, and the Casio CZ-101/1000 and CZ-1.

188. ---. "Atari Music: Steinberg *SynthWorks DX/TX*." *Music, Computers & Software* June 1988: 68-69. Updated editor/librarian for the Atari ST. Features include faster screen update; DX11, TX7, TX216, TX816, and TX802 compatibility; and multiedit functions for working with multiple synthesizer setups.

189. ---. "MCScope System: Atari ST MIDI System." *Music, Computers & Software* Apr. 1988: 58-60. Jingle writer and arranger Billy Arnell discusses why he works with an Atari ST for music composition rather than an IBM or Macintosh SE. Price, dependability, built-in MIDI interface, and simple operating system are among the reasons mentioned.

190. ---. "ShorTakes." Rev. of *Edit 8000,* from Savant Audio. *Music, Computers & Software* Feb.-Mar. 1988: 77. Editor/librarian for the Korg DW8000 and EX8000.

191. "The Atari ST: Putting It All Together: A Complete Picture of Computer Music's Rising Star." *Music, Computers & Software* Aug. 1987: 42+ In-depth evaluation of the Atari ST including the new Mega ST. Includes a sidebar entitled "Guide to Atari Music Software."

192. Bachand, Ray. "*Master Tracks Pro*: MIDI Power from Passport." *STart: The ST Quarterly* 2.5 (1988): 57-60. MIDI sequencer. Features include display elapsed time of any section, select count-in, conductor track, song editor, SYSEX librarian, and keyboard mapper.

193. Baggetta, Albert. "*Shakuhachi Keyboard*: Re-Create the Haunting Tones of the Japanese Bamboo Pipe on Your Atari." *Analog Computing* May 1987: 23-24. BASIC program for synthesizing Shakuhachi sounds.

194. Bajoras, Tom. "Save Your Synthesizer Sounds: *MIDISAVE*, a Casio and Yamaha Patch Librarian." *STart: The ST Quarterly* Summer 1987: 80-87. Command-oriented program written in Alcyon C that works with many different brands of synthesizers. Includes an explanation of how synthesizers handle MIDI information.

195. Barbour, E. "Why Buy a MIDI Sequencer When You Could Get an Atari ST Instead?" *Electronic Musician* June 1986: 42-43.

196. "BASIC Sound on the Atari ST." *Compute!* Mar. 1986: 110-12. Description of how to get started with ST sound using the WAVE and SOUND commands in Atari ST BASIC.

197. Bass, Patrick. "ST Sound: Hearing the AY-3-8910 Chip." *Antic: The Atari Resource* Nov. 1985: 16-18.

198. Baugh, S. M. "*Sound Effects Editor* Takes the 'Error' Out of Trial-And-Error Sound Effects." *Analog Computing* May 1987: 11-14. Sound effects program in BASIC.

199. Belian, Barry. "The Atari Musician." *Compute!* May 1983: 214-16. Two programs for the Atari that compute pitch values for chords and scales.

200. Brilliant, Lee S. "Bits 'n' Pieces: Pops." *Analog Computing* Nov. 1988: 54+ Description of how to build a device that gives the ST stereo sound using the POPS (POly Phonic Sound) adapter. Includes a schematic, program listing, and parts list.

201. Cecil, Malcolm. "Atari 520ST: The MIDI PC." *Electronic Musician* June 1986: 37-40. Features a built-in MIDI interface.

202. ---. "The Ultimate MIDI Dream Machine." *ST-Log: The Atari ST Monthly Magazine* May 1987: 9-10. Description of "Stage L," one of the largest MIDI installations in the world. It is located on the Paramount film lot in Hollywood California and is used exclusively for creating electronic effects for motion pictures and television.

203. Cowart, R. "Keyboard Report: Atari 520ST Computer." *Keyboard Magazine* Feb. 1986: 116+ Features a built-in MIDI interface (in/out), a three-voice square wave sound generator, RS-232C modem port, and mouse. It is based on the Motorola 68000 16/32 bit microprocessor, the same chip used in the Apple Macintosh.

204. Daniel, Walter. "*MIDIPrint* for the Atari ST." *Electronic Musician* June 1987: 74-75. MIDI data analyzer. Originally conceived as a C-64 program, the author includes the necessary changes so that it will run on the Atari ST.

205. Davies, Rick. "*ADAP* Soundrack." *Music Technology* Sep. 1986: 86-87. A look at *ADAP* (*Analog/Digital Audio Processor*), a hardware/software package that turns the Atari 520 ST or 1040 ST into a powerful sampling system.

206. ---. Rev. of *Keyboard Controlled Sequencer*, from Dr. T. *Music Technology* Feb. 1987: 92-94. Divided into three parts i.e., Track Mode (functions as a multitrack recorder), Open Mode (emulates older *KCS* programs), and Song Mode (chains sequences together for playback). Features include 48 tracks, punch-in/out, and MIDI echo.

207. Dimond, Stuart Dudley III. Rev. of *Guitar Wizard*, from Baudville and *MIDI Recording Studio*, from Dr. T. *Atari Explorer: The Official Atari Journal* Jan.-Feb. 1988: 26+ *Guitar Wizard* is an instructional program for the Atari 800 XL/XE; *MIDI Recording Studio* is a MIDI sequencer for the ST.

208. Duberman, David. Rev. of *SoftSynth*, from Digidesign. *ST-Log: The Atari ST Monthly Magazine* Aug. 1988: 84-85. A "software synthesizer" that uses the computing power of the ST to create sounds that can be played back on a variety of samplers.

209. Eddy, Andy. Rev. of *MIDIPLAY*, from Electronic Music Publishing House. *ST-Log: The Atari Monthly Magazine* May 1987: 12-13. Sequencer for the Atari ST that allows one to play music using the ST's three voices.

210. "Electronic Music Swings on the Air Waves." *Personal Computing* May 1983: 53. Brief description of how a songwriter uses an Atari 400 to generate and compose music.

211. Faris, Charles. "Sound Chip: A Look at MIDI Through the Eyes of Some of Today's Top Producers and Performers." *Atari Explorer: The Official Atari Journal* May-June 1988: 90-93. Comments on MIDI from Mark Droubay, Jeffrey Delman, Bo Tomlyn, Jimmy George, and Hank Donig.

212. Foster, Frank. "Professional Musicians and the Atari ST: The Inside Story on How Atari Won the War Against IBM, Apple, and Commodore." *ST-Log: The Atari ST Monthly Magazine* May 1987: 17-20. Peter Gabriel, the Pointer Sisters, Tangerine Dream, and others discuss why the Atari ST is their choice for music applications. Reasons mentioned include the built-in MIDI interface and the variety of software available.

213. Franco, Nina. "Holiday Greetings." *Antic: The Atari Resource* Dec. 1983: 47. Presents a program that displays a colorful picture and plays a seasonal tune in four-part harmony. For the Atari 800.

214. Frederick, D. "Keyboard Report: *DX-Droid* Voicing and Librarian Software for the Atari ST." *Keyboard Magazine* July 1986: 140+ Editor/librarian for the Atari ST and Yamaha DX7 synthesizer.

215. Friedland, Nat. Rev. of *Colortone Keyboard*, from Waveform Corp. *Antic: The Atari Resource* June 1985: 77.

216. ---. "Play It Again, Atari!: They Laughed When I Sat Down at the 800 XL." *Antic: The Atari Resource* June 1985: 30-33. Description of *Virtuoso* from Enhanced Technology Associates and *MIDITrack II* from Hybrid Arts.

217. Gershin, Scott. Rev. of *ADAP (Analog/Digital Audio Processor)*, from Hybrid Arts. *Music Technology* Oct. 1987: 37-41. Stereo sampling sound processor.

218. ---. "Compu-Mates R100 *DrumDroid*." *Music Technology* Feb. 1988: 63. Drum machine software for the Atari ST and the Kawai R100 drum machine. *DrumDroid* allows the user to view drum patterns in a gridwork of squares that represent MIDI clocks.

219. ---. "In Brief." Rev. of *Perfect Patch*, from Aegix. *Music Technology* Sep. 1987: 38. Editor/librarian for the Atari ST and Yamaha DX7 synthesizer.

220. ---. Rev. of *Sound Works*, from Steinberg and *Soundfiler*, from Drumware. *Music Technology* Feb. 1988: 73+ Visual waveform editing programs for the Akai S900 and the Atari ST.

221. Giambra, Angelo. "*The Musician*: Type-In Music Construction Software." *Antic: The Atari Resource* June 1985: 37+ Three-voice composition program in BASIC.

222. Giwer, Matt. "Adding Sound Effects to Atari." *Compute!* Feb. 1985: 109-11. Five short programs in BASIC for building notes, chords, and harmonics.

223. ---. "*Atari Sound Experimenter*." *Compute!* July 1983: 200+ Presents a program in BASIC that gives the user more control of the volume, distortion, and frequency of sounds within the four independent sound channels of Atari 8-bit computers via the SOUND and POKE instructions.

224. Gotcher, Peter. "Technology: Computers for Keyboardists, Choosing a Computer: A Closer Look at the Atari ST." *Keyboard Magazine* Aug. 1987: 102. The author states that at less than half the price of a Macintosh, a better value is hard to find.

225. Guber, Sol. Rev. of *Music Painter*, from Atari. *Antic: The Atari Resource* Aug. 1986: 50.

226.   Gutierrez, Glenn.   *"Drum   Synth/Bass   Synth*:   Powerful AUDCTL Rhythm Section." *Antic: The Atari Resource* Feb. 1985: 26+ Two programs that let the Atari become a drum machine or an electronic bass synthesizer.

227.   Hague, James.   *"Atari   Sound   Commander."*   *Compute!* Nov. 1986: 61-63. A set of machine language subroutines to be used with BASIC for sound and music production. The subroutines will run in the background while other BASIC events are in progress. For Atari 8-bit systems.

228.   Hallas, Aaron.   Rev. of *MIDIDraw*, from Intelligent Music. *Music Technology* Nov. 1988: 70-71. Intelligent software for the Atari ST in which music is composed and performed according to the characteristics of a picture drawn on the screen.

229.   Harms, Ken.   *"Sounder."* *Antic: The Atari Resource* Feb. 1983: 50+ An Atari PILOT program that expands the sound capability of the standard Atari PILOT sound commands. For the Atari 800.

230.   ---.   "Sweet Toots: Logo Sounds as Good as It Looks." *Antic: The Atari Resource* Nov. 1983: 56-62. Description of the sound capabilities built into Atari Logo. Includes a sound generation program.

231.   Havey, Paul.   "Musical Atari Keyboard." *Compute!* Aug. 1983: 204-07.   Presents a program that makes the Atari a musical instrument. Sounds include bells, piano, and organ.

232.   Herzberg, Larry.   *"MIDIMON."* *ST-Log: The Atari ST Monthly Magazine* Aug. 1988: 22-25. Program that provides analysis of MIDI output from a synthesizer, drum machine, sequencer, or other type of controller. Available through the August 88 disk version of *ST-Log* or the *ST-Log* SIG on Delphi.

233.   Jablonski, Dennis.   "Dr. T's *KCS* Made Easy." *Electronic Musician* Sep. 1988: 32+ In-depth discussion of the sequencing structure of *Keyboard Controlled Sequencer* from Dr. T. The author explains how its unique data structuring can allow MIDI sequences to be "called" in the manner of a computer subroutine from random points in other sequences.

234.   Jackson, Charles.   "Random Music: Can an Atari Make a Melody?" *Antic: The Atari Resource* Nov. 1983: 50-54.   General discussion of the sound capabilities of Atari computers.

235.   Jeffries, Tom.   "The Ins, Outs, and Thrus of MIDI." *STart, the ST Quarterly* Spring 1987: 48-57. Overview of MIDI technology and the Atari ST. Includes a list of music software for the ST.

236. ---. "*MIDI Driver*: Program ST's Musical Instrument Digital Interface." *Antic: The Atari Resource* Mar. 1986: 54+ Presents a MIDI driver program in Hippo C and Alcyon C.

237. Jenkins, Chris. Rev. of *Omni-Banker*, from Paradigm Software. *Music Technology* June 1988: 75. A desk accessory for the Atari ST that allows the user to store sound patches from a variety of synthesizers.

238. Joel, George. Rev. of The Drumesiser. *Antic: The Atari Resource* Nov. 1983: 109. A cartridge for the Atari 800 that allows the computer to be used as a musical instrument.

239. Johnson, Charles F. "Catching the ST Sound Wave: An Overview of MIDI Software for Your Atari ST." *ST-Log: The Atari ST Monthly Magazine* May 1987: 67-68. Descriptive list of MIDI sequencers, patch librarians (*DX-Android* and *CZ-Android*), and scoring software for the Atari ST.

240. ---. Rev. of *Keyboard Controlled Sequencer*, from Dr. T's Music Software. *ST-Log: The Atari ST Monthly Magazine* May 1987: 47-48. Features include real and step time recording, sequence editing, 48 tracks, and auto-punch.

241. ---. Rev. of *MIDISoft Studio*, from MIDISoft Corp. *ST-Log: The Atari ST Monthly Magazine* May 1987: 48. Sequencer for the Atari ST. Features include real and step time recording, transposition, 32 tracks, and support for all 16 MIDI channels.

242. ---. "An Overview of 8-Bit MIDI Software." *Analog Computing* May 1987: 55-56. Comprehensive list of music software for the Atari 800/XL and 130/XE. Items discussed include sequencers and patch librarians. All products listed are from Hybrid Arts.

243. ---. Rev. of *SMPTE-Track*, from Hybrid Arts. *ST-Log: The Atari ST Monthly Magazine* May 1987: 48-49. Sequencer for the Atari ST. Features the ability to synchronize to an external drum machine or tape player.

244. Johnson, Jim. "The Atari ST Power User, Pt. I: The Hardware." *Electronic Musician* Nov. 1988: 29+ In-depth discussion of the ST and related hardware e.g., hard drives, RAM upgrades, modems, and monitors. Includes a directory of hardware manufacturers.

245. ---. "The Atari ST: A Musician's View." *Music, Computers & Software* Aug. 1987: 46. The ST is considered an excellent computer for music applications because of its built-in MIDI ports and one Meg of RAM.

246. ---. "*Chord*: An Algorithmic Composing Program in Atari ST BASIC." *Electronic Musician* Apr. 1988: 22+ A program written in modular form that creates chord progressions and plays them over MIDI. Progressions may be saved as a sequence in the format used by Dr. T's *Keyboard Controlled Sequencer*.

247. ---. "First Take: Atari ST Public Domain Patch Editors and Librarians." *Electronic Musician* Feb. 1988: 113-14. *CZLIB, DXLIB, FB-Patch*, and *DX7-Patch*. (GEnie)

248. ---. Rev. of *Keyboard Controlled Sequencer*, from Dr. T. *Music, Computers & Software* June 1987: 70-72. Features include 48-track sequencing, real and step time recording, 128 simultaneous independent sequences, and auto-punch.

249. ---. "ShorTakes." Rev. of *ESQ-apade*, from Caged Artist. *Music, Computers & Software* Oct. 1987: 72-73. Editor/librarian for the Ensoniq ESQ synthesizers and the Atari ST.

250. ---. "The ST Power User, Pt. II: The Software." *Electronic Musician* Dec. 1988: 22+ In-depth discussion of current music software for the ST. Includes popular public domain programs.

251. ---. "Take the Hex Off Your Data: *MIDI View*." *STart: The ST Quarterly* Feb. 1988: 75-77. Description of a program that translates MIDI information that arrives at the ST's MIDI port and prints the explanation on the screen in plain English. *MIDI View* uses the rules set down in the MIDI 1.0 specification.

252. ---. Rev. of *Xsyn Series*, from Beam Team. *STart: The ST Quarterly* Feb. 1988: 92-93. A series of patch editors with a single master patch editing program to be used with a number of separate modules for specific synthesizers. This review focuses on modules for the CZ101, DX21, and FB-01.

253. Kaller, Richard. Rev. of *CZ-Android*, from Hybrid Arts. *ST Applications: The Atari ST Journal* Mar. 1987: 34. Patch editor/librarian and sound generator for the Casio CZ synthesizer and the Atari ST.

254. ---. Rev. of *MIDITrack ST*, from Hybrid Arts. *ST Applications: The Atari ST Journal* June 1986: 72. MIDI sequencer.

255. Krutz, Jamie. "The Atari Arrives." *Electronic Musician* Apr. 1988: 64+ In-depth discussion of the Atari ST and its music capabilities. Includes a list of MIDI software and manufacturers of music products for the ST.

256. ---. Rev. of *The Copyist*, from Dr. T. *Electronic Musician* Dec. 1987: 78-79. Scoring program, version 1.4.

257. ---. "First Take: HyperTek/Silicon Springs Atari ST *OmniRes Monitor Emulator*." *Electronic Musician* Mar. 1988: 91+ Program that allows one to run low and medium (color) resolution software on a high resolution (monochrome) Atari ST system.

258. ---. "First Take: MIDIMouse Music Atari ST *Fast Tracks ST* 1.0." *Electronic Musician* Mar. 1988: 101. Sequencing software for the ST. Features 100,000 note capacity on a 1040 ST, punch-in/out, looping, variable count down feature, transposition, and GEM user interface.

259. ---. "First Take: Savant Audio Atari ST *Edit-8000* and Synergy Resources Atari ST *SynthView*." *Electronic Musician* Mar. 1988: 90-91. Brief descriptions of two sequencer/editor/librarian programs for the Atari ST.

260. ---. Rev. of *GenPatch*, from Hybrid Arts. *Electronic Musician* Dec. 1987: 80-81. Generic patch librarian that backs up patches from any MIDI synthesizer to an Atari ST.

261. ---. "MIDI Beat." Rev. of *DX-Heaven*. *ST Applications: The Atari ST Journal* Aug. 1987: 25-27. Patch editor/librarian for the Yamaha DX7 synthesizer and the Atari ST.

262. ---. "MIDI Beat." Rev. of *Xsyn*. *ST Applications: The Atari ST Journal* Aug. 1987: 27-30. Integrated DX/TX7 patch editor for the Yamaha DX7 and TX7 synthesizers and the Atari ST.

263. ---. "A Report from NAMM." *ST Applications: The Atari ST Journal* Aug. 1987: 52-58. Overview of music products for Atari computers presented at the National Association of Music Merchants Expo.

264. ---. Rev. of *SMPTE-Track*, from Hybrid Arts. *STart: The ST Monthly* Oct. 1988: 57-59. Sequencer for the Atari ST.

265. Lasky, Michael. Rev. of *Bank Street Music Writer*, from Mindscape. *Antic: The Atari Resource* Sep. 1985: 73-74. Music composition software that allows users with little or no musical background to create original music. Features include time signature check, tone shape, and a built-in collection of ready-to-play scores.

266. Leytze, David. "Short Takes: *SynthWorks ESQ-1*, Editor & Librarian for the Atari ST." *Keyboard Magazine* Aug. 1988: 157+ For

the Ensoniq ESQ-1 synthesizer from Steinberg. Capable of containing two banks of 40 sounds in memory at the same time.

267. Lindgren, Richard K. "*Banjo Picker*: Play Bluegrass Music like a Bionic Earl Scruggs!" *Antic: The Atari Resource* Oct. 1985: 28+ BASIC program that lets the Atari simulate a banjo.

268. Manoliu, Mihai. Rev. of *Big Band Orchestral Composer*, from Imagine Music Group. *Music Technology* Nov. 1988: 72-73. Produces big band arrangements of chord progressions provided by the user. The program can also generate its own progressions or melodies. Compatible with *Studio 24* (sequencer from Imagine).

269. ---. Rev. of *Big Band Orchestral Composer*, from Imagine Music Group. *STart: The ST Monthly* Mar. 1989: 49-50. Supports color and monochrome monitors and can arrange chords or melodies in 14 different musical styles e.g., Rock, Ballad, Blues, Swing, Reggae, etc. Requires a MIDI equipped synthesizer.

270. ---. Rev. of *CZ Voice Master*, from MIDIMouse. *Music Technology* July 1988: 78. An editor/librarian for the Atari ST and the Casio CZ series of synthesizers. Includes 13 sound banks.

271. ---. Rev. of *Master Tracks Pro*, from Passport. *Music Technology* Apr. 1988: 71. MIDI sequencer for the Atari ST. Features include 64 tracks for real or step time recording, transposition, and quantize function.

272. Many, Chris. Rev. of *D50 Command*, from Compu-Mates. *Music Technology* May 1988: 70-71. Patch editor/librarian/sound design software for the Atari ST and the Roland D50 synthesizer. Uses a patch generator that produces excellent sound and includes a graphic envelope display.

273. ---. "*EZ-Track ST*." Rev. of *EZ-Track ST*, from Hybrid Arts. *Antic: The Atari Resource* Dec. 1986: 97-98. 20-track, polyphonic MIDI sequencer. Features include real and step time recording, copy, mix, and a tempo range of .5 to 480 beats per minute.

274. ---. "Hybrid Arts' *MIDITrack ST*." Rev. of *MIDITrack ST*, from Hybrid Arts. *Music Technology* June 1987: 68-70. MIDI sequencer for the Atari ST. Features include global transposition, direct link to SMPTE, micro editing, and MIDI thru channel selection.

275. ---. "*Music Studio*." Rev. of *Music Studio*. *Antic: The Atari Resource* Sep. 1986: 20-21. Music composition software for the ST. Features include a music editor, sound engineering function (for the creation of instrumental sounds and sound effects), scoring capabilities, and MIDI compatibility.

276. ---. Rev. of *SuperScore*, from Sonus. *Music Technology* Sep. 1988: 79-81. Sequencer/notation software for the ST. Features include seven predefined score layouts, score size options, sequencing mode containing 24 separate sequences (32 tracks each), and standard quantize, transpose, bouncing, etc.

277. Mastel, Vern. "Simple Synthesizer: Make a Musical Peripheral for Your Atari." *Antic: The Atari Resource* Nov. 1983: 42-46. Demonstrates how to build a piano-type keyboard that can be used with Atari computers as a simple music synthesizer.

278. McBain, Craig. "Logo: Turtle Piano: Easy Logo Keyboard Music." *Antic: The Atari Resource* June 1985: 10+

279. "MIDI Comparison Charts." *STart: The ST Quarterly* Feb. 1988: 96-99. Comparison of important features of popular MIDI programs for the ST. The charts were compiled from reviews and charts that appeared in previous issues of *STart*. Includes a list of manufacturers with addresses and phone numbers.

280. Meyer, Chris. Rev. of *SampleMaker* 1.51, from Dr. T. *Music Technology* Jan. 1989: 62-64. Sound synthesis program for the Atari ST. Sounds can be created and edited for use with the Prophet 2000 or 2002, Akai S900, Ensoniq Mirage, E-mu Emax, and the Casio FZ1. Includes illustrations.

281. Moorhead, Jan. "Catch the Waveforms, Save a Thousand Sounds." Rev. of *K3PO + Synth-Droid*, *Casio Synth-Droid*, and *DW8000 Synth-Droid*, from Compu-Mates. *STart: The ST Quarterly* Feb. 1988: 90-93. Patch editors for the ST and the Kawai K3, Casio CZ, and Korg DW8000 synthesizers. All three programs are GEM-based.

282. ---. Rev. of *Creator* and *Notator*, from C-Lab Software. *STart: The ST Monthly* Jan. 1989: 75-77. Sequencing and notation software respectively. *Creator* has a resolution of 192 ppqn and impressive quantization features. *Notator* is identified as a "subset" of *Creator* and runs in monochrome only at the present time.

283. ---. Rev. of *Masterscore* and *Pro-24 Sequencer*, from Steinberg/Jones. *STart: The ST Monthly* Nov. 1988: 63-66. *Pro-24 Sequencer* operates in an environment similar to a conventional tape recorder. *Masterscore* is designed as a companion program for notation.

284. ---. Rev. of *MIDISoft Studio*, from MIDISoft. *Antic: The Atari Resource* July 1987: 69-70. MIDI sequencer for the ST. Features include 32 tracks, auto-rewind, mouse control, step time recording, track editing, and regional editing.

285. ---. "A New Face on the ST MIDI Marketplace." *STart: The ST Quarterly* Feb. 1988: 94-95. The inside story on Compu-Mates, a new company which handles a line of low-cost ST MIDI hardware and music software.

286. ---. Rev. of *Notator* and *Creator*, from C-Lab Software. *Electronic Musician* Jan. 1989: 108+ Integrated sequencing/notation software for the Atari ST. Features include keystroke commands that can be used for mouse functions, tape recorder emulation, ghost tracks, and an editing screen that includes a MIDI note list, piano-roll style graphics display, and traditional notation.

287. ---. "Synths, Samplers and Drums: A Shopping List of Music Hardware." *STart: The ST Quarterly* Feb. 1988: 82-89. Descriptions, specs, and important features of most popular synthesizers, samplers, and drum machines. A list of manufacturers with addresses and phone numbers is included.

288. "Music Service Software's *Data Dumpstor ST*." Rev. of *Data Dumpstor ST*, from Music Service Software. *Music, Computers & Software* May 1987: 63-65. Universal MIDI system exclusive data storage program for the ST.

289. Naman, Mard. "Dirty Dancing on the ST." *STart: The ST Monthly* Feb. 1989: 61-63. Interesting account of how Brian Tankersley used *SMPTE-Track* from Hybrid Arts to prolong the hit "Do You Love Me," originally 2.5 minutes, to 6 minutes for the movie *Dirty Dancing*.

290. ---. "Making Tracks with MIDI: A Profile of Tangerine Dream." *STart: The ST Monthly* Oct. 1988: 67-69. General discussion of Tangerine Dream, a twenty year old electronic music group, and the equipment they use. Mentions products from Steinberg Software and C-Lab Software.

291. ---. "Making Tracks with MIDI: Mick Fleetwood of Fleetwood Mac." *STart: The ST Quarterly* Summer 1988: 70-71. Mick Fleetwood describes how he uses the *ADAP* system (*Analog/Digital Audio Processor* from Hybrid Arts) and MIDI in the recording studio.

292. ---. "A Portrait of a Rock Musician." *STart: The ST Quarterly* 2.5 (1988): 53-55. Rock musician Dave Mason describes how he uses the Atari 1040 ST in music production.

293. ---. "Rock 'n' Roll with Atari: Music Stars and Your Favorite Computer." *STart: The ST Quarterly* Feb. 1988: 68-73. Top recording artists comment on how Atari ST computers help them in their work. Participating musicians include B. B. King, Mick Fleetwood, the Pointer Sisters, Dave Mason, and others.

294. O'Donnell, Bob. Rev. of *MT32 Editor/Librarian*, from Dr. T. *Music Technology* Feb. 1988: 66. Voice editing software for the Roland MT32 and Atari ST.

295. ---. Rev. of *SynthWorks ESQ-1*, from Steinberg. *Music Technology* Apr. 1988: 66-67. A voice editing and storage program for the Atari ST and the Ensoniq ESQ-1.

296. ---. "*Transform Xsyn*: Sound Editing Programs." Rev. of *Transform Modular Music System*, from Beam Team. *Music Technology* Nov. 1987: 36-39. A group of programs referred to as *Xsyn* modules, all of which are available from within the main "Manager" program. Includes sequencing, scoring, editing, and printing capabilities.

297. Panak, Steve. "Music Made Easy: *Music Studio* and *Music Construction Set*." Rev. of *Music Studio*, from Activision and *Music Construction Set*, from Electronic Arts. *STart: The ST Quarterly* Feb. 1988: 111-13. Music composition and notation software for the ST.

298. Pierson-Perry, Jim. Rev. of *Colleen Music Creator*, from Colleen Limited. *Antic: The Atari Resource* Mar. 1988: 13. Music composition program -- essentially an upgrade of *Pokey Player*.

299. ---. "Dr. T's *Musical Workstation*: From Random Thoughts to Finished Score." *STart: The ST Quarterly* Summer 1988: 73-76. Description of the *Multi-Program Environment*, an enhanced version of *Keyboard Controlled Sequencer*, Level II from Dr. T. that controls all compatible software e.g., *The Copyist*. Includes many helpful illustrations.

300. ---. Rev. of *DXMate*, from Synchro-Systems. *Antic: The Atari Resource* Feb. 1988: 59. GEM-based patch editor/librarian for the ST and the Yamaha DX series of synthesizers.

301. ---. "Home Recording on a Budget: Setting up Your Own MIDI Studio." *STart: The ST Quarterly* Feb. 1988: 79+ Helpful hints on home recording and the equipment needed. Topics discussed include Atari ST software and synthesizers. The author emphasizes the advantages of buying equipment in modules. Includes a list of manufacturers.

302. ---. Rev. of *Matrix 6 Tricks*, from Dr. T. *STart: The ST Monthly* Dec. 1988: 59-61. Librarian/editor for the Oberheim Matrix 6 synthesizer and Atari ST. This is the only patch editor currently available for the Matrix 6 and ST. Runs in Dr. T's *Multi-Program Environment*.

303. ---. Rev. of *MIDI Magic*, from Micro-W. *Antic: The Atari Resource* Mar. 1987: 73. Reads music disks and sends the data to a MIDI compatible instrument. For the Atari ST.

304. ---. Rev. of *MIDI Recording Studio*, from Dr. T. *Antic: The Atari Resource* Sep. 1987: 57-58. Entry-level MIDI sequencer. Features include real time entry and music editing capabilities.

305. ---. "MIDI Resources: Guide for ST Electronic Musicians." *Antic: The Atari Resource* June 1988: 52+ Resources include books, magazines, bulletin board services, and various organizations that deal specifically with music applications of the Atari ST.

306. ---. "The Musical ST, Pt. II: MIDI Patch Editors." *STart: The ST Quarterly* Fall 1987: 70+ Discussion and evaluation of *CZ-Patch*, *CZ-Android*, *DX-Heaven*, and *Perfect Patch*.

307. ---. "The Musical ST: Consumer MIDI Software, Tools, and Toys." *STart: The ST Quarterly* Summer 1987: 51-58. Includes a bibliography and addresses for publishers of music software for the ST. There is also a listing of public domain software and electronic bulletin boards.

308. ---. "The Professional MIDI Machine and How It Grew." *STart: The ST Monthly* Nov. 1988: 20-25. Historical account of MIDI and the Atari ST and how they have developed over the past few years. Discusses applications e.g., sample editing and transcription, and includes a directory of manufacturers.

309. ---. Rev. of *SoftSynth ST* and *Sound Designer ST*, from Digidesign; *ST Sonic Editor*, from Sonus; and *Soundworks Mirage*, from Steinberg/Jones. *STart: The ST Monthly* Feb. 1989: 67-72. Sample editors for the ST and Ensoniq Mirage sampler. Includes illustrations.

310. ---. Rev. of *SoftSynth*, from Digidesign. *STart: The ST Monthly* Oct. 1988: 87-89. Software-based synthesis.

311. ---. "The ST/MIDI Connection: New Releases." *STart: The ST Monthly* Feb. 1989: 64-66. Brief descriptions of twelve new music/MIDI programs for the Atari ST. Products mentioned include *Take Note* (Thinkware), *Song Files* (Golden MIDI), and *Master Tracks Jr.* (Passport).

312. ---. "The ST/MIDI Connection: The Now and Future MIDI." *STart: The ST Monthly* Jan. 1989: 79-81. Overview of new products including *Phantom* (Dr. T.) a SMPTE sync box, *Video Jambox* (Southworth) a MIDI-to-SMPTE interface, and *Keys* (Dr. T.) notation/sequencing software for the education market.

313. ---. "Super CZ: Real Time MIDI Special Effects." *Antic: The Atari Resource* June 1988: 51-54. Overview of the Casio CZ synthesizer. Features include keyboard split, voice overlay, and four independent voices. Described as an excellent working companion for the Atari ST.

314. Rue, Dan. Rev. of *D-10/20/110/MT-32 Editor Librarian*, from MusicSoft. *Music Technology* Dec. 1988: 61. For the Atari ST and the Roland L/A series of synthesizers.

315. ---. Rev. of *KI Ed-Lib*, from Drumware. *Music Technology* Nov. 1988: 72. Editor/librarian for the ST and the Kawai KI.

316. Rychner, Lorenz. Rev. of C-Lab *Creator*, from Digidesign, Inc. *Music Technology* Apr. 1988: 78-81. MIDI sequencer for the Atari ST. Features include system exclusive dumps of voice data, system exclusive parameter access for programming during play, and selective MIDI merge.

317. ---. Rev. of *GenWave/12*, from Drumware. *Music Technology* July 1988: 90-93. Visual waveform editor for the Atari ST. Allows the user to import sample data from the Akai S900, Emax, E-mu SP1200, and the Prophet 2000/2. Features include zoom, looping, and Fast Fourier Transform.

318. ---. Rev. of *KCS* (*MPE*, *PVG*, and the *Copyist*), from Dr. T. *Music Technology* Aug. 1988: 70+ Enhanced version of *Keyboard Controlled Sequencer* that includes a *Multi-Program Environment* (enables the user to load up to four of Dr. T's editor/librarian programs simultaneously) a *Programmable Variations Generator* (allows the user to alter existing sequences) and *The Copyist* (notation software).

319. ---. "Micro Reviews." Rev. of *K5 Editor/Librarian*, from Dr. T. *Music Technology* Oct. 1988: 84. Voice editor for the Kawai K5 and the Atari ST.

320. ---. Rev. of *S900 Pro Sample Editor*, from Dr. T. *Music Technology* Oct. 1988: 80-83. Can be used to slice out loops and download them to a Kawai K5 or Prophet VS.

321. Ryder, Michael. "Atari Sound Development System." *Compute!* July 1986: 69-75. Presents a program that lets one design sounds on the screen with the joystick and keyboard using features built into the Atari's sound chip. For Atari 400/800, XL, and XE.

322. Scarborough, John. "Atari's Sound System." *Compute!* Jan. 1983: 48-50. Discussion of various methods of bypassing the Atari

800's SOUND command and producing high quality sound from television speakers or the built-in speaker of the Atari.

323.   Sharp, Daniel, and Joe West.   "MIDIMate and *MIDITrack II.*" Rev. of MIDIMate and *MIDITrack II*, from Hybrid Arts.   *Whole Earth Review* Winter 1985: 111.   MIDI interface and sequencer respectively for the Atari 800 XL or the 65 ME.

324.   Snow, David.   "*Beat-It*: A Drum Sensor Interface for the Atari ST."   *Electronic Musician* Dec. 1988: 87+   Discussion of how to turn a synthesizer into a drum machine with the Atari ST. Includes a schematic, program listing in LDW BASIC, and parts list.

325.   ---.   "*Drumbox*, the CZ/ST Connection."   *Electronic Musician* Feb. 1988: 32+   A program written in ST BASIC that generates and plays random rhythmic patterns on a CZ synthesizer.

326.   ---.   The *MIDI Music Box*: More Cheap Thrills for the Atari ST. *Electronic Musician* Mar. 1989: 58+   Presents an algorithmic composition program for the Atari ST. Includes source codes in LDW BASIC and Assembly.

327.   Stover, Kirk.   "*CZ-101 Patch Librarian*: Expand Yor Keyboard Horizons - Save Every Sound You'd Like."   *ST-Log: The Atari ST Monthly Magazine* May 1987: 29-37.

328.   Tapper, Larry.   "Guide to Atari Music Software."   *Atari Explorer: The Official Atari Journal* July-Aug. 1988: 34-37. Descriptive list of current music software. Includes a directory of publishers.

329.   Tedsen, Fred.   "16-Bit Atari Music."   *Compute!* Mar. 1983: 214-20.   Subroutines that can be added to Atari BASIC to expand the SOUND command to 65,000 different frequencies.

330.   Thomas, Tony.   Rev. of *EZ-Score Plus*, from Hybrid Arts.   *Music, Computers & Software* Oct. 1988: 76-77.   Scoring software for the ST. Features include pop-up menus; the ability to map the modulation wheel, pitch bend wheel, sustain pedal; and MIDI controllers. Compatible with files generated by *EZ-Track*, *SMPTE Track*, or *SYNC Track*.

331.   Trask, Simon.   "Steinberg *Pro 24*: Software for Atari ST Computers."   Rev. of *Pro-24 Sequencer*, from Steinberg/Jones.   *Music Technology* Nov. 1986: 60-63.   Multitrack MIDI recording system.

332.   Vail, Mark.   "Keyboard Report: Dr. T's *PVG Programmable Variations Generator & Master Editor*."   *Keyboard Magazine* July 1988: 174+   Editing enhancement for the *Keyboard Controlled*

Sequencer, Level II. Features include ornamentation, track blending, pitch mapping, chord arpeggiation, and tempo utilities. For the Atari ST or Mega ST.

333. Walnum, Clayton. "BASICally Melodic: How to Tease BASIC into Giving You the Music You Want." *Analog Computing* May 1987: 37-40.

334. ---. Rev. of *Music Painter*, from Atari Corp. *Analog Computing* July-Aug. 1987: 85-86.

335. White, Jerry. "16-Bit Soundpower: How the Pros Enhance Atari Music." *Antic: The Atari Resource* Sep. 1985: 38+ Contains a BASIC program that demonstrates 16-bit sound on any Atari computer.

336. ---. Rev. of *Music Construction Set*, from Electronic Arts. *Antic: The Atari Resource* Dec. 1984: 80-81. Music composition software that allows the user to customize instruments and play through any MIDI equipped synthesizer.

337. ---. Rev. of *Songwriter*, from Scarborough Systems. *Antic: The Atari Resource* Nov. 1984: 78.

338. Wiegers, Karl. "Guess That Song? How Many Notes Do You Bid." *Antic: The Atari Resource* July 1985: 24+ Musical quiz program in BASIC.

339. ---. "Pick a Chord: Your Atari Can Play Most of Them." *Antic: The Atari Resource* Nov. 1983: 47-49. Presents a program for the Atari 800 that allows the user to hear twelve different chords in any key.

340. Wiffen, Paul. Rev. of *ADAP* (*Analog/Digital Audio Processor*), from Hybrid Arts. *Music Technology* Jan. 1987: 76. Sound sampler for the Atari ST.

341. Williamson, C. Rev. of *KCS* Level II, from Dr. T. *Electronic Musician* Sep. 1988: 84+ *Keyboard Controlled Sequencer* for the Atari ST. Features include a "Track Mode" for recording, an "Open Mode" for editing, a *Progammable Variations Generator* for altering existing sequences, and a *Multi-Program Environment* that allows the user to switch between programs.

342. Witt, Richard. "The Simplest Atari Notation Program You'll Ever See." *Electronic Musician* Feb. 1989: 98-103. Descriptive overview of *Transcribe*, a program written in ST BASIC that can transcribe sequences recorded on the *SST Sequencer* from Sonus. It can also be used with *Chord*, an algorithmic composition program by Jim Johnson. Includes program listing.

343.   Yap, Roger.   Rev. of *Music Construction Set*, from Electronic Arts.   *Antic: The Atari Resource* Feb. 1988: 59.   Music composition/notation software for the ST.

344.   Yost, Gary.   "*MIDI Music System*."   Rev. of *MIDI Music System*, from Synthetic Software.   *Antic: The Atari Resource* June 1986: 56.

Commodore

345. Aikin, Jim. "Keyboard Report: *Moog Song Producer*, Dr. T's *Keyboard Controlled Sequencer*, and *Musicdata MIDI Sequencer* for the Commodore 64." *Keyboard Magazine* Sep. 1985: 82+

346. Rev. of *Algorithmic Composer*, from Dr. T. *Keyboards, Computers & Software* Dec. 1986: 60-61. Computer assisted composition software for the C-64/128.

347. Alonso, Robert. "SID Plays Bach: Tap Some of the Musical Power Hidden Inside Your 64 to Play Bach in Machine Code." *Commodore: The Microcomputer Magazine* Sep.-Oct. 1985: 106-09.

348. Anderton, Craig. "20 Great Achievements in Twenty Years of Musical Electronics 1968-1988." *Electronic Musician* July1988: 28+ The Commodore 64 and its SID chip are included in the list of "20 Great Achievements." Introduced in the early 1980s, the C-64 went far beyond the musical ability of most personal computers.

349. ---. "Personal Computers Become Personal Composers: Music Software for the Commodore-64." *Record* Aug. 1984: 50. Brief overview of music software available for the C-64.

350. Bagley, James. "*Mozart Magic*." *Compute!* Oct. 1986: 89-91. Program for the C-128 that composes minuets in the style of Mozart. The program is based on a musical game devised by Mozart.

351. Baird, J. "CZ Meets C-64: Six Inexpensive Librarians and Editors That Can Turn Your Casio into a Powerhouse." *Musician* Nov. 1986: 52+

352. Bateman, Selby. "Commodore's 64 and 128: Marvelous Music Machines." *Compute!'s Gazette for Commodore Personal Computer Users* Aug. 1987: 18-21. Music capabilities of the C-64/128.

353. Benford, Tom. "Commodore 64 Music Keyboard Buyer's Guide."
Commodore: The Microcomputer Magazine July-Aug. 1985: 76-79.
Overview of music hardware and software available for the C-64.

354. Brooks, David. Rev. of *The Advanced Music System*, from
Firebird Software. *Commodore Magazine* Feb. 1987: 44-46. Music
composition and editing software for the C-64. Uses traditional
notation, a MIDI compatible keyboard, and can handle compositions
in up to six parts.

355. ---. "The Best of Music Products." *Commodore Microcomputers*
Nov.-Dec. 1986: 132. A guide to the best music products of 1986 for
Commodore computers. Products chosen include: *Keyboard
Controlled Sequencer* and *Sampler-64*.

356. ---. Rev. of *Keyboard Controlled Sequencer*, from Dr. T.
Commodore Magazine Nov. 1987: 38+ Sequencer for the C-64.

357. ---. "Making Music with MIDI: By Combining a Commodore
with MIDI Technology, Almost Anyone Can Produce
Professional-Sounding Music." *Run: The Commodore 64/128 User's
Guide* July 1987: 38-42. Includes a list of publishers of MIDI software
for Commodore computers.

358. ---. Rev. of *Master Composer*, from Access Software.
Commodore: The Microcomputer Magazine July-Aug. 1985: 28+
Music composition software for the C-64.

359. ---. "MIDI Programming, Pt. I." *Commodore Magazine* Aug.
1987: 88+ Includes a program that introduces users to the MIDI
interface.

360. ---. "MIDI Programming, Pt. II: Monitoring MIDI
Information." *Commodore Magazine* Sep. 1987: 74-77. Includes a
program called *MIDIHacker* that can receive MIDI data.

361. ---. "Scale Tunings for SID." *Commodore: The Microcomputer
Magazine* Mar.-Apr. 1985: 91-97. Just, Meantone, and Equal
Temperament.

362. Butterfield, Jim. "Commodore 64 Music: *Happy Birthday*."
Compute! Oct. 1984: 177-78. Presents a program in BASIC that plays
Happy Birthday.

363. Campbell, Alan Gary. Rev. of *DX/TX Librarian* and *C Z
Librarian*, from Triangle Audio. *Electronic Musician* Jan. 1988: 81.
Patch librarians for the C-64/128. Compatible with Passport or
Sequential (Dr. T.) interfaces.

364. ---. "Questions and Answers." *Electronic Musician* Oct. 1987: 44+ Discussion of how to unstick a C-64 keyboard spacebar and other problems. Gives addresses for repairs.

365. Campbell, Tom, and Larry McClain. "*MusiCalc* Can Make the Commodore 64 Play Sweetly But not Without a Lot of Effort on Your Part." Rev. of *MusiCalc*, from Waveform Corp. *Popular Computing* Nov. 1984: 158-62. Music composition software for the C-64.

366. Chandler, James. Rev. of *ES1 Librarian*, from Valhala. *Electronic Musician* Jan. 1988: 79. Librarian software for the Ensoniq ESQ-1 and C-64/128. Does not include any patch editing features.

367. ---. "First Take: *X-LIB* Patch Librarian for Yamaha DX/TX Synths and the Commodore 64." *Electronic Musician* Mar. 1988: 91. Incompatible with the Yamaha FB-01 Sound Module.

368. ---. Rev. of *Jiffy DOS/64*, from Fellows Inc. *Electronic Musician* Jan. 1988: 81-82. Firmware quickload program for the C-64.

369. ---. "*Keyfrets*: Keyboard to Guitar Voicing Translator." *Electronic Musician* Aug. 1988: 74+ Program listing for the C-64 that remaps what is played on a keyboard to sound like a guitar.

370. "Commodore Hornblower: Inside the SID Chip." *Home Computer Magazine* Mar. 1985: 54-55. Brief but informative description of the SID chip and its tone generating capabilities.

371. Cross, Hubert. "*Sound Manager*." *Compute!'s Gazette for Commodore Personal Computer Users* Jan. 1988: 62+ A program that allows the user to design sounds for use in other programs.

372. Daniel, Walter. "Alternate Scales on the Commodore 64: A Tuning Demonstration Program." *Electronic Musician* Oct. 1987: 38+ Program that explores Equal Temperament, one form of Just Intonation, and Pythagorean tuning.

373. Di Silvestro, Laile L. "The Magic of Music Videos: A Review of the Sight and Sound *Music Video Kit*." Rev. of *Music Video Kit*, from Sight and Sound Music Software. *Home Computer Magazine* Aug. 1985: 42-43. Integrated sound and graphics package for the C-64.

374. Dowty, Tim. "Using the *EM* Interface: A MIDI Echo/Delay." *Electronic Musician* Aug. 1986: 29-32. A program in BASIC for the C-64 that allows one to experiment with the sonic possibilities of MIDI echo. The schematic for the *EM* interface appears in *Electronic Musician*, May 1986.

375. Freiberger, Paul. "Learning to Play Music on the C-64." *InfoWorld* 14 Nov. 1983: 32-33. Introduction to *MusiCalc 1* for the C-64.

376. Greenwald, T. "Keyboard Report: *Algorithmic Composer* and *KCS 128*." *Keyboard Magazine* Oct. 1986: 142+ Music composition (*Algorithmic Composer*) and sequencing software (*Keyboard Controlled Sequencer*) for the C-64/128. Programs may be used together.

377. Guerra, Bob. Rev. of *Super Score*, from Sonus. *Commodore Microcomputers* May 1988: 34. Allows the user to string together up to 16 sequences. Also includes many editing features and is compatible with *Super Sequencer*, also from Sonus.

378. Higginbottom, Paul. "Life Beyond SID: A Review of Passport Design's MIDI Hardware and Software." *Commodore: The Microcomputer Magazine* Mar.-Apr. 1985: 47-48. Reviews five products from Passport including *MIDI/4 Sequencer* for the C-64.

379. Iovine, John. "Building a MIDI Interface Device for the Commodore 64 and 128." *Commodore Magazine* Mar. 1989: 48+ Excellent article that explains the basics of MIDI technology. Includes illustrations, a schematic for the MIDI interface, a listing for the interface program, and a list of required parts and Radio Shack part numbers.

380. ---. "Sound Digitizer II." *Commodore Magazine* Nov. 1988: 52+ Description of how to make a sound digitizer for the C-128. Includes a detailed schematic, a list of required parts and Radio Shack part numbers, and a program listing in BASIC.

381. Jaco, Jerry. "Working with SID." *Compute!* Oct. 1983: 277-88. In-depth discussion of the C-64's SID (Sound Interface Device) chip.

382. Johnson, Jim. Rev. of *Sampler-64* and *Com-Drum*, from Micro Arts Products. *Keyboards, Computers & Software* Dec. 1986: 51-52. *Sampler-64* includes sound sampling and editing software, a microphone, and a monitor adapter cable. *Com-Drum* is a drum machine program.

383. Kerkhoff, Jim. "*Random MIDI*." *Electronic Musician* Dec. 1987: 20-23. Program written in COMAL (Common Algorithmic Language) that generates random pitches and velocities and then converts them into the appropriate MIDI Note-On and Note-Off commands. For the C-64.

384. Koberstein, Wayne. "The Music of Sound, Pt. II: Music Software for the C-64 vs. Casio's CT-6000 Keyboard." *Home Computer Magazine* May 1985: 40-43.

385. Lane, John. "Programming 64 Sound, Pt. I." *Compute!* June 1984: 134-39. Presents methods for controlling the SID chip with BASIC. Covers waveforms and sound envelopes.

386. ---. "Programming 64 Sound, Pt. II." *Compute!* July 1984: 124-29. Programming music and sound on the C-64 in BASIC. Includes four program listings.

387. Lehrman, Paul D. "Say Hellow to SID: Commodore 64's Sound Interface Device." *High Fidelity/Musical America* Dec. 1983: 69-72. General overview of the sound chip used in the C-64.

388. Lewis, Bill. "KCScope." Rev. of *Valhala Sound Library*, from Valhala. *Keyboards, Computers & Software* Feb. 1987: 71+ 757 patches for Yamaha's DX/TX synthesizers. For C-64/128.

389. Lisowski, James A. "Hear the Scales." *Electronic Musician* Oct. 1987: 42. Presents a program in BASIC that allows one to hear scales in Equal Temperament, Pythagorean tuning, or Just Intonation.

390. Mace, Scott. "Sophisticated Synthesizers Target Personal Computers." *InfoWorld* 6 Feb. 1984: 59-60. Describes a six-voice synthesizer from Sequential Circuits for the C-64.

391. Malone, Don. *"Dr. Sound* for the 64." *Compute!* Sep. 1986: 89-93. An algorithmic note sequencer that plays notes according to parameters the user selects in real time using the SID chip.

392. Mansfield, Richard. Rev. of *Music Sequencer*, from Sequential Circuits. *Compute!* Jan. 1985: 104-08. Sequencer for the C-64/128.

393. ---. Rev. of *Synthy 64. Compute!* Oct. 1983: 152-54. Music composition program for the C-64.

394. Milano, D. "Music Expo '85; Everything's Coming up Software." *Keyboard Magazine* Sep. 1985: 30-34.

395. Monaghan, Dan. "Synthesis." *Compute!* May 1987: 62-68. Presents a program that turns the C-64's keyboard into a musical keyboard.

396. Mulvaney, Paul G. "Automatic Irish Jigs on a Commodore 64." *Keyboard Magazine* Mar. 1987: 91+ Includes a program called *MIDI*

Jig Generator in BASIC that plays Irish Jigs. A Passport MIDI interface and a MIDI keyboard are required for playback.

397. Nelson, Philip. "Advanced Sound Effects on the 64." *Compute!* Feb. 1985: 129-33. Presents several ways one can create unusual sound effects with the C-64's built-in synthesizer chip. Includes a program called *Sound Effects Generator*.

398. ---. "Exploring the SID Chip." *Compute!'s Gazette for Commodore Personal Computer Users* Aug. 1987: 22-24. General overview of the SID (Sound Interface Device) chip found in the C-64.

399. ---. "128: Sound and Music, Pt. II" *Compute!* Sep. 1985: 113-16. Discussion of the Filter, Sound, and Play commands of the C-128.

400. ---. "Sound and Music on the Commodore 128, Pt. I." *Compute!* Aug. 1985: 76-78. Demonstrates the use of the Volume, Tempo, and Envelope statements in the C-128's advanced BASIC.

401. Petersen, Marty. Rev. of *Synthesound 64. InfoWorld* 9 Apr. 1984: 44-45. Music-generating software for the C-64.

402. Picard, Ronald. "64 Sound Tester." *Compute!* Nov. 1983: 187. Presents a program called *Sound Test* that allows one to explore the attack, decay, sustain, and release features of the C-64's sound system.

403. Pierce, Chuck. "Reader Tips: *Commodore MIDI File Editor*." *Keyboard Magazine* Sep. 1988: 20+ Sequencers for the C-64 without a step editing function often present problems when attempting to record machine-perfect synth lines and complex rhythm patterns. This program allows the user to load a sequencer file, examine it, edit, and resave the modified version.

404. Russell, B. "Computers and Music: Music Software for the Commodore 64." *Canadian Musician* 8.4 (1986): 82+

405. ---. "Dr. T's Sequencer for Commodore 128." Rev. of Dr. T's Sequencer. *Canadian Musician* 8.6 (1986): 32-33. Enhanced version of the C-64 program. Has the ability to store more notes and sequences, and allows for keyboard splitting.

406. Sandberg-Diment, E. "Mastering Melodies." *Science Digest* July 1984: 82-83. Evaluation of *MusiCalc I* from Waveform, music composition software for the C-64. Features include 32 built-in instrumental sounds and melodies. Includes a very brief description of *MusiCalc II Scorewriter* that allows one to connect various digital sound-effect devices and transcribe compositions into standard musical notation.

407. Schulak, Barbara. "Songs in the Key of C-128: Entering Music Is an Exercise in Harmony with *Music Editor*." *Run: The Commodore 64/128 User's Guide* Oct. 1988: 49+ Presents a program (*Music Editor*) that facilitates transcribing written music into strings that can be used by the C-128 Play Statement.

408. Speerschneider, Roger. "Dynamusic." *Compute!'s Gazette for Commodore Personal Computer Users* Aug. 1987: 62+ Programs for the C-64 and C-128 that allow the user to create music that plays in the background while another program runs.

409. Steed, Mike. "*SYSound*." *Compute!* Sep. 1984: 146-48. Program for creating sounds on the C-64.

410. Stockford, James. "*CZ-Rider*." Rev. of *CZ-Rider*, from Dr. T. *Whole Earth Review* Winter 1985: 111. Patch editor/librarian for the Casio CZ-101 or CZ-1000 MIDI keyboard, C-64/128, and Roland MIDI interface.

411. ---. "Dr. T's MIDI Sequencer Program." Rev. of Dr. T's MIDI Sequencer. *Whole Earth Review* Winter 1985: 110. MIDI sequencer for the C-64. Features include real and step time recording.

412. Tarr, Greg. "*Basically Music*: A Complete Composition Tool for the 64." *Compute!'s Gazette for Commodore Personal Computer Users* Mar. 1988: 73+ A program in BASIC that gives the user complete control over the 64's sound chip.

413. Teverbaugh, Rick. Rev. of *The Music Shop*, from Broderbund. *Commodore: The Microcomputer Magazine* July-Aug. 1985: 27. Music composition software for the C-64. Features include pull-down menus, step edit, notation capabilities, MIDI compatibility, and music printing.

414. Tobenfeld, Emile. "A General-Purpose Sequencer for MIDI Synthesizers." *Computer Music Journal* 8.4 (1984): 43-44. Description of the author's implementation of a MIDI sequencer for the C-64 that allows use of the computer keyboard as an instrument of real time control. It also allows the user to construct a musical composition out of smaller elements using as many levels of nesting as desired.

415. Todd, Mike. "Music Maker." *Practical Computing* Dec. 1984: 152-54. Introduces two programs, *Note Editor* and *Play a Song* for composing and playing three-part songs.

416. Wadie, Jonathan. "Commodore 64 *Polyphonic 64*." *Personal Computer World* (U.K.) Feb. 1986: 215-17. BASIC program that has 8 built-in instrumental sounds for the C-64.

417. West, Joe. "A Keyboard for *MusiCalc*...the *Colortone Keyboard*." Rev. of the *Colortone Keyboard*, from Waveform Corp. *Whole Earth Review* Mar. 1985: 99. A membrane keyboard with software for the C-64.

IBM

418. Aikin, Jim. "Keyboard Report: *Cakewalk* Sequencer for the IBM PC." *Keyboard Magazine* Dec. 1987: 144+ Brief overview of *Cakewalk* from Twelve Tone Systems. Features include 256 tracks, online help, auto-rewind, event filters, timed auto-save, and step-entry recording.

419. ---. "Keyboard Report: *SampleVision*, S900 Editor for the IBM." *Keyboard Magazine* Aug. 1988: 124+ Sample and program editor for the Akai S900. Features include cut-and-paste editing, GEM-based mouse or keyboard operation, graphic envelope editing, and Fourier analysis display.

420. ---. "Keyboard Report: *Score* Notation Software." *Keyboard Magazine* July 1988: 156+ Notation/printing software for the IBM PC from Passport Designs. Features include automatic stemming, beaming and aligning, online help screens, user macro definitions, and automatic page layout. Requires Roland MPU-401 MIDI interface.

421. Andreas, Michael. Rev. of *MIDI-Manager 7*, from Performance Computer Concepts. *Music Technology* Oct. 1988: 68-71. Integrated sequencer/librarian package consisting of a circuit board, a remote MIDI Inter-Connect Box, a 50-pin connecting cable, and software.

422. Banes, Vince. "Audio-Frequency Analyzer: Build IBM PC Accessories to Analyze Your Stereo." *Byte* Jan. 1985: 223-50. Demonstration of how to build a device that allows one to monitor the frequency response of a stereo using an IBM PC.

423. Bassett, Rick, Jonathan Matzkin, and Charles Petzold. "A MIDI Musical Offering." *PC Magazine* 29 Nov. 1988: 229+ In-depth coverage of MIDI software for the IBM PC/PS2. Includes informative sidebars on FM synthesis, MIDI terminology, and online MIDI bulletin boards. Illustrated.

424. Charbeneau, Travis. Rev. of *Sideman 81Z*, from Voyetra. *Music, Computers & Software* Oct. 1988: 78-79. Editor/librarian for the Yamaha TX81Z FM sound module and the IBM PC.

425. ---. "System: The IBM." *Music, Computers & Software* Aug. 1988: 49-51. General overview of the IBM and its music potential. Stresses the importance of third party manufacturers and mentions specific software e.g., *Personal Composer* (Jim Miller) and *Sequencer Plus* (Voyetra).

426. Cummings, S. "Keyboard Report: Octave Plateau *Sequencer Plus* Software for the IBM PC." *Keyboard Magazine* Nov. 1985: 98+ The author states that *Sequencer Plus* files can be transcribed into conventional notation using *The Copyist* from Dr. T.

427. De Furia, Steve. "Software for Musicians: *MIDISave*: A Generic MIDI Data Storage Program." *Keyboard Magazine* July 1988: 134+ A librarian program written in Turbo Pascal for the IBM PC and clones. Requires a MPU-401 MIDI interface. *MIDISave* is designed to work with all types of MIDI devices and can be altered for use with other computers.

428. DiNucci, Darcy. "*Tune Trivia*." *PC World* June 1985: 129-33. Description of *Tune Trivia*, a music game from Sight and Sound Music Software.

429. Doerschuk, Bob. "Bob James Takes on the Traditionalists with His High-Tech Treatment of Scarlatti." *Keyboard Magazine* Apr. 1988: 66+ The author describes how Bob James utilizes an IBM PC and *Texture* (sequencer) for recording piano compositions by Scarlatti, the subject of his second Masterworks album.

430. Doyle, Frank. "MCScope." Rev. of *Sequencer Plus Mark III*, from Voyetra. *Music, Computers & Software* Oct. 1987: 79-80. Professional quality sequencer that includes an interface to *Patch Master*, Voyetra's patch librarian and network organizer.

431. ---. "MCScope: Software." *Music, Computers & Software* Feb.-Mar. 1988: 78-79. Brief overview of *ProMIDI Studio System*, a MIDI sequencer from Systems Design Associates. Features include the ability to record and playback directly to and from the computer's disk.

432. ---. "ShorTakes." Rev. of *TX81Z Graphic Editing System*, from Bacchus. *Music, Computers & Software* Dec. 1987: 64+ Object-based editing system for the Yamaha TX81Z tone generator. Features include icons, overlapping/movable windows, mouse operation, and graphic control panels.

433. Edwards, Gary A. "MIDI Column: *M.E.S.A.* Critique." *Computer Shopper* Jan. 1989: 295+ Descriptive overview of *Music Editor, Scorer and Arranger* from Roland Corp.

434. Einhorn, R. "*Texture* Version 2." *Electronic Musician* May 1986: 74+ MIDI sequencer for the IBM PC. Features include punch-in and punch-out, overdubbing, tape sync, note-by-note editor, and global editing commands.

435. Freff. "Keyboard Report: Yamaha C1 & C1/20 Music Computers." *Keyboard Magazine* Feb. 1989: 152-55. The C1 includes two 720 K 3.5" floppy disk drives -- the C1/20 includes one floppy and a 20 MB hard disk. Features include the ability to support an external CGA color or Hercules monochrome monitor and a 10 MHz 80286 microprocessor.

436. ---. "Making Music with the Well-Synthesized PC." *PC: The Independent Guide to IBM Personal Computers* Dec. 1983: 338-50. Emphasis is on the MIDI interface. The author states that this could well be the "found chord" of computerized music. Other topics include synthesizers and various electronic musical instruments.

437. ---. "Short Takes: Roland *PC Desktop Music Studio* MIDI Starter Kit." *Keyboard Magazine* Nov. 1988: 156. Includes an MT-32 sound module, MPU-IPC PC/MIDI interface, and *EASE* software (*Easy Arranging and Sequencing Environment*).

438. Gilby, Ian. Rev. of *Sequencer Plus MK I, II*, and *III*, from Voyetra Technologies. *Electronic Musician* Mar. 1988: 92+ In-depth review of *Sequencer Plus* for the IBM PC. The program comes in three versions which vary in price and capabilities and a chart is included that compares the various features of each one.

439. Goldstein, Burt. "First Take: Bacchus *TX802 Graphic Editing System* for the IBM PC." *Electronic Musician* Aug. 1988: 82-83. A program from Bacchus that puts the parameters of the Yamaha TX802 synthesizer on the IBM's monitor. Allows for much easier and faster control of the instrument. Compatible with the IBM Music Feature.

440. ---. "Reader Tips: Enhancing Your IBM Sequencer with Macros." *Keyboard Magazine* Jan. 1988: 18+ Practical examples of how a macro collection can streamline many sequencing tasks.

441. Goldstein, Burt, and Freff. "More Power for the IBM PC." *Keyboard Magazine* Oct. 1988: 58+ In-depth discussion of IBM/MS-DOS and music applications. States that Yamaha is

committed to the IBM standard and that "everything the typical musician with a PC needs to know about [MS] DOS can be learned in less than an hour."

442. Gray, Stephen B. "*SongWright IV*: Prints and Plays Music." *Computer Shopper* Jan. 1989: 108-09. General overview of a program from SongWright Software that uses the PC's keyboard as a musical instrument. Includes illustrations.

443. Greenwald, T. "Keyboard Report: IBM Sequencers: *48 Track PC II* and *Forte*." *Keyboard Magazine* Aug. 1987: 122+ *48 Track PC II* is from Robert Keller and features 48 simultaneous polyphonic tracks, 600 ppqn resolution, and MIDI sync. *Forte* is from LTA Productions and features 16 tracks, real and step time input, MIDI or FSK sync, and 10-character track names.

444. ---. "Keyboard Report: Sight and Sound *MIDI Ensemble* Software." *Keyboard Magazine* Feb. 1986: 128+ MIDI sequencer for the IBM PC. Features include real time and step time entry, 255 tracks (8 simultaneous), one text page per sequence, and many user-configured possibilities. Requires Roland MPU-401 and color graphics card.

445. ---. "Keyboard Report: *Texture* 2.0 Sequencer for the IBM PC." *Keyboard Magazine* Oct. 1986: 138+ MIDI sequencer for the IBM PC. Features include record and edit buffers, automated punch-in and punch-out, variable resolution to 1/192 beat, and DOS subdirectory capability.

446. Grupp, Paul. "Compatibles: Inside a Trio of Musical Clones." *Music, Computers & Software* June 1987: 66-67. Description of several IBM compatible music systems. Companies discussed include Professional Music Systems (Durham, NC), The Teknecom Group (Dallas, TX), and The Personal Computer Store (San Antonio, TX).

447. ---. "MCScope." Rev. of *48 Track PC II*. *Music, Computers & Software* Aug. 1987: 65+ MIDI sequencer for the IBM PC. Features include 48 independent tracks, 50,000 event capacity, and resolution of 24-600 ppqn.

448. ---. "A New Kind of Music Box: The IBM Personal System/2, Model 30." *Music, Computers & Software* Oct. 1987: 38+ Description and evaluation of the new IBM PS/2 Model 30 and its potential as a musician's computer. Includes a list of current music software and information about the new IBM Music Feature.

449. ---. "ShorTakes." Rev. of *Lighthouse*, from Bering Data Systems. *Music, Computers & Software* Aug. 1987: 76-77. MIDI

sequencer for the IBM PC. Features include 8 tracks, pull-down menus, and mouse-based operation. Requires the Roland MPU-401 MIDI interface.

450. ---. "IBM: The Musician's Choice?" *Music, Computers & Software* May 1987: 34+ Discussion of the IBM PC and its potential music applications. The author states that cost and reliability make the PC a good investment. Other topics include music software, monitors, memory, and speed.

451. ---. "OP-4001 IBM PC MIDI Interface." *Electronic Musician* June 1986: 78-79. General overview of a MIDI interface from Voyetra.

452. Harris, Craig R. "A Composer's Computer Music System: Practical Considerations." *Computer Music Journal* 11.3 (1987): 36+ Discussion of the various factors that contribute to the development of a small but powerful computer music workstation. Computers discussed include an Advanced Logic Research (ALR) Dart, and an Altos 986. Both run on Intel processors.

453. "The IBM PC Music Feature." *Computer Buyer's Guide and Handbook* May-June 1987: 37. Brief description of a music synthesizing card to be used with the PC or PS/2 Model 30. Features are basically the same as the Yamaha FB-01 sound module e.g., can produce 8 different timbres simultaneously.

454. "IBM Personal System/2." *Music, Computers & Software* Aug. 1987: 92. Brief description of the PS/2 Model 30 and its potential music applications.

455. Isaacson, Matt. Rev. of *Cakewalk*, from Twelve Tone Systems. *Music Technology* Nov. 1987: 75-79. Sequencing software for the IBM PC. Features 256 tracks, online help, auto-rewind, event filters, step-entry recording, and timed auto-save.

456. ---. Rev. of *Concepts: One*, from MIDIConcepts. *Music Technology* June 1988: 83-87. MIDI sequencer for the IBM PC and compatibles. Features include 32 tracks and automated punch-in and punch-out.

457. ---. Rev. of *Forte II*, from LTA Productions. *Music Technology* Nov. 1988: 83-87. MIDI sequencer for the IBM PC. Compatible with the Roland MPU-401, IBM Music Feature, and Yamaha C1 computer.

458. Kubicky, Jay. "A MIDI Project: A MIDI Interface with Software for the IBM PC." *Byte* June 1986: 199-208. Description of how to build a computer music interface for the IBM PC. Includes an overview of MIDI protocol and a detailed schematic.

459.   Langdell, James.   "Music: The PC's New Frontier."   *PC Magazine* 29 Apr. 1986: 187+ Evaluation of *Sequencer Plus* from Octave Plateau Electronics, *Personal Composer* from Standard Productions, *MIDI Ensemble* from Sight & Sound, and *Music Processing System* from Roland.

460.   ---.   "Singing in the RAM."   *PC Magazine* 7 Aug. 1984: 57. Overview of a program that plays five compositions with several voices.

461.   Latimer, Joey.   Rev. of the C1 Music Computer, from Yamaha. *Compute!* Dec. 1988: 74+ Weighs less than 19 pounds and uses a high-density backlit display. The author states that the display is very sharp if the user is right in front of the machine. As one moves to the side, however, the contrast deteriorates quickly.

462.   Leytze, David.   "Keyboard Report: Music Feature for the IBM PC."   *Keyboard Magazine* Oct. 1987: 128+ Overview of the IBM Music Feature, a music synthesizing card for the PC or PS/2 Model 30. Features include Yamaha FB-01 sounds and functions, 240 preset voices, and 96 user-programmable voices.

463.   ---.   "Short Takes."   Rev. of *MIDI Starter System*, from Music Quest.   *Keyboard Magazine* June 1988: 158.   Peripheral card and MIDI sequencing software for the beginner. Menu-driven and can record up to eight tracks of MIDI data.

464.   Lipson, Stefan B.   Rev. of *Windows* 2.3, from Microsoft.   *Music Technology* Apr. 1988: 67.   General discussion of a menu-driven environment for the IBM PC with only brief references to music applications.

465.   Maki, Jim.   "System: The Yamaha C1 Computer."   *Music, Computers & Software* Dec. 1988: 48+ The author states that along with the impressive array of music related features, the C1 will run most IBM business software. MS-DOS 3.3 and two utility programs are supplied with the C1 i.e., a bulk save program and a MIDI monitor utility.

466.   Many, Chris.   Rev. of *48 Track PC II*, from Robert Keller.   *Music Technology* July 1987: 38-41.   MIDI sequencer for the IBM PC. Features include 600 ppqn resolution, pitch wheel editing, an online help screen, mouse support, and tools for film and video scoring.

467.   ---.   "IBM Music Feature: Yamaha *PlayRec* Sequencer."   Rev. of the IBM Music Feature, from IBM and *PlayRec*, from Yamaha. *Music Technology* Oct. 1987: 48-51.   The IBM Music Feature is a card

for the IBM PC and PS/2 computers that allows the computer to be used as a Yamaha FB-01 sound module with eight polytimbral voices. *PlayRec* is a sequencer package to be used with the IBM Music Feature.

468. ---. Rev. of *Music Printer Plus*, from Temporal Acuity Products. *Music Technology* Dec. 1988: 62-65. Notation software for the IBM PC. Features include step time MIDI input, mouse support, IBM Music Feature compatibility, MIDI volume control for crescendos and diminuendos, and support for trills and grace notes. Includes examples of printed score output.

469. ---. Rev. of *Oberon Music Editor*, from Oberon Systems. *Music Technology* Nov. 1987: 40-42. Music scoring and editing program based on a music typesetting program for mini-computers.

470. ---. Rev. of *Personal Computer Music System*, from Ad Lib Inc. *Music Technology* Feb. 1988: 58-59. A musical starter system for the IBM PC and compatibles that includes an audio plug-in card and sequencing software.

471. ---. "Roland *MESA: Music Editor, Scorer and Arranger*." Rev. of *MESA*, from Roland. *Music Technology* Aug. 1987: 79+ Integrated sequencing, scoring, and printing software for the IBM PC.

472. ---. Rev. of *Score*, from Passport Designs. *Music Technology* May 1988: 77+ Music notation software for the IBM PC. Described as "one of the most comprehensive music manuscript programs available to date." Modular in design (scoring, printing, page layout, justification, and drawing).

473. ---. Rev. of *Tape 'n' Step*, from the MIDI Connection. *Music Technology* July 1988: 78-79. Entry-level sequencer for the IBM PC. Features include 16 track recording (one track per MIDI channel), step recording, copy, delete, looping, and transposition.

474. Marans, Michael. "Keyboard Report: Voyetra *Sequencer Plus Mark III* IBM Sequencer Software." *Keyboard Magazine* Jan. 1989: 134+ Version 2.0 of a sequencer for the IBM and compatibles. Features include 64 tracks, extensive editing, menu operation, transposition, and punch-in/out. Requires a MIDI interface and at least 512 K of RAM.

475. Matzkin, Jonathan. "Make Your Own Melodies: Systems for Amateurs and Virtuosos." *PC Magazine* 26 Jan. 1988: 416+ Systems discussed include the Ad Lib *Personal Computer Music System* and Music Magic Synthesizer. A sidebar discusses the MIDI standard.

476. Meyer, Chris. "Future Possible: The AudioFrame Explained, Pt. I: The Architecture." *Music Technology* Sep. 1988: 22-26. First part of a four-part series covering the AudioFrame Digital Audio Workstation being developed at WaveFrame in Boulder, Colorado. The AudioFrame consists of two main units, a Compaq 386 running under Microsoft *Windows* 2.0 and a large rack-mountable black box called the Digital Audio Rack (DAR).

477. ---. "Future Possible: The AudioFrame Explained, Pt. II: The Present." *Music Technology* Oct. 1988: 44-47. Overview of the hardware and software components of the AudioFrame system. The author discusses the 16-voice digital sampling synthesizer, memory expansion modules, input/output (hardware), and the *SoundProcessor* and *EventProcessor* (software).

478. ---. "Future Possible: The AudioFrame Explained, Pt. III: Mixing and Recording." *Music Technology* Nov. 1988: 34-39. Discussion of how the AudioFrame could significantly enhance, or possibly replace, standard mixing consoles and tape recorders with on-screen/software controls that can be moved with a mouse.

479. ---. "Future Possible: The AudioFrame Explained, Pt. IV: Sound Modeling." *Music Technology* Dec. 1988: 48-52. After a brief overview of the various methods by which standard instrumental sounds may be reproduced e.g., normal synthesis, sampling, and additive resynthesis, the author discusses sound modeling, a process that attempts to reproduce sounds with a set of mathematical equations. Includes a sidebar entitled "Conversation with Roger Powell."

480. "MIDI Meets DOS in a Laptop." *Byte* Nov. 1988: 67. Brief description of the new IBM compatible Yamaha C1 laptop computer. It is designed specifically for musicians featuring 11 MIDI ports (2 in, 1 thru, and 8 out).

481. Milano, D. "Keyboard Report: *Texture* MIDI Sequencer Software." *Keyboard Magazine* July 1985: 90+ Features include auto-punch, up to 1/192 ppqn resolution, tape sync, note-by-note editing, and global editing commands. Requires MPU-401 or Voyetra OP-400/4000 MIDI interface.

482. Miller, Dennis. Rev. of *SampleVision*, from Turtle Beach Softworks. *Music Technology* Jan 1989: 67+ Generic sampling program for the IBM PC. Features include a "Mac-like" operating environment, color support, and extensive editing and looping capabilities. Compatible with most popular samplers.

483. Miller, J. "*Personal Composer*." *Computer Music Journal* 9.4 (1985): 27-37. In-depth discussion of *Personal Composer*, an IBM PC-based integrated software package for music processing. Includes many helpful illustrations.

484. Mocsny, Daniel. "MS-DOS Music: Dominant Functions *Tiff* 1.11." *Music, Computers & Software* Aug. 1988: 58-60. 64-track MIDI sequencer for the IBM PC/XT/AT and compatibles. Requires a MPU-401 interface, 512K, and a hard drive. It is designed for musicians "with at least reasonably good playing skills, as it has neither step entry nor an event editor."

485. ---. "MS-DOS Music: LTA Productions *Forte II*." *Music, Computers & Software* June 1988: 70-71. 32-track sequencer for the IBM PC. Features include tape sync, tempo control, data filtering, and MIDI mapping/channel assignment. The program is key-driven and mouse support is not expected in the near future.

486. ---. "ShorTakes." Rev. of *Personal Computer Music System (PCMS)*, from Ad Lib. *Music, Computers & Software* Apr. 1988: 68. Half-sized music synthesizer card (11 voice multitimbral). Includes *Visual Composer* software, *Juke Box* software (playback), *Instrument Maker* software (sound design), and *Championship #1* and *Basic Concepts* software (music theory instruction).

487. Musica, Ciani. "MCS Sound Design." *Music, Computers & Software* Feb.-Mar. 1988: 82-84. Suzanne Ciani describes the equipment she uses in live performance. Her setup includes an IBM clone (CMS computers) and *Texture* sequencing software from Magnetic Music.

488. Newquist, Harvey. "Micro Reviews." Rev. of *Ensoniq Master Editor/Librarian*, from SoundQuest. *Music Technology* Oct. 1988: 85. Software for the PC that allows the user to control most of the features of the Ensoniq ESQ1 and SQ80 synthesizers.

489. ---. Rev. of *MIDI Starter System*, from Music Quest Inc. *Music Technology* June 1988: 76-77. Hardware/software MIDI package intended for beginners. Includes a MIDI interface, sequencer, DX editor/librarian and CZ editor/librarian, and a MIDI trace utility for visual monitoring.

490. ---. Rev. of *PC Desktop Music Studio,* from Roland Corp. *Music Technology* Aug. 1988: 76-77. An integrated package that includes the MT32 multitimbral sound module, *EASE Songmaker Software* (sequencer and notation), a MPU-IPC MIDI interface card, and a MIDI cable. For the IBM PC/XT/AT.

491.   ---.   Rev. of The Yamaha C1 Music Computer.   *Music Technology* Dec. 1988: 72-75.   Features include IBM compatibility, two faders built into the keyboard, SMPTE sync ports, and a built-in music notation font for scoring. The C1 weighs 18 pounds and 12 ounces and requires continuous AC current. The author includes a list of compatible music software.

492.   ---.   Rev. of *FDSoft*, from Lyre.   *Music Technology* Apr. 1988: 72-74.   An additive synthesis program for the IBM PC that can resynthesize samples received over MIDI.

493.   Osteen, Gary.   "Synchronized Recording with Virtual MIDI Tracks."   *Electronic Musician* Feb. 1988: 62+   The author describes his experience with synchronizing seven tracks of tape recorded music with a computer sequencer (*Texture*).

494.   Peters, Constantine.   MS-DOS Music: MIDI Concepts *Sequencers I, II*, and *III*."   *Music, Computers & Software* Jan. 1989: 58-59.   A series of MIDI sequencers for the IBM and compatibles ranging in price and level of sophistication. All require at least 512K of RAM.

495.   ---.   "MS-DOS Music: Music Quest MQX-32 MIDI Interface Card."   *Music, Computers & Software* Dec. 1988: 58+   Features include two independent controllable MIDI-out ports and SMPTE or Chase Lock Synchronization. Works well with *Personal Composer*, *Cakewalk*, and *Forte*. MPU-401 compatible.

496.   ---.   "MS-DOS Music: Temporal Acuity *Music Printer Plus*."   *Music, Computers & Software* Nov. 1988: 62-64.   Music processing software for the IBM PC, XT, AT, PS/2 or compatible. Features include high quality printout and MIDI performance. Although it lacks a real time sequencer for input, it does include Logitec mouse support, extensive online help, and an 800 help line.

497.   Poole, Lon.   "Programming Sound in BASIC."   *PC World* July 1983: 176-84.   Explores the full range of sounds the PC can produce and provides listings for several melodies. Excerpt from *Using Your IBM Personal Computer*, a book by Lon Poole.

498.   Porter, Martin.   "16-Bit Seduction of Roger Powell."   *PC Magazine* 3 Apr. 1984: 156-60.

499.   Rosch, Winn L.   "Tecmar Arranging PC Compositions: Ohio Firm Developing Advanced Music Synthesizer for PC Family."   *PC Magazine* 25 Dec. 1984: 41.   Preview of a system board for the IBM PC, XT, and AT that will include control software capable of manipulating up to 16 timbres simultaneously.

500. Rychner, Lorenz. Rev. of *TX802 Graphic Editing System*, from Bacchus Software Systems. *Music Technology* May 1988: 70. Editor/librarian software for the IBM PC or PS/2 and the Yamaha TX802 or DX7II. Features include custom screen and window configurations, and simultaneous display of up to 64 voices.

501. Scholz, Carter. Rev. of *48 Track PC* 3.0, from Robert Keller. *Electronic Musician* Nov. 1988: 86+ MIDI sequencer for the IBM PC. The author states that one of its most impressive features is its timing resolution i.e., 600 ppqn.

502. ---. "Big Blue Does MIDI: A Survey." *Electronic Musician* Apr. 1988: 46+ General discussion of the music capabilities of the IBM PC and PS/2 computers. Topics discussed include MIDI interfaces, sequencers, scoring software, and other music software. Includes a list of products, prices, and manufacturers.

503. ---. Rev. of *Cakewalk Professional*, from Twelve Tone Systems. *Music Technology* Jan. 1989: 65. The author stresses that this is not the "next version" of *Cakewalk* 2.0. *CP* is a new program designed to work with the Music Quest MQX32 MIDI interface with 2 ports (32 MIDI channels). It can also be used with any MPU-compatible MIDI interface.

504. ---. Rev. of CMIDI, from CMIDI. *Music Technology* Dec. 1988: 60-61. MIDI programming language for the IBM PC. Compatible with Microsoft's Quick C and Borland's Turbo C.

505. ---. Rev. of *FDSoft*, from Lyre Inc. *Electronic Musician* Dec. 1988: 114+ Sample editor for the IBM. Features include additive synthesis, resynthesis, harmonic analysis, and spectral editing.

506. ---. "First Take: Ad Lib Music Synthesizer." *Electronic Musician* May 1988: 83-84. Brief description of Ad Lib, a plug-in synthesizer card for the IBM PC. Intended for beginners, it is capable of sounding nine different monophonic instruments at once through a headphone jack.

507. ---. "First Take: Dominant Functions *Tiff* Sequencing Software." *Electronic Musician* June 1988: 100. Inexpensive MIDI sequencer for the IBM PC. Features exclude quantizing, step entry, and individual note editing. Hard disk required.

508. ---. "First Take: Magnetic Music *Pyramid* Voice Editor/Librarian for the DX/TX." *Electronic Musician* Sep. 1988: 72-73. For the Yamaha DX/TX synthesizers and the IBM PC. Features pull-down menus, editable note memory of 16 notes, and a utility that allows the user to browse or auto-search through files and print lists of voices.

509. ---. "First Take: Music Quest *MIDI Starter System.*" *Electronic Musician* July 1988: 132. System includes a half-size MIDI interface card, an 8-track sequencer, voice editors for several synthesizers, and a MIDI trace utility.

510. ---. "First Take: *PC Desktop Music Studio.*" *Electronic Musician* Jan. 1989: 94-95. Integrated package from Roland Corp. consisting of an MT-32 sound module, MPU-IPC MIDI interface, MIDI cables, and *EASE* (*Easy Arranging and Sequencing Environment*) software.

511. ---. Rev. of *FWAP!*, and *TrackGenie*, from LTA Productions. *Electronic Musician* Mar. 1989: 84-87.   Drum machine and algorithmic composition programs respectively. Both programs can run in conjunction with *Forte II*, a sequencer from LTA Productions, or can be used as stand-alone applications.

512. ---. Rev. of *MusiCard*, from Music Magic. *Electronic Musician* Dec. 1987: 86+ In-depth review of a plug-in synthesis board with software for the IBM PC. One card provides up to 16 multitimbral stereo voices and as many as four cards can run on one system. Input can be through a MIDI keyboard or the computer keyboard.

513. ---. Rev. of *Personal Composer* 2.0, from Jim Miller. *Electronic Musician* Sep. 1988: 92+ Scoring/sequencing software for the IBM PC/PS2. Includes several modules designed to work together i.e., score editor, recorder, event editor, and a DX/TX7 editor/librarian. The program occupies 1MB of hard disk space and requires the Roland MPU-401 interface or the IBM Music Feature.

514. ---. Rev. of *Score*, from Passport Designs. *Electronic Musician* Sep. 1988: 76+ Professional-level music publishing software. *Score* is PostScript compatible and is described as being the most powerful scoring program currently available. Includes illustrations and a printed excerpt from the *Concord Sonata* by Charles Ives. Although loaded with features, the program is also described as being very complex and difficult to learn.

515. ---. "Six Power Sequencers for the IBM." *Electronic Musician* Jan. 1989: 57+ Sequencers discussed are *Cakewalk* (Twelve Tone Systems), *48 Track PC* (Robert Keller), *Sequencer Plus* (Voyetra), *Personal Composer* 2.0 (Jim Miller), *Texture* (Magnetic Music), and *Forte II* (LTA Productions). Includes a feature comparison chart.

516. ---. "*SPXFILE*: An SPX90 Librarian." *Electronic Musician* June 1988: 44+ An IBM/clone program in Turbo Pascal that can upload or download all SPX90 user memory. The Yamaha SPX90, a digital multieffects unit, has had problems with the MIDI out. This article presents a quick and effective solution.

517. "Send in the Clones." *Music, Computers & Software* May 1987: 38+ A discussion of companies marketing PC compatibles specifically for music applications.

518. Sirota, Warren. "MIDI: The Music Interface." *PC World* Oct. 1985: 208-15. Nuts and bolts description of MIDI. Discusses the Roland MPU-401 PC to MIDI Card and other interfacing devices. Also a good explanation of the MIDI specification 1.0.

519. ---. "PCjr. Strikes a Chord." *PC World* July 1984: 204-09. Description of the music capabilities of the PCjr. including how to produce three-voice chords. The author also describes how to connect the PCjr. to a stereo system.

520. ---. "Three-Part Harmony." *PC World* Aug. 1984: 200-06. Three-voice programming for the PCjr.

521. Stockford, James. "*Personal Composer*." Rev. of *Personal Composer*. *Whole Earth Review* Winter 1985: 111. MIDI sequencing/notation software for the IBM PC. Features include automatic transposition, MIDIgraphic editing, score editing, and playback.

522. ---. "*Sequencer Plus*." Rev. of *Sequencer Plus*. *Whole Earth Review* Winter 1985: 111. Song files can be transcribed into conventional notation by using *The Copyist* from Dr. T. *Sequencer Plus* is available at three levels of sophistication (Mark I, II, & III) and may be upgraded from lower versions.

523. Stone, Michael. Rev. of *Tiff* Sequencer, from Dominant Functions, Inc. *Music Technology* Feb. 1988: 70-71. Inexpensive sequencer for the IBM PC. Features 64 tracks and requires DOS 2.1 or higher, 320 K of memory, and an MPU-401 or compatible interface.

524. ---. Rev. of *TX81Z Graphic Editing System*, from Bacchus. *Music Technology* Sep. 1987: 44-46. Graphic editing system for Yamaha's TX81Z's and the IBM PC.

525. Swearingen, Donald. "MIDI Programming: Processing the MPU-401 Track Data Stream." *Byte* June 1986: 211-24. Various software algorithms, constructed in Turbo Pascal for an IBM PC, are used to process a MIDI data stream. The various procedures include scaling MIDI velocity values, transposition of MIDI pitches, changing MIDI channel data, and quantizing timing values.

526. Tamm, A. C. "IBM PC Display Systems for the Musician." *Electronic Musician* July 1986: 52+

527.   Tello, Ernie.   Rev. of *Personal Composer* 2.0, from Jim Miller/Personal Composer.   *Music Technology* July 1988: 95-98. Updated sequencer/notation software for the IBM PC/PS 2. Features include 32 tracks, an event editor, IBM Music Feature support, extensive scoring capabilities, and a patch editor/librarian for the Yamaha DX7 and TX7 synthesizers.

528.   Trivette, Donald.   "Music for Amateurs."   *Compute!* Jan. 1985: 138-40.   General discussion of how the IBM PC and PCjr. can be used in music applications.

529.   Tully, Tim.   Rev. of *PlayRec*, from Yamaha.   *Electronic Musician* Dec. 1987: 83-84.   Sequencing software to be used with the IBM Music Feature. Features 48 preset voices, 16 tracks, and simple voice-editing.

530.   Vail, Mark.   "Short Takes: Dominant Functions *Tiff* MIDI Sequencer for IBM PCs and Compatibles."   *Keyboard Magazine* May 1988: 155.   Brief description and evaluation. Records and plays 64 tracks of MIDI data including pitch-bend, modulation wheel, after-touch, and program change.

Macintosh

531. Aikin, Jim. "Keyboard Report: *TurboSynth* Sample Synthesizer for the Mac." *Keyboard Magazine* Oct. 1988: 139+ Modular synthesis and sample processor software for the Macintosh from Digidesign. Features include waveform drawing and editing, filtering, amplitude contouring, and frequency shifting.

532. ---. "Short Takes: *Opcode D-50 Editor/Librarian*." *Keyboard Magazine* May 1988: 144-45. Compared with *Dr. T's D-50 Editor/Librarian*. Opcode's product is a bit more expensive but it allows the user to open various windows so different parameters can be edited by merely switching back and forth.

533. Aker, Sharon Zardetto. "Of Mice and Music." Rev. of *ConcertWare*, from Great Wave and *Professional Composer*, from Mark of the Unicorn. *A+* Oct. 1985: 132-38. *ConcertWare* is a music composition program with three parts i.e., *Instrument Maker*, *Music Writer*, and *Music Player* that allows one to enter music and play it back using a variety of instrumental sounds. *Professional Composer* is a sophisticated music transcription program.

534. ---. "Power Basic, Pt. XIII: *Music Writer*: You and Your MS BASIC Programs Can Now Make Beautiful Music Together." *Nibble Mac: The Magazine for Macintosh Enthusiasts* 3.7 (1988): 71+ Program for writing Sound statements that can be stored as text files and imported to any program.

535. ---. "Quick Clicks." Rev. of *Jam Session*, from Broderbund. *MacUser* July 1988: 113+ Interactive software that allows one to use the Macintosh keyboard as a musical instrument and play along with supporting harmonies. No previous knowledge of music is required.

536. Anderton, Craig. Rev. of *Alchemy* 1.2, from Blank Software. *Electronic Musician* Feb. 1989: 114+ Sample editor for the Macintosh Plus, SE, or II. Features include a unique "overview" window that displays a longer (but smaller) portion of a sample along the top of the screen. The article is well illustrated and includes a sidebar entitled "SCSI Data Transfer."

537. ---. "Editing on the Macintosh." *Electronic Musician* Apr. 1988: 102. Brief discussion of *MPX820 Editor/Librarian* from Opcode. Designed to work in conjunction with the MPX820 MIDI-automated audio mixer from Akai Professional.

538. ---. "First Take: Digital Music Service's *TX81Z Pro*." *Electronic Musician* Feb. 1988: 113. Comprehensive editor/librarian for Yamaha's TX81Z and the Macintosh.

539. ---. "First Take: *MacDrums* by Coda Music Software." *Electronic Musician* Feb. 1988: 112-13. Drum machine software for the Macintosh that includes 35 different sampled sounds. Designed as an entry-level program that is easier to use than a drum machine but not as powerful.

540. ---. "*Master Tracks Pro* for the Mac." Rev. of *Master Tracks Pro*, from Passport Designs. *Electronic Musician* Aug. 1987: 68+ Multitrack MIDI sequencer for the Macintosh. Features include 64 tracks, conductor track for setting meter and tempo, song editor, sysex librarian, and zoom in/out on data.

541. Austin, K. "*The Mac/Mirage Interface*: Sound Lab Software." *Electronic Musician* Feb. 1986: 50-52. Sampling program.

542. ---. "Southworth's *Total Music*." Rev. of *Total Music*, from Southworth. *Electronic Musician* Jan. 1986: 60+ Integrated sequencer/notation software. Features include the ability to record from two keyboards at once, punch-in and punch-out, and simultaneous playing of 8 tracks at a time. Comes with a MIDI interface card.

543. Barnett, David. "A Beautiful Duet." Rev. of *MIDIMac Sequencer* 2.5, from Opcode and *Deluxe Music Construction Set*, from Electronic Arts. *Macworld* Mar. 1987: 142-43. Sequencing and music composition/printing software respectively.

544. ---. "Musical Interlude: *Performer* 1.22." Rev. of *Performer* 1.22, from Mark of the Unicorn. *Macworld* Dec. 1986: 140. Sequencer and editor. Compatible with *Professional Composer* from Mark of the Unicorn for score transcription.

545. ---. "Play It Again, Mac!" *MacUser* Mar. 1986: 75+ In-depth discussion of *Deluxe Music Construction Set*, from Electronic Arts. Features include music input with traditional notation and MIDI compatibility. Includes illustrations.

546. ---. "Software City: New Mac Sequencers from Opcode and Mark of the Unicorn." *Musician* Dec. 1986: 72+

547. Beamer, Scott. "Wiring Your Mac for Sound." *Macworld* Apr. 1988: 117-18. Brief description of MacRecorder from Farallon, a sound digitizer for the Macintosh.

548. Bell, Bryan. "New Music." *Macworld* June 1987: 111. Brief overview of six products shown at the National Association of Music Merchants Convention.

549. Bell, Jack. "Make Music with Macintosh." Rev. of *MusicWorks*, from Hayden Software. *Personal Computing* May 1985: 178. Music composition software that allows one to compose using either conventional staff notation or a grid that emulates a piano keyboard.

550. Bernardo, Mario Sergio. "*ConcertWare* + and *SongPainter*: Two Software Packages for Making Music on the Macintosh." Rev. of *ConcertWare* +, from Great Wave and *SongPainter*, from Rubicon. *Byte* June 1986: 273-76.

551. Biedny, David. "MIDI to the Macs: You, Mac and MIDI Lead a Symphony from the Podium." *MacUser* Dec. 1985: 91. Excellent overview of MIDI technology and related terms e.g., sequencing, quantizing, and patch libraries. Includes brief descriptions of products for the Macintosh e.g., *Total Music, StudioMac, MusicWorks, MIDIMac Sequencer*, and *ConcertWare + MIDI*.

552. ---. "Roll over Beethoven: Three Innovative Programs Offer Different Ways of Using Your Mac to Write and Generate Music. Each One Commands Its Own Audience." *MacUser* Oct. 1985: 84+ Descriptive overview of *MusicWorks* (Hayden), *ConcertWare* (Great Wave), and *Professional Composer* (Mark of the Unicorn).

553. ---. "Six-Part Harmony: Is It the Real Thing Or Is It Just *Studio Session*?" *MacUser* Dec. 1986: 110+ In-depth discussion of *Studio Session*, a music composition program that features six-voice playback, traditional notation display, and over 80 instrumental sounds. Includes illustrations.

554. Birchall, Steve. "Do, Re, Mouse: *Music Mouse* Gives You Computer-Assisted Improvisation and Leaves You Free to Jam."

MacUser May 1987: 136-40. Evaluation of *Music Mouse*, a real time performance application that lets the user become involved in playing music by using the mouse as a musical instrument.

555. Branst, Lee, and Ed Dorobek. "No Musical Stone Unturned." *Music Technology* Apr. 1988: 84-87. Interview with Carl Stone, electronic musician. Describes how Stone uses the Macintosh and software such as *Jam Factory*, *Performer*, and *Opcode Sequencer* in his musical activities.

556. Breen, Christopher. "Pick a Pack of MIDI." *MacUser* Dec. 1988: 41. Brief overview of *MIDIPack*, a program from CTM Development that allows the user to quickly alter parameters such as tempo, instrumentation, and overall length of a sequence.

557. Burger, Jeff. Rev. of *One-Step*, from Southworth. *Music Technology* July 1988: 86-87. Inexpensive MIDI sequencer for the Macintosh. Features include 16 tracks, global editing, solo, record, looping, and punch-in/out.

558. Burgess, Jim. "Getting More Miles Per Mac." *Music Technology* June 1987: 26-27. Tips on how to increase the speed and efficiency of the Macintosh.

559. ---. Rev. of *HyperCard*, from Apple. *Music Technology* Nov. 1987: 20-22. Interactive "database-type" program that can be used to look for and store text, custom graphics, digitized photographs, and sampled sounds.

560. ---. "Intelligent Music *Jam Factory*: Software for the Macintosh." Rev. of *Jam Factory*, from Intelligent Music. *Music Technology* Feb. 1987: 36-38. *Jam Factory* is a music composition program that allows the user to record, manipulate, control, and interact with the performance in real time.

561. ---. "Intelligent Music *M*: Software for the Apple Macintosh." Rev. of *M*, from Intelligent Music. *Music Technology* Mar. 1987: 44-46. A music processor that accepts input from a variety of sources and permits real time manipulation of a performance by controlling a wide range of variables.

562. ---. "Intelligent Music *UpBeat*: Software for the Macintosh." Rev. of *UpBeat*, from Intelligent Music. *Music Technology* Aug. 1987: 60-63. A flexible program for computer-based sequencing and drum pattern programming.

563. ---. Rev. of *Master Tracks Pro*, from Passport Designs. *Music Technology* July 1987: 74-77. MIDI sequencer for the Macintosh.

564. ---. "The New Macintosh." *Music Technology* May 1987: 15-17. In-depth discussion of the Macintosh SE and II. The SE is considered an expandable high-performance Mac Plus. It uses the same microprocessor (Motorola 68000) as the original Macintosh but runs about 15-20% faster than the Plus. The Macintosh II features a 68020 32-bit microprocessor, color with 640 x 480 pixel resolution, and four-voice stereo sound generation.

565. ---. Rev. of *Performer* 2.2, from Mark of the Unicorn. *Music Technology* Jan. 1988: 68+ Sequencer for the Macintosh 512, Plus, or SE. Features a timing accuracy of 480 ppqn, track looping on each track, and compatibility with *Professional Composer*, a notation program also from Mark of the Unicorn.

566. Butler, Chris, and Bill Lewis. "David Van Tieghem: A Percussionist Finds the Perfect Axe for the Modern Composer... A Mac." *Music, Computers & Software* Apr. 1988: 22+ Interesting discussion of how composer David Van Tieghem uses a Macintosh SE and Opcode's sequencer in his musical activities.

567. Clement, Thomas J. "Micro Reviews." Rev. of *Sound Designer Universal* 1.3, from Digidesign. *Music Technology* Oct. 1988: 84-85. Sample editing software that supports a wide variety of samplers e.g., Akai S900, X7000, and S700; Casio FZ1 and FZ10M; and Ensoniq Mirage and EPS.

568. Coale, Kristi. "I Want My M3TV." *MacUser* Dec. 1988: 40. Brief overview of *The Open Door: Macintosh, MIDI, and Music*, a VHS video from Apple Computer Co. The video is interesting but consists mainly of interviews with musicians who use the Macintosh in their music acitvities. It contains little information regarding specific programs and techniques.

569. Combs, Jim. "Apple Music: Great Wave *Concertware + MIDI*." *Music, Computers & Software* Aug. 1988: 54-55. A low-cost, integrated sequencer/transcriber for the Macintosh. Consists of three programs i.e., *Music Writer*, *Music Player*, and *Instrument Maker*. *Music Writer*, the recorder/transcriber, can record 8 tracks with up to 8 note polyphony per track.

570. ---. "Mac II/SE." *Music, Computers & Software* June 1987: 39+ Description and evaluation of the new Macintosh computers with special attention given to the Macintosh II. The author states that the open architecture and more sophisticated sound chip give the Mac II tremendous potential as a musician's tool.

571. Cummings, S. "Keyboard Report: Mark of the Unicorn *Performer* Sequencer for the Macintosh." *Keyboard Magazine* May

1986: 124+ High-end MIDI sequencer with features that include multitrack recording, error-correction commands, step time recording, and 50,000 note capacity.

572. ---. "Keyboard Report: Opcode Systems *MIDIMac Sequencer* for the Macintosh." *Keyboard Magazine* Nov. 1985: 92+ Features include 66,000 note capacity, simultaneous playback of up to 16 sequences, independent loop for each track, and two kinds of quantization with 18 resolutions. If used with *Switcher*, the program has the ability to interact with *MIDIMac Patch Editor/Librarian*.

573. ---. "Keyboard Report: Southworth *Total Music* Macintosh Software." *Keyboard Magazine* Dec. 1985: 114+ Sequencer/notation software for the Macintosh. Features include auto punch-in and punch-out, 99 tracks, simultaneous playing of 8 tracks at a time, and automatic beaming.

574. ---. "Music for Beginners: A Guide to Playing, Recording, and Learning Music on the Mac." *Macworld* April 1989: 124-129. Excellent overview of music and the Macintosh. Topics discussed include sequencing and scoring software, MIDI, and synthesizer basics. The author also includes helpful illustrations of various MIDI configurations ranging from simple to complex.

575. Davies, Rick. "Digidesign *SoftSynth* & *Burner*: Software for the Apple Macintosh." Rev. of *SoftSynth* and *Burner*, from Digidesign. *Music Technology* Sep. 1986: 60-62. *Burner* allows the user to create samples and burn sample data into EPROMs for use in drum machines. *SoftSynth* uses additive synthesis to create sound samples on the Macintosh.

576. ---. Rev. of *MacDrums*, from Coda. *Music Technology* Apr. 1988: 66. Drum machine software for the Macintosh. The program provides a library of 35 digitized drum sounds and may be used as a drum pattern programmer for MIDI drum voices.

577. ---. Rev. of *TX81Z Editor/Librarian*, from Beaverton Digital Systems. *Music Technology* Feb. 1988: 67. Voice editing program for the Yamaha TX81Z and the Macintosh.

578. De Furia, Steve. "Software for Musicians: A MIDI Channel-Mapping Program to Build On." *Keyboard Magazine* Feb. 1989: 118+ Presents a program written in Lightspeed Pascal and MIDIPascal for the Macintosh. The author states that "with a little work" it can be adapted for use on other computers.

579. ---. "Software for Musicians: Compiling Stand-Alone Applications for the Macintosh." *Keyboard Magazine* Sep. 1988: 131. The technique described employs MicroSoft BASIC/MIDIBASIC.

580. ---. "Software for Musicians: Installing MIDIBASIC as a Code Resource." *Keyboard Magazine* Oct. 1988: 132. Offers a solution to the legal problem of how one can incorporate MIDIBASIC routines in a MIDI program and still distribute it to people who do not have access to MIDIBASIC.

581. ---. "Software for Musicians: MIDI Program Example: Turning Our Microtuning Librarian into an Editor." *Keyboard Magazine* Dec. 1987: 128. Revision of a program presented in the October 1987 issue of *Keyboard Magazine*. See #584.

582. ---. "Software for Musicians: More MIDIBASIC for the Mac: Subroutines for Last Month's Micro-Tuning Librarian." *Keyboard Magazine* Nov. 1987: 126. Subroutines presented allow one to name microtuning files and save them to disk. See #584.

583. ---. "Software for Musicians: Over the Wires and Thru the Goods." *Keyboard Magazine* Dec. 1988: 120+ Presents a program called *THRU DISPLAY* that turns a Macintosh into a MIDI thru data display. The program is written in Lightspeed Pascal with routines from Altech's MIDIPascal code library.

584. ---. "Software for Musicians: Programming Example: Microtuning Editor/Librarian." *Keyboard Magazine* Oct. 1987: 117. A MIDIBASIC program that requests a Yahama device to transmit its microtuning edit buffer to the Mac.

585. ---. "Software for Musicians: Designing a Music Spreadsheet from Scratch." *Keyboard Magazine* Feb. 1988: 129-30. Discusses designing a music spreadsheet using MS BASIC. Includes a MIDIBASIC program that may be helpful in a variety of musical calculations e.g., duration, tempos, etc.

586. ---. "Software for Musicians: Son of Designing a Program from Scratch." *Keyboard Magazine* Mar. 1988: 129. Continuation of last month's article concerning a "Music Math Program." Includes updated subroutines to a MIDIBASIC program that calculate a variety of musical values. See #585.

587. ---. "Software for Musicians: The Last Will and Testament of Music Math." *Keyboard Magazine* Apr. 1988: 127. Updated subroutines for a MIDIBASIC program that figure a variety of musical calculations e.g., sample loop sizes, durational values, etc. See #585 and #586.

588. Deutsch, Larry-Stuart. "Sound -- the Easy Way." Rev. of MacRecorder, from Farallon Computing. *Macworld* June 1988: 150-51. Sound recording, editing, mixing, and special effects system for the Macintosh. Features include a sound digitizer, *SoundEdit*

software for recording, and *HyperSound* software for storing sounds in *HyperCard* applications.

589.   Doerschuk, Bob.   "Disabilities Diminish with MIDI." *Keyboard Magazine* July 1988: 32-33. Teddy Pendergrass and Johnnie Wilder Jr. describe how they have been able to continue their musical careers despite their handicaps with a Macintosh and related MIDI equipment.

590.   ---.   "William Aura: New Age by Choice." *Keyboard Magazine* Oct. 1988: 43-44. Studio musician William Aura discusses how he became involved in the "New Age Movement." His equipment includes a Macintosh Plus and Opcode software. He states that "Opcode is much more new age than *Performer. Performer* seems best for people who start at the beginning of a song and play all the way through."

591.   Dolen, William.   "Making (Sound) Waves with Macintosh." *Call A.P.P.L.E.* Dec. 1985: 40-44. Waveform synthesis program written in BASIC.

592.   ---.   "Your Well Tempered Music Synthesizer." *Call A.P.P.L.E.* Feb. 1986: 14-16. Tutorial on tuning the Macintosh when using it as a music synthesizer.

593.   Donovan, Joe.   "Clannad: Wrapping Gaelic Traditions Around MIDI and the Macintosh Computer." *Music, Computers & Software* Oct. 1988: 32-33. Discussion of how the Irish rock band, Clannad, uses the Macintosh and *Performer* in their musical activities.

594.   ---.   "Stanley Jordan Hammers On." *Music, Computers & Software* Aug. 1988: 34+ Jordon states that he uses Opcode's patch editors and librarians along with an Apple Macintosh, *Performer*, and *Deluxe Music Construction Set* "to compose music in the form of sequences or in printed-out notation."

595.   Elliott, Kevin.   "Note Cards: *HyperCard* Could Become the Ultimate Musical Instrument like the Song Says, 'Be It Ever So Humble, There's No Place like Home.'" *MacUser* Oct. 1988: 309+ Overview of *HyperCard* stacks for music applications. Most of the ones described e.g., *HyperTunes, Sound Scripter,* and *Hyper-Song,* are free or relatively inexpensive. *HyperTunes* is interesting as it displays a keyboard and note values for rapid input of sound scripts.

596.   Floeter, Valerie A., and Alan D. Floeter.   "Mac Music Makers." Rev. of *ConcertWare,* from Great Wave Software; *MusicWorks,* from Hayden Software; and *MacMusic,* from Utopian Software. *Nibble* Aug. 1985: 122-30.

597. Frederick, D. "Keyboard Report: Airdrums, Rhythm Stick, *Music Mouse*: Make Mine MIDI, But Hold the Keys." *Keyboard Magazine* Jan. 1987: 131+ Brief discussion of *Music Mouse*, a MIDI performance program for the Macintosh that allows the user to use the mouse as a musical instrument in real time.

598. Freff. "Keyboard Report: Opcode Systems Yamaha Editor/Librarians for the Mac." *Keyboard Magazine* Jan. 1989: 128-32. Overview of editor/librarians for the DX/TX, TX81Z/DX11/DX21, FB-01, and SPX90. Features include graphic editing, the ability to link different instruments and instrument files, playback, and algorithms for the creation of sounds.

599. ---. "MIDI for the Macintosh: The First Generation of Products." *A+* Feb. 1986: 116+ Includes a list of product information e.g., programs and addresses of publishers.

600. ---. "Patchwork: Editors and Librarians Can Be a Synthesizer's Best Friends. They'll Organize and Enhance All Your Batches of Patches." *MacUser* Feb. 1989: 234+ Excellent coverage of four editor/librarians for the Macintosh and Roland D-50 synthesizer i.e., *Opcode D-50*, *Valhala D-50*, *Dr. T's D-50*, and *Beaverton D-50*. Features of each program are discussed in detail. Includes illustrations.

601. ---. "Rhythm 'n' Views: What a Difference a Year Makes." *MacUser* Dec. 1988: 223+ Brief overview of the 1988 NAMM (National Association of Music Merchants) Expo.

602. ---. "Rhythm 'n' Views: What It Isn't, What It Is." *MacUser* Sep. 1988: 265-66. Introduction of a new column dealing with the Macintosh and music. The column intends to address primarily the music potential of the Macintosh as a musical instrument "in its own right" as well as MIDI applications.

603. ---. "Rhythm 'n' Views: Winning Hearts and Minds (and Wallets)" *MacUser* Jan. 1989: 223-24. Interesting discussion of how Apple Computer Company is gradually moving deeper into the music market. The author states that the Macintosh has a great deal of potential for success in the music business but prices will have to drop before it can surpass Atari and IBM as the number one selling computer for music applications.

604. ---. "Software City (*Total Music*; *Sound Designer*)" Rev. of *Total Music* and *Sound Designer*. *Musician* Jan. 1986: 86.

605. Gibson, Robert S. T. "Aural Fixation." *MacUser* Apr. 1988: 186+ In-depth evaluation of *SoundWave* from Impulse, a sound digitizer

for the Macintosh that allows one to customize menus, record new sounds, and edit existing sounds. Is not compatible with *Switcher*.

606. Goehner, Ken. "A Little Byte Music." Rev. of *Studio Session* 1.0. *Macworld* Nov. 1987: 158-59. Music composition software from Bogas Productions. Contains an editor and a player that can produce up to six voices of digitized sound.

607. Gotcher, Peter. "Mac the Axe." *Electronic Musician* Feb. 1986: 18-21. MIDI, transcription, and signal processing.

608. ---. "Keyboard Clinic #11: Advanced Applications for *Sound Designer*." *Keyboard Magazine* Feb. 1988: 68+ In-depth discussion of *Sound Designer* from Digidesign. Topics include re-enveloping, controlled clipping, wavetable synthesis, and removing DC offsets.

609. Greenwald, T. "Intelligent Music: *Jam Factory* and *M*." *Musicians' Equipment Guide* Summer 1987: 71+ Evaluation of two patch generators for the Macintosh.

610. ---. "Keyboard Report: *Jam Factory* and *M*, Automated Improvisation Software." *Keyboard Magazine* Feb. 1987: 141+

611. ---. "Keyboard Report: *Master Tracks Pro*, Passport Sequencer for the Macintosh." *Keyboard Magazine* July 1987: 142+ Features include on-screen transport controls, 64 tracks of real time input, and step-editing.

612. ---. "Keyboard Report: *UpBeat* Intelligent Drum Machine Programmer." *Keyboard Magazine* Oct. 1987: 152+ Sequencer, visual editor, and automatic variation generator for drum machines and synthesizers from Intelligent Music.

613. ---. "*MIDIMac*: Opcode Sequencer for the Mac." *Keyboard Magazine* Mar. 1987: 134-40. Version 2.5. Features include real time recording of tempo changes, song pointer synchronization with SMPTE/MIDI interfaces, and independent track looping. Compatible with *Deluxe Music Construction Set* and *Professional Composer*.

614. Hallerman, David. Rev. of MacRecorder, from Farallon Computing. *Family & Home Office Computing* May 1988: 62. Sound digitizer for the Macintosh that is capable of sampling sounds at four different rates i.e., 5.5 KHz to 22 KHz. Includes two programs for control, *SoundEdit* and *HyperSound*.

615. Heid, Jim. "Getting Started with Music: Scoring and Sequencing, Mastering MIDI, and Outfitting Your Mac to Make Music." *Macworld* Nov. 1987: 283+ General overview of music

software available for the Macintosh. A list of music software, MIDI interfaces, and manufacturers is included.

616. ---. "Is It Live Or Is It Mac?" *Macworld* Aug. 1986: 124-27. Discussion of new digitizers, sound editors, sound libraries, and other audio products available for the Macintosh.

617. ---. "Making Tracks." Rev. of *MegaTrack* Version XL, from Musicworks. *Macworld* Sep. 1986: 172-76. MIDI sequencer for the Macintosh. Features include an unlimited track capacity, 32 MIDI channel assignments, variable zoom, extensive graphic editing features, and expandable note capacity.

618. ---. "Musical Wares." *Macworld* Feb. 1986: 93-99. General discussion of music products for the Macintosh including software, synthesizers, and MIDI interfaces. Also includes a sidebar that explains the Musical Instrument Digital Interface (MIDI).

619. Heinbuch, Dean. Rev. of *TX81Z Editor/Librarian*, from Beaverton Digital Systems. *Electronic Musician* July 1988: 138-39. Version 1.2 of a random patch generator for the Macintosh and the Yamaha TX81Z.

620. Holsinger, Erik. "Film Scoring Simplified." *Macworld* Sep. 1987: 158-60. Description of *Cue: the Film Music System*, 1.0. from Opcode and *Clicktracks*, 2.0 from Scores Unlimited. Software packages that "aid in film scoring by providing cue sheets and converting film tempos to musical tempos."

621. "HyperTips: Sounds and Graphics: Sound and Graphics Add More Than Pizzazz to Your Stacks." *Nibble Mac: the Magazine for Macintosh Enthusiasts* 3.3 (1988): 28-30. Description of how one can use sound and graphics in *HyperCard* stacks. Excerpt from *HyperCard Power: Techniques and Scripts* by Carol Kaehler.

622. Iams, Paul. "Making Macbeth: The Mac Musician." *MACazine* Mar. 1987: 52-55. Interesting account of how the author used *Studio Session* (Bogas Productions) to create a music demo for his six year-old daughter, Beth. A copy of the demo can be purchased from the author. Includes illustrations.

623. Ito, Russell. "Audible Motion." *MacUser*, Mar. 1989: 116-118. Interesting discussion of "MIDIDancer," a MIDI system that turns motion into music using position sensors, radio transmitters, a radio receiver, and a Macintosh to play various synthesizers. The position sensors are attached to the dancer's arm and leg joints while he or she performs.

624. Kelly, Kevin. "*ConcertWare*." Rev. of *ConcertWare*, from Great Wave Software. *Whole Earth Review* Winter 1985: 111. Music composition software for the Macintosh. Features include sound design and conventional staff notation.

625. Kempton, David. "Southworth's *JamBox/4+*" Rev. of *JamBox/4+ Electronic Musician* Oct. 1987: 86+ SMPTE/MIDI interface for the Macintosh. Features include merging of four separate MIDI inputs, SMPTE synchronization, MIDI interface, and synchronization to an audio click track or other percussive audio source.

626. King, Chris. Rev. of MacRecorder, from Farallon Computing. *HyperLink Magazine* Apr.-May 1988: 42-44. Sound digitizer for the Macintosh. The author states that sounds can be imported from other Macintosh applications e.g., *SoundCap* and *Studio Session* and saved on cards.

627. Kovach, Mark A. "ShorTakes." Rev. of *Drumfile*, from Blank Software. *Music, Computers & Software* June 1987: 68-69. Drum machine software for the Macintosh.

628. Latimer, Joey. Rev. of *Jam Session*, from Broderbund. *Family Computing* Apr. 1988: 73-74. The author states that *Jam Session* recordings can be played on other Macs without the program. Also recommends the use of external speakers and an amplifier.

629. Lavroff, Nicholas. "Playing It By Eye." Rev. of *SongPainter*, from Rubicon Publishing. *Macworld* Sep. 1985: 109-10. Music software that uses graphic images to represent musical selections.

630. ---. "Roll over Mozart." Rev. of *MusicWorks*, from Hayden Software and *ConcertWare*, from Great Wave Software. *Macworld* June 1985: 72-79. Music composition software for the Macintosh.

631. Lehrman, Paul D. "First Take: Capsule Comments: *HB Music Engraver* Scoring Software for the Macintosh." *Electronic Musician* Oct. 1988: 90+ Professional-level publishing/transcription software. Has no direct musical input or output via MIDI. However, the author states that this will probably be added in future versions.

632. ---. "Iddy-Bitty MIDI." *MacUser* June 1988: 206-11. In-depth look at Apple's MIDI interface for the Macintosh and Apple IIGS. The interface has only one MIDI output; however, it can be used with several MIDI instruments because most synthesizers are equipped with a MIDI thru-port. Has a 1-MHz clock rate and is compatible with most MIDI software currently available. Includes a descriptive list of manufacturers of other MIDI interfaces for the Macintosh.

633. ---. "MIDI and the Macintosh." *Computer Shopper* Mar. 1988: 156+ Overview of music software available for the Macintosh. Products discussed include *Q-Sheet* and *Cue*.

634. ---. "MIDIBASIC 2.0: Music Power to the People." *Electronic Musician* Oct. 1987: 80-85. Discussion and evaluation of MIDIBASIC from Altech Systems, a "set of BASIC Library routines for accessing MIDI within BASIC." Requires an MS-BASIC interpreter or compiler, or a ZBASIC compiler.

635. ---. "Multitracking MIDI Master: *Master Tracks Pro*: The Cleanest, Clearest, Most Comprehensive and Easiest to Use MIDI Sequencer Yet." *MacUser* Dec. 1987: 180+ In-depth discussion of *Master Tracks Pro* from Passport Designs.

636. ---. "Music between the Keys: *M* and *Jam Factory* Take You to Parts of the Musical Spectrum You Never Knew Existed." *MacUser* Oct. 1987: 146+ Automated improvisation software for the Macintosh.

637. ---. "Music for the Masses: So You Want to Write Your Own MIDI Program? MIDIBASIC Is the Way to Go." *MacUser* Aug. 1987: 126+ Macintosh MIDI command library.

638. ---. "Quick Clicks." Rev. of *Deluxe Music Construction Set*, from Electronic Arts. *MacUser* June 1988: 110+ Music composition/notation software for the Macintosh. The user can enter up to 48 voices on 8 staves and play the music through the Macintosh (4 voices only) or via MIDI and an external synthesizer. Not compatible with the Mac II.

639. ---. "Quick Clicks." Rev. of *UpBeat*, from Intelligent Music. *MacUser* May 1988: 94+ Program that turns the Macintosh into a front panel for a highly complex drum machine. An unlimited number of rhythmic patterns are available and a "jamming" feature allows the user to play along with a running pattern.

640. ---. "Scroll over Beethoven." *MacUser* July 1988: 210+ Informative article that deals with compatibility problems one may encounter when integrating music software, specifically *Deluxe Music Construction Set* and *ConcertWare +*, with traditional graphics software such as *PageMaker*, *SuperPaint*, or *MacDraw*.

641. ---. "The Write Staff: A New Generation of Desktop Music Publishing Tools Is Bringing Composers and Arrangers New Ways to Score." *MacUser* Oct. 1988: 164+ Excellent article on music notation software for the Macintosh. Focuses primarily on *HB Music Engraver* from HB Imaging and *Music Publisher* from Graphic Notes. Other programs discussed include *Finale* from Coda Music Software, and *NoteWriter* and *Encore* from Passport Designs.

Includes sidebars on *Deluxe Music Construction Set* from Electronic Arts and *ExampleKrafter* from MusiKrafters Music Services. Also includes a directory of publishers.

642. Levine, Michael, and Bob Kinkel. Rev. of *Q-Sheet*, from Digidesign. *Electronic Musician* May 1988: 98+ MIDI event-sequencing program intended for the automation of studios making audio for video, and sound effect sequencing for video and film. Uses SMPTE/MIDI time code.

643. Levy, S. "Whose Music Is It, Anyway?" *Macworld* Aug. 1988: 37+ General discussion of new music software for the Macintosh. Programs discussed include *Jam Session* from Broderbund, *Studio Session* from Bogas Productions, and *Music Mouse* from Opcode.

644. Lewis, Bill. "Apple Music: *Alchemy* for the Macintosh." *Music, Computers & Software* Nov. 1988: 58-59. Networking software designed to facilitate data sharing between multiple or incompatible samplers. Supports the Ensoniq Mirage and EPS, EMU E-Max and SP-1200, Akai S-900, Casio FZ-1 and FZ-10, and the Roland S-550.

645. ---. Rev. of *M*, from Intelligent Music. *Music, Computers & Software* Oct. 1988: 72-73. Review of version 2. Changes include an improved operating screen laid out in six areas i.e., Patterns, Variables, Conducting, Cyclic Variables, MIDI, and Snapshot.

646. ---. Rev. of *Music Mouse. Keyboards, Computers & Software* Feb. 1987: 72-73. Interactive music software that turns the Macintosh into a musical instrument. Requires no keyboard skills or knowledge of music notation and is suitable for children.

647. ---. "ShorTakes." Rev. of *MIDIScope*, from Kurzweil Music Systems. *Music, Computers & Software* Aug. 1987: 77. Analyzes incoming MIDI data streams. Can be downloaded free from the *MCS* Music Forum data library on CompuServe or PAN's Synth and MIDI Forum.

648. ---. "System: The Macintosh." *Music, Computers & Software* June 1988: 52+ General overview of the Macintosh and music products currently available. Includes a list of addresses for manufacturers of music software.

649. Leytze, David. "Keyboard Report: *Performer* 2.3, Updated MIDI Sequencing Software for the Mac." *Keyboard Magazine* July 1988: 168+ From Mark of the Unicorn. Features include 32 channel operation, multiple-channel recording on up to 300 tracks, and individual event editing. Compatible with the Macintosh II.

650. ---. "Short Takes: *MacDrums* Macintosh Drum Machine Software." *Keyboard Magazine* May 1988: 145+ Inexpensive drum machine software that plays samples through the internal sound chip in the Macintosh. Includes 35 different sampled percussion sounds.

651. ---. "Short Takes: MacRecorder, Macintosh Sound Recorder & Editor." *Keyboard Magazine* Aug. 1988: 155+ Sound digitizer from Farallon Computing for the Macintosh. May be used to install sounds into *HyperCard* stacks.

652. Litterst, George F. "Digitized Sound Made Easy: MacRecorder." *MACazine* Aug. 1988: 64-67. The author states that he experienced some difficulty running *HyperSound* under *MultiFinder*. Includes illustrations and a helpful sidebar on connecting the MacRecorder to older Macs.

653. ---. "MacMusic Comes of Age: Biggest Hits of 1987." *MACazine* Dec. 1987: 82-85. Descriptive overview of various products including *Jam Session* (Broderbund), *Different Drummer* (Primera Software), *Ovaltune* and *Strawberry Ovaltune* (Opcode), *ExampleKrafter* (MusiKrafters), several MIDI interfaces, and MIDI related books.

654. ---. "Notes on Mac Music." *MACazine* Apr. 1988: 80-82. Overview of several popular music programs for the Macintosh i.e., *Jam Session* from Broderbund, *MacDrums* from Coda Music Software, and *MIDIMac Sequencer* 2.5 from Opcode.

655. ---. "The Well-Tempered Mac." *MACazine* Feb. 1987: 14-15. Brief discussion of various topics including *High Score* from Advanced Music Notation Systems (notation software), networking for Mac musicians, MIDI interfaces, and music related clip art.

656. ---. "The Well-Tempered Mac." *MACazine* June 1987: 62+ Overview of *MIDIWrite* and MIDIBASIC from Altec Systems. *MIDIWrite* displays MIDI information as it comes into the Mac as hexadecimal and decimal readouts and includes an English translation. MIDIBASIC is a MIDI programming tool.

657. ---. "The Well-Tempered Mac." *MACazine* Mar. 1987: 56+ Descriptive overview of *Performer* 1.22 from Mark of the Unicorn. The author discusses how *Performer* works with *Professional Composer* and states that both programs are compatible with *Switcher*. Includes illustrations.

658. ---. "The Well-Tempered Mac." *MACazine* May 1987: 17+ Descriptive overview of *M* and *Jam Factory* from Intelligent Music, and *Music Mouse* from Opcode. Includes illustrations.

659. ---. "The Well-Tempered Mac: Does the Mac Put Musicians Out of Work?" *MACazine* Sep. 1987: 83-85. Interesting account of how the 61-piece orchestra of the Merrimac Lyric Opera in Boston was replaced (May 22) with two Kurzweil 250 Sampling Keyboards and a Macintosh Plus.

660. Macdonald, Gerry. "System: The Mac Plus." *Music, Computers & Software* Oct. 1988: 61-64. The author gives an overview of how he uses the Mac in his profession (record producer). Topics include software (*Performer* 2.3 and *Professional Composer*), basic procedures for writing arrangements, and problems encountered along the way.

661. "Macintosh Music." *Changing Times* May 1986: 91. Brief discussion of *Deluxe Music Construction Set* and *ConcertWare +*, music composition/notation software for the Macintosh.

662. Mansfield, Ernie, and Freff. "Keyboard Report: *HB Music Engraver* Scoring Software for the Macintosh." *Keyboard Magazine* Dec. 1988: 134+ Features include up to 50 staves with up to 8 voices per staff, files of up to 1000 measures, automatic stemming and beaming, and a comprehensive set of notation symbols. MIDI playback not yet available.

663. Many, Chris. Rev. of *Cue* 2.0, from Opcode. *Music Technology* May 1988: 83-85. Software designed to assist composers in the mathematics and administration of writing music for film. Features include custom score paper design and flexible tempo mapping. Includes sample screen output.

664. ---. Rev. of *D50 Librarian & Patch Editor*, from Zero One Research. *Music Technology* Nov. 1988: 73. Full-featured programs that function as desk accessories.

665. ---. Rev. of *D50 Librarian*, from Opcode. *Music Technology* Apr. 1988: 82. New version of Opcode's Librarian software for Roland's D50 and D550 synthesizers. The program uses the same documentation as the DX7 or CZ librarian with a supplement for D50 use.

666. ---. Rev. of *Q-Sheet*, from Digidesign. *Music Technology* Jan. 1988: 38-42. An event sequencer for film and video cue lists that can automate any MIDI device in sync to SMPTE.

667. Matsuoka, Doug. "Yes, There Is Life after MIDI: Get More Out of Your Computer." *Keyboard Magazine* Mar. 1988: 34+ Discussion of how musicians can use the Macintosh for various applications that may be helpful in music production e.g., databases, word processing, and communications.

668. McGuiness, Timothy. "Box of Magic." *Electronic Musician* Dec. 1987: 42+ The author discusses the reaction received from musicians in China where he demonstrated his Kurzweil 250, Macintosh, MIDI connections, and associated equipment.

669. McNeill, Dan. Rev. of *Jam Session*, from Broderbund. *Compute!* Oct. 1988: 66. Performance software that allows the user to play along with given accompaniment by pressing keys on the Macintosh keyboard. Includes digitized instrumental sounds and 19 prerecorded songs to play along with.

670. Merkin, Robby. "Scoring." *Music, Computers & Software* June 1988: 79-80. Discussion of the techniques and equipment used by composer Alan Menken and the author while composing music for *Act II*, (NBC-TV pilot). Merkin's equipment list included a Macintosh Plus, a Southworth MIDI interface, and Mark of the Unicorn's *Performer* 1.1.

671. Meuse, Steve. "ShorTakes." Rev. of MIDIBASIC 2.0, from Altech. *Music, Computers & Software* Oct. 1987: 73+ Macintosh MIDI command library for Microsoft's MS-BASIC and Zedcor's ZBASIC compiler.

672. Meyer, Chris. Rev. of *SoftSynth* Version 2.0, from Digidesign. *Music Technology* Mar. 1987: 23. Program that uses additive synthesis to create musical sounds.

673. Milano, D. "Keyboard Report: *Alchemy* Sample Editing & Networking Mac Software." *Keyboard Magazine* June 1988: 142-44. Recommends two Megs of RAM. Features include stereo sampling, harmonic resynthesis, stereo pan level adjustment, and multiple sample display. From Blank Software.

674. ---. "Keyboard Report: Coda *Finale*, Music Notation & Transcription Software for the Mac." *Keyboard Magazine* Feb. 1989: 142+ Descriptive overview of *Finale* including excellent illustrations and examples of score printout from a Linotronic, a LaserWriter, and an ImageWriter. Features include the ability to save scores as EPS (Encapsulated PostScript) files for use in other programs. The author states that an IBM version is being developed.

675. ---. "Keyboard Report: Digidesign *SoftSynth* Additive Synthesis for the Mac." *Keyboard Magazine* Dec. 1986: 149+ After the user specifies a group of harmonics, envelopes, etc., *SoftSynth* creates digital sound that can be transferred to a digital sampler for playback.

676. ---. "Keyboard Report: *DMP7 Pro Editor/Librarian* Mac Software." *Keyboard Magazine* Apr. 1988: 158-59. Interactive

automation software from Digital Music Services for the Yamaha DMP7 mixer and the Macintosh. Features include graphic display of all DMP7 controls, snapshot memories, update memories, and grouping functions.

677. ---. "Keyboard Report: *Q-Sheet* Event Sequencer & MIDI Automation Mac Software." *Keyboard Magazine* Nov. 1987: 153+ *Q-Sheet* allows the user to preprogram program change information to occur at a specified moment during a song or video. *Q-Sheet* can also be patched to control a Yamaha DMP7 allowing the user to control the mixdown from the Macintosh keyboard. From Digidesign.

678. ---. "Short Takes." Rev. of *One-Step*, from Southworth. *Keyboard Magazine* June 1988: 160. MIDI sequencer for the Macintosh. Features include 16 track recording and graphic editing in the style of Macintosh paint programs.

679. ---. "Keyboard Report: *MIDIPaint* Southworth Mac Sequencer Software." *Keyboard Magazine* Oct. 1987: 142+ Features include graphic and numeric note editing, 16,000 tracks, independent looping on 400 multitrack sequences, and SMPTE direct time lock.

680. "MSBasic Sound." *Nibble Mac: The Magazine for Macintosh Enthusiasts* 3.1 (1988): 36-42. Demonstration of how to make simple sounds with the SOUND command and combine SOUND commands to get multivoice melodies.

681. Nemvalts, Kalle. "Sequences That Swing with *Performer*." *Electronic Musician* Mar. 1988: 60+ In-depth discussion of the new quantizing capabilities of *Performer* 2.1 from Mark of the Unicorn. The main focus of the article deals with problems encountered when one tries to quantize swing rhythms.

682. Newquist, Harvey. Rev. of *GM70 Companion*, from Snap Software. *Music Technology* June 1988: 66-67. A patch editor/librarian for the Roland GM70 guitar-to-MIDI converter and the Macintosh. Also available for the IBM PC.

683. O'Donnell, Bob. Rev. of *Finale*, from Coda Music Software. *Music Technology* Dec. 1988: 66-71. Sophisticated music notation software for the Macintosh. Features include support for up to 128 staves, tools for creating custom music symbols, and real time MIDI input that can be transcribed instantly into music notation. The author includes sidebars that describe the various parts of the program i.e., *Hyperscribe*, *Transcribe*, and *Tools*.

684. ---. "Steps in Time." *Music Technology* Feb. 1988: 18-21. Interview with Peter Erskine, drummer for Weather Report & Steps

Ahead. Erskine describes his activities as a synthesist, composer, producer, and his home MIDI studio which includes a Macintosh.

685. O'Donnell, Craig. "Apple's NAMM Debut." *MacUser* Apr. 1988: 38. Brief overview of products for Apple computers exhibited at the Winter National Association of Music Merchants exposition. Products mentioned include Apple's MIDI interface and music software from Digidesign, Passport, and Graphic Notes.

686. ---. Rev. of DASCH, from Western Automation. *Electronic Musician* Dec. 1986: 82+ Disk Acceleration Storage Control Hardware.

687. ---. "Insights on *HyperCard*: How to Digitize and Script Sounds in *HyperCard* Stacks." *Macworld* June 1988: 219+ Includes many helpful illustrations and a directory of "Sound Sources" for *HyperCard* sounds.

688. ---. "*Macworld* News: New Music High." *Macworld* Mar. 1988: 107+ Brief discussion of digital signal processing and the Macintosh. Mentions *DMP7 Pro* from Digital Music Services, a full-function editor/librarian/interactive controller for Yamaha's DMP7 Digital Mixer.

689. Parisi, Deborah. "Wind on Film." *Music Technology* Nov. 1988: 57-61. Interview with Tom Scott on studio basics and wind synthesis in film scoring. Software used by Scott includes *Performer* and *Cue*. Includes a schematic of Scott's equipment setup.

690. Pogue, David. Rev. of *Finale*, from Coda Music Software. *Macworld* Feb. 1989: 222-23. Professional-level sequencing/transcription/notation software. Features include the ability to notate music in many styles (ancient to avant-garde) and laser printer output.

691. "Quick Clicks." Rev. of *Performer* 2.2 and *Professional Composer* 2.1, from Mark of the Unicorn. *MacUser* Jan. 1988: 94+ *Performer* is a MIDI sequencer. *Professional Composer* is notation software that can be used with *Performer*.

692. Redmon, Nigel. "The MIDI Stack: *HyperCard* for Musicians." *Music, Computers & Software* Jan. 1989: 36+ General overview of *HyperCard* and how it can be used in music/MIDI applications. Topics include *HyperCard's* database capabilities and *HyperMIDI*, a shareware stack that contains a toolkit of XCMDs for MIDI communications via *HyperCard*.

693. Reveaux, Anthony. "Digital Sound for the Mac." *A+* May 1986: 106-13. Discussion of *SoundCap* from MacNifty Central and *Natural Sound* from Magnum Software. Sound digitizers for the Macintosh.

694. Rich, Robert. Rev. of *Alchemy*, from Blank Software. *Music Technology* June 1988: 70-73. Sample editing software for the Macintosh. Features include compatibility with a variety of samplers, stereo sample editing, resampling, digital EQ, and many visual waveform editing functions.

695. ---. Rev. of *TurboSynth*, from Digidesign. *Music Technology* Sep. 1988: 72-75. Synthesis software for the Macintosh that allows the user to create sample generating algorithms. Patches may be exported to a sampler for playback. However, the author mentions there are some problems when running the program under System 6.0.

696. Rietmann, Kearney. "Open Window." *Macworld* Nov. 1984: 124-28. Demonstration of a method of writing music scores on the Macintosh.

697. Roberts, Jim. "John Colby: Scoring Musical Points with ESPN." *Keyboard Magazine* May 1987: 18. John Colby, the music director for ESPN, uses a Macintosh to help create music for the cable television sports network.

698. Rona, Jeff. "Take Your Cue: Film Scoring Software from Opcode." Rev. of *Cue*, from Opcode. *Electronic Musician* Oct. 1988: 108-11. Requires a Mac Plus, SE, or II; MIDI interface; SMPTE-to-MIDI converter recommended. Designed to facilitate various mathematical tasks involved in film scoring.

699. ---. "Technology: Computers On-Line." *Keyboard Magazine* Feb. 1988: 138. Brief overview of *HyperCard* and its music applications.

700. Stone, Greg. "It Was Love at First Sight with Hayden Software's *MusicWorks*." Rev. of *MusicWorks*. *A+* May 1985: 112-14. Music composition/notation software for the Macintosh.

701. Swearingen, Donald. Rev. of *Master Tracks Pro*, from Passport Designs. *Byte* Nov. 1987: 212+ MIDI sequencer for the Macintosh. Features include a keyboard mapper for control of the sequencer from a MIDI keyboard. Requires the Passport MIDI interface and one MIDI equipped instrument.

702. Swigart, Rob. "They're Playing Our Song." Rev. of *Professional Composer*, from Mark of the Unicorn and *Deluxe Music*

Construction Set, from Electronic Arts. *Macworld* Feb. 1986: 109-12. Music composition/notation software for the Macintosh. Both programs are compatible with the *Opcode Sequencer*.

703. Tolleson, Robin. "Billy Cobham Piecing Together the Picture -- Byte-By-Byte." *Down Beat* Apr. 1988: 58-59. Billy Cobham (jazz/rock drummer) discusses his latest album "Picture This" and how he used a Mac Plus, *Performer*, and *Professional Composer* to create it.

704. Tully, Tim. "First Take: Altech Systems' 1 x 3 MIDI Interface and 2 x 6 MIDI Interface for the Macintosh." *Electronic Musician* Sep. 1988: 73-74. The 1 x 3 features one MIDI in/three MIDI outs. The 2 x 6 features two MIDI ins/six MIDI outs. Both are 1.0 MHz units and work with the Mac 512, Plus, SE, and II. The 1 x 3 requires a DB-9 adapter for use with the 512.

705. ---. "Quick Clicks." Rev. of *Cue*, from Opcode. *MacUser* Feb. 1989: 80-81. Program that facilitates the task of composing for film by assisting in the various timing computations required. Compatible with the Macintosh II and *MultiFinder*.

706. ---. "Simpler Samplers: Is It Live Or Is It MIDI Hex? Only Your Sampler Knows for Sure." *MacUser* Oct. 1988: 148+ Detailed overview of four sampling programs i.e., *Alchemy* from Blank Software, and *Sound Designer*, *SoftSynth*, and *TurboSynth* from Digidesign. Includes two sidebars that discuss the sampling process and its historical development.

707. ---. Rev. of *TurboSynth*, from Digidesign. *Electronic Musician* Nov. 1988: 106-09. Modular synthesis software for the Macintosh. Allows the user to develop sounds for most popular samplers by altering waveforms and linking the processed waveforms to various modules e.g., envelopes, filters, etc.

708. Unger, Brian. "Apple Music: Yamaha *DMP7 Pro*." *Music, Computers & Software* June 1988: 64-65. Discussion of *DMP7 Pro*, a program that emulates all of the controls of the Yamaha DMP7 mixing console. Features include graphic channel name and pan windows.

709. Williams, Wheat III. Rev. of *Music Publisher* 1.01, from Graphic Notes. *Music Technology* Aug. 1988: 60-63. Notation software for the Macintosh. Features include custom score design, "Presto," a 36-key keypad for note entry, automatic beaming, and precise entry of slurs and crescendos. The author states that although this version does not support MIDI, *Music Publisher* is expected to become MIDI compatible in the near future.

710. Yavelow, C. "Berklee School of Music." *Macworld* June 1987: 109-11. Interesting overview of the music LAN at the Berklee College of Music. The system includes a 3Com EtherMac network.

711. ---. "A Concert in PostScript." Rev. of *ConcertWare + MIDI*, from Great Wave Software. *Macworld* Jan. 1988: 163-65. Music composition/notation software for the Macintosh. Compatible with PostScript's Sonata font.

712. ---. "Digital Sampling on the Macintosh." *Byte* June 1986: 171-83. Description and explanation of digital synthesis. Includes a list of available software.

713. ---. "From Keyboard to Score: An Introduction to Music Processing and Evaluations of Six Packages That Put Your Performances on Paper." *Macworld* Dec. 1986: 108+ Evaluations include *MusicWorks, ConcertWare + MIDI, Deluxe Music Construction Set*, and *Professional Composer*.

714. ---. "*High Score*." *Macworld* Nov. 1986: 81. Discussion of *High Score*, a coprocessor that gives users the ability to format music for publication-quality printing. From Music Notation Systems.

715. ---. "Low-Cost MIDI Interface Quartet." Rev. of the Apple MIDI Interface, from Apple Computer Co.; MIDIface II, from Austin Development; Professional Plus, from Opcode; and the Passport MIDI Interface, from Passport Designs. *Macworld* Aug. 1988: 139+ Comparison of four inexpensive MIDI interfaces for the Macintosh. Includes specifications and illustrations.

716. ---. "Mac Power User = Power Muser, Pt. I." *Electronic Musician* Apr. 1988: 72+ First of a three-part series discussing the various ways to use the Macintosh as a productivity tool that can save time for creativity. Part 1 discusses power desk accessories e.g., *DeskPaint* and *JamBox*. Includes a list of manufacturers.

717. ---. "Mac Power User = Power Muser, Pt. II." *Electronic Musician* May 1988: 56+ Discussion of utilities that can turn the Macintosh into a "higher-performance machine." Topics covered include FKeys, INITS, CDEVS, print spoolers, quasi-multitasking applications, and hard disk utilities.

718. ---. "Mac Power User = Power Muser, Pt. III: Advanced Techniques." *Electronic Musician* June 1988: 53+ In-depth discussion of how one may begin to customize program code, automate longer tasks using macros, and start taking advantage of *HyperCard*. Includes a list of "power products" and manufacturers.

719. ---. "*Macworld* News: Grand Finale." *Macworld* June 1988: 105+ Preview of *Finale*, an integrated MIDI sequencer and notation program from Coda Music Software. Features instant notation of music as it is played in real time.

720. ---. "MIDI and the Apple Macintosh." *Computer Music Journal* 10.3 (1986): 11-47. Comprehensive overview of the Macintosh and MIDI. Topics include MIDI interfaces and sequencing software (e.g., *Performer*, *Total Music*, *MIDIMac Sequencer*, *ConcertWare* +, and others). Includes bibliography.

721. ---. "Music Processing: The Next Generation." *Macworld* July 1988: 102-11. Excellent article on the present state of music processing. Paul Sadowski, proprietor of Music Publishing Services in New York, discusses how and why his firm uses the Macintosh for music publishing. Products discussed include *Finale*, *HB Music Engraver*, *High Score*, and *Music Publisher*. Includes illustrations.

722. ---. "Music Software for the Apple Macintosh." *Computer Music Journal* 9.3 (1985): 52-67. Overview of *ConcertWare*, *MacMusic*, *MusPrint*, *MusicWorks*, *Professional Composer*, *Song Painter*, and *Music Character Set*.

723. ---. Rev. of *Performer* 2.2, from Mark of the Unicorn. *Electronic Musician* May 1988: 92+ MIDI sequencer. Features include editing and synchronization capabilities, the ability to convert performance data into conventional music notation (using *Professional Composer*), and flexible SMPTE implementation.

724. ---. "Top of the Charts: On Stage and in the Studio, the Mac Is Number One with Music Professionals." *Macworld* Aug. 1987: 138-45. Discussion of Macintosh applications in sound design, film music, and performance. Presents profiles of several well-known composers, engineers, and programmers who use the Macintosh in music production.

725. Yelton, G. "Budget MIDI for the MAC." Rev. of *MIDI Composer*, from Assimilation; *Deluxe Music Construction Set*, from Electronic Arts; and *ConcertWare* + *MIDI*, from Great Wave Software. *Electronic Musician* Aug. 1986: 72+

726. ---. "Mark of the Unicorn's *Professional Composer*." *Electronic Musician* Mar. 1986: 60+ Advanced music transcription software. Compatible with the *Opcode Sequencer* and *Performer*.

727. ---. "Opcode's *MIDIMac Patch Librarian*." *Electronic Musician* Mar. 1986: 68-69. Apple's *Switcher* allows this program to interact with the *MIDIMac Sequencer* from Opcode.

728. ---. "*SoundCap*: A Low Cost Mac Sampler." *Electronic Musician* May 1986: 70-73.

729. ---. "The State of the Macintosh: A Musical Perspective." *Electronic Musician* Apr. 1988: 56+   In-depth discussion of the evolutionary stages of the Macintosh and its growing list of music applications. Topics discussed include MIDI, hard disks, large screen monitors, and various music software packages.

730. ---. "Opcode's *MIDIMac Sequencer* 2.5 for the MAC." Rev. of *MIDIMac Sequencer* 2.5, from Opcode. *Electronic Musician* Nov. 1987: 110+   Records up to 26 sequences per song file with a total recording capacity of up to 24,000 notes on a Macintosh 512K, 16 tracks per voice. Other features include recorded tempo changes and selectable MIDI adapter clock speed.

731. Young, Jeffrey. "Peerless Itzhak Perlman." *Macworld* June 1985: 160-63.   Perlman's thoughts on how computer technology is affecting music production, recording, education, and musicians in general.

732. Zicarelli, David. "*M* and *Jam Factory*." *Computer Music Journal* 11.4 (1987): 13-29.   An in-depth description and evaluation of *M* and *Jam Factory*, interactive composing software from Intelligent Music. Architecture and some of the algorithms employed are discussed in detail. Includes illustrations and bibliography.

733. Zilber, Jon. "Can We Talk? With MacRecorder, Applications and *HyperCard* Stacks Come Alive with the Digitized Sound of Music -- Or Speech. Say Good-Bye to the Sounds of Silence." *MacUser* June 1988: 214+   In-depth look at MacRecorder from Farallon Computing. Includes two programs i.e., *HyperSound* and *SoundEdit*. *HyperSound* can take any digitized sound and turn it into a *HyperCard* button. *SoundEdit* provides special effects and mixing capabilities. Includes many helpful illustrations.

734. ---. "Interactive Cultures: The Mac Brought Art to the Business World. It Also Helps the Art World Get Down to Business." *MacUser* Oct. 1988: 100+   In-depth discussion of how the Macintosh is being used in the graphic arts and music. Topics include MIDI, SMPTE and film scoring, sequencers, and powerful new integrated programs e.g., *Finale* from Coda Music Software. Includes an extensive directory to music products for the Macintosh.

735. ---. "Mac Your Own Kind of Music." *MacUser* May 1988: 34-35. Brief overview of music products for the Macintosh exhibited at the Macworld Expo. in San Francisco. Products include *Finale* from Coda, an integrated sequencer and notation package that can follow changes in tempo.

736. ---. "New on the Menu: For a Song." *MacUser* May 1988: 46. Brief description of *Music Publisher* from Shaherazam, a graphics oriented notation program.

737. ---. Rev. of *Performer* 2.2 and *Professional Composer* 2.1, from Mark of the Unicorn. *MacUser* Jan. 1988: 102-03. *Performer* 2.2 features the ability to change tempo or meter and nested loops. *Professional Composer* 2.1 supports PostScript's Sonata font, various chord symbol fonts, and command key equivalents.

Tandy

738. Alford, Roger. "Fastdance: Three Seconds of Your Favorite Tunes." *80 Micro* Apr. 1984: 196-201. Demonstration of how to build a tune generator board for the TRS-80 Models I and III. Includes a schematic and illustrations.

739. Alsop, Brian H. "Polyphonic Play -- Multi-Voice Music on the Tandy 1000." *PCM: The Personal Computer Magazine for Tandy Users* Apr. 1987: 20-24. Presents a program in GW BASIC that plays a short version of the *Minuet in G* by J. S. Bach.

740. Augsburg, Cray. "The CoCo Comes to Life with the Sounds of *Lyra.*" *The Rainbow* Dec. 1986: 133. Evaluation of *Lyra*, an eight-voice music editor for the Color Computer.

741. Barden, Bill. "The Sounds of Science." *PCM: The Personal Computer Magazine for Tandy Users* Sep. 1985: 11-24. BASIC program listings for producing different sounds on the Tandy 1000.

742. Bell, Jack. "Classical Music Mosquito." *Personal Computing* Feb. 1985: 22. A description of how programmer Robb Murray uses his TRS-80 for music composition. "Classical Mosquito" is a recording of the computer as it plays various musical parts simultaneously. It has sold over 600 copies.

743. Bernico, Bill. "Graphing Great Guitars." *The Rainbow* June 1988: 56+ Presents a program called *Graphic Guitars* that allows the user to design guitars with the Color Computer.

744. Boots, Greg. "Print That Tune!" *The Rainbow* June 1988: 52-55. Presents a program called *Print Tune* that allows the user to print the complete "PLAY" statement for any specified tune. For the Color Computer.

745. Brothers, Hardin. "Sounding Off on the 1000." *80 Micro* Jan. 1988: 82-88. An in-depth look at the music capabilities of the Tandy 1000 sound chip. Includes 5 program listings that demonstrate different aspects of sound generation.

746. ---. "Sounding Off on the 1000: Encore." *80 Micro* Feb. 1988: 91+ Discussion of ways to make the sound chip in the Tandy 1000 sound less mechanical.

747. Burke, Val. "Playin' the Blues." *The Rainbow* June 1988: 20+ Presents a program that plays a 12-bar blues progression while displaying graphics. For the Color Computer.

748. Clemens, Gary W. "Sounding Out Tandy's Sound/Speech Cartridge." Rev. of Sound/Speech Cartridge, from Tandy. *Hot CoCo* June 1985: 73-76.

749. Davis, Merton. "The Sound of *Musikon*." *80 Micro* Apr. 1984: 138+ Music composition software for the TRS-80 Models I and III.

750. Devlin, Joe. Rev. of Synther 7. *Creative Computing* Dec. 1983: 98-101. Music synthesizer for the TRS-80 Color Computer.

751. Engelhardt, David. "Going for a Song." Rev. of *TuneSmith*, from Blackhawk Data Corp. *80 Micro* Aug. 1986: 118.

752. Freese, Peter. "*Music-80*." *80 Micro* Mar. 1983: 310-24. A music generation program for the TRS-80 Model I.

753. Frischein, Ben. "Harmony and Me." *80 Micro* Nov. 1983: 265-69. Presents a program for the TRS-80 Model 100 that allows one to compose, play, save, and load music files.

754. Gibson, Don Phillip. "Tandy Tunes: Make Beautiful Music Together with Your Tandy 1000." *80 Micro* Dec. 1986: 89-93. Presents a program for making music with a Tandy 1000.

755. Grammer, Eric. Rev. of *Musica*, from Speech Systems. *Hot CoCo* Oct. 1984: 101-02. Allows the user to compose music containing four voices/timbres with the Color Computer.

756. ---. "*MusiWriter* Musings." Rev. of *MusiWriter*, from Tesseract Software Systems. *Hot CoCo* May 1985: 76-77.

757. Huang, David. "Internal Sound." *The Rainbow* June 1988: 99-100. Description of a circuit that allows the user to produce sound internally on the Color Computer. Includes a helpful schematic.

758.   Huben, Carl.   "Young Programmer's Contest: *Music Composer*." *80 Micro* Feb. 1983: 104-07. First place program in the 11-13 age group. The program composes songs with up to 200 notes on the TRS-80 Color Computer.

759.   Keefe, Robert W.   "*Music Maker*." *PCM: The Personal Computer Magazine for Tandy Users* Jan. 1987: 99+ Presents a program in Turbo Pascal that plays music in up to three voices on the Tandy 1000.

760.   Kirley, Dennis.   "*Melody Maker*: Pleasant Diversion and Tune Maker for the 100." Rev. of *Melody Maker*, from Custom Software. *PCM: The Personal Computer Magazine for Tandy Users* May 1985: 71-72. Music composition software for the TRS 80, Model 100.

761.   Ludwick, Gary.   "Let There Be Music." Rev. of Orchestra-90 Stereo Music Synthesizer, from Tandy/Radio Shack. *80 Micro* Mar. 1985: 114-16. For the TRS 80, Models III and IV.

762.   Matthews, Becky F.   "CoCo Goes Country." *The Rainbow* June 1988: 36+ Presents a program that plays "Rockytop" as it displays a skyline of Nashville.

763.   Mueller, John E.   "Uncovering the MIDI Section." *The Rainbow* June 1987: 36-37. General introduction to MIDI.

764.   Nickel, Harold.   "The CoCo Composer." Rev. of *Piano*. *The Rainbow* June 1987: 114-16.

765.   Ogsapian, John.   "Tuning in CoCo Tuner." Rev. of CoCo Tuner, from Real Time Specialties. *Hot CoCo* Aug. 1985: 74-76. Converts a computer into an auditory and stroboscopic tuner for a musical instrument. (Hardware)

766.   Plaster, Gip Wayne.   "From Scales to Mozart." *The Rainbow* Jan. 1988: 72-73. Presents a program that produces about three minutes of music using four major loops and three PLAY statements.

767.   Platt, Joseph D.   "The Sweet Strains of CoCo." *The Rainbow* June 1987: 94-95. Transposition refinements for *Music +*.

768.   Ramella, Richard.   "Bit Parade: Compose Melodies on Your Portable and Integrate Them into Your BASIC Programs." *PCM: The Personal Computer Magazine for Tandy Users* Dec. 1985: 30-31.

769.   ---.   Rev. of *Professor Pressnote's Music Machine*, from Tandy. *Hot CoCo* May 1985: 25-26.

770. Ray, James. "Create the Sounds of Music with the *Music Studio*." Rev. of *Music Studio*, from Activision. *PCM: The Personal Computer Magazine for Tandy Users* Feb. 1987: 127-28. Music composition and editing software for the Tandy 1000, 1200, or 3000. Supports up to three voices and is MIDI compatible.

771. Shaw, Chris. "An Orchestra in Your 100." *Portable 100/200* Oct. 1985: 40+ Presents *Music*, a program in BASIC for the TRS-80 Model 100 that allows the user to record short pieces and play them back.

772. Shelton, Garry L. "Color Composer." *The Rainbow* June 1988: 42+ Presents a program for the Color Computer called *Song Writer*, a music processor that enables the user to create and edit music compositions.

773. Spiller, Jeremy. "Synthesizer Sound-Off." *The Rainbow* June 1988: 102+ Presents a program in BASIC called *SuperPlay* that installs a machine language algorithm within the BASIC interpreter and turns the "PLAY" command into a digital synthesizer.

774. Stajduhar, Jerry. "*The Music Machine*: Make Melodies to Soothe the Savage Hacker." *PCM: The Personal Computer Magazine for Tandy Users* May 1986: 33-40. Music composition software for the Tandy 1000.

775. Thompson, Ernie. "Blast from the Past." *The Rainbow* June 1988: 96-98. Presents a program called *Jukebox* that plays various ragtime selections on the Color Computer.

776. Thompson, Matthew. "Steppin Out with My CoCo." Rev. of *Bells and Whistles 2*. *The Rainbow* June 1987: 58+

Part II
Nonspecific and Other Computers

777.   Aikin, Jim.   "Keyboard Report: FB-01 Editor/Librarian Software." *Keyboard Magazine* Oct. 1987: 135+ Discussion of *FB Pro* from Digital Music Services for the Macintosh, *SynthWorks* from Steinberg for the Atari ST, *4-Op Deluxe* from Dr. T. for the Atari ST, *FB-01 Command* from Command Development for the C-64, and *FB-01 Design* from Sonus for the C-64.

778.   ---.   "Mechanical, Analog, Digital Sequencer History in a Nutshell." *Keyboard Magazine* June 1987: 46-47.   Brief historical outline of sequencers. The author also comments on the idea of a uniform file format proposed by Dave Oppenheim.

779.   ---.   "Plug in Here: The ABC's of Techno-Music Literacy." *Keyboard Magazine* June 1988: 34+ Description of some key concepts of present-day music technology. Topics include MIDI, sampling, sequencers, computer applications, and music software. Concludes with a list of electronic music terms and definitions.

780.   ---.   "Sequencer Basics: A Guide for the Mystified." *Keyboard Magazine* June 1987: 36+ In-depth discussion of sequencers. The author makes the distinction between hardware and software sequencers and explains various terms e.g., inputting, playback, editing, and timing.

781.   ---.   "Keyboard Report: Roland *MPS* Sequencing/Notation Software." *Keyboard Magazine* Apr. 1986: 124-29. *Music Processing System*. Features include 8 tracks, auto punch-in/out, transcription of MIDI data into standard notation, and transposition on playback. Requires 320K RAM, color/graphics compatible monitor, Roland MIF-IPC interface card, and Roland MPU-401 MIDI Processing Unit.

782. Anderson, John, and Ted Drude. "Making Waves: A Roundup of Audio Digitizers." *Computer Shopper* Mar. 1988: 72+ Brief overview of sound digitizers available for all popular microcomputers.

783. Anderton, Craig. Rev. of *Atari ST Matrix 12/Xpander*, from MIDIMouse; *MIDIMac*, from Opcode; and *Xpandit #1*, from the MIDI Station. *Electronic Musician* Dec. 1987: 79-80. Patch librarians.

784. ---. "First Take: Snap Software *GM70 Companion*." *Electronic Musician* June 1988: 100-01. Sends and receives System Exclusive data to and from the GM70. Library windows contain a listing of all patches and four windows may be viewed at once. For the IBM PC and Macintosh.

785. ---. "Making Your Micro Musical." *Electronic Musician* Aug. 1986: 18-19. General discussion of the personal computer as a musical instrument. Focus is on internal sound chips of various computers and MIDI.

786. ---. "The Ultimate Sample Organizer." *Electronic Musician* Feb. 1989: 50+ General overview of what a database program is and how it can help catalog samples and facilitate the general organization of any recording studio or MIDI setup. The program used for demonstration and illustrations is Microsoft *Works* for the Macintosh but the ideas presented apply to database applications in general.

787. ---. "Using Your Sequencer as a MIDI System Analyzer." *Electronic Musician* Dec. 1988: 28+ Discussion of how to create sequences that generate a stream of MIDI data that can monitor or test all types of MIDI equipment.

788. ---. "What's in a Sequencer?" *Electronic Musician* Aug. 1988: 18+ Description of the most common sequencer functions and typical applications e.g., automated punch-in/punch-out, track vs. channel, programmable tempo changes, etc. Intended to help the reader evaluate which sequencer is best for his or her specific needs.

789. ---. "The MIDI Recording Studio: How to Buy It, How to Set It Up, and How to Run It." *Musician* Aug. 1985: 74-77.

790. ---. "Personal Computers Become Personal Composers." *Record* July 1984: 46-47.

791. Anderton, Craig, et al. "Special Report: The 1988 Summer NAMM Show." *Electronic Musician* Sep. 1988: 16+ Overview of the 1988 National Association of Music Merchants Expo. Products

discussed include the *Feel Factory*, a program for the Macintosh that alters the "feel" of sequenced music from Filmsonix and the new Yamaha C1 laptop computer, an IBM compatible with two MIDI inputs, eight outputs, and SMPTE in/out.

792. Armbruster, G. "The Information Source of the Future Is On-Line Now: Electronic Bulletin Boards." *Keyboard Magazine* Dec. 1985: 12+

793. Baird, J. "Roger Linn, the Missing Link: Musicians and Computers Meet in the Mind of a Modest Revolutionary." *Musician* Aug. 1985: 86+

794. Baker, J. R. "Bach, Beethoven, Brahms & Bytes: Orchestrating Classical Music with Computers & Sequencers." *Music, Computers & Software* Apr. 1988: 43-46. Describes the preliminary stages of recording, performing, notating, and mixing with MIDI. Includes references to specific software packages and illustrations.

795. Balthrop, William K. "Razzle Dazzle: A Few Quick Tricks Tune Your TI-99/4A into Dazzling 3-Part Harmony." *Home Computer Magazine* Mar. 1985: 38-39.

796. Barnett, David. "Keeping Score: Word Processor-Like Manipulations Greatly Speed up Assembling a Page of Music." *Music, Computers & Software* June 1987: 55+ Description of effective notation packages available for a variety of computers. Discusses catagories of software, methods of input, editing, and output.

797. Bateman, Selby. "Making Music with MIDI." *Compute!* Jan. 1986: 24-34. Excellent introduction to MIDI. The author explains how "MIDI is turning musical instruments into computer peripherals." He also states that the MIDI specification from the International MIDI Association is the primary source to consult for technical details.

798. ---. "The New Music." *Compute!* May 1987: 18+ General discussion of music, computers, and MIDI. Includes a glossary of electronic music terms and cites professional musicians who are taking advantage of MIDI.

799. Beall, Garm. "Application Tips: Get the Most Out of Your Sequencer: New Dimensions for 11 Major Devices." *Keyboard Magazine* June 1987: 74+ Description of *MIDIMac Sequencer* from Opcode for the Macintosh, *Sequencer Plus* from Voyetra for the IBM PC, *Master Tracks Pro* from Passport Designs for the Atari ST, and eight others.

800. Benoit, Ellen. "Music's Black Box." *Forbes* 13 Aug. 1984: 102. General introduction to MIDI and its potential in the music industry.

801. Berger, Myron. "High C's from IC's: Composing Capabilities of a Personal Computer." *High Fidelity/Musical America* June 1983: 48-49. General overview of *Music Composer* for the Atari and *Electric Duet* for the Apple II. Includes illustrations.

802. Bermant, Charles. "Computing Is Just a Song." *Personal Computing* Oct. 1987: 182-83. John Kay (Steppenwolf) describes how he uses the Compaq Deskpro and Zenith Z-183 laptop in live performance.

803. Bonner, P. "The Sound of Software: New Programs Help You Understand Music and Turn Your Computer into an Instrument." *Personal Computing* June 1984: 94+ General introduction to music software and a guide to publishers.

804. Bradfield, David. "First Take: Zero One Research's *Roland D-50 Editor* and *D-50 Librarian*." *Electronic Musician* Jan. 1989: 99-101. Desk accessories for the Macintosh and IBM PC that provide access to the D-50's sound library while another program is in use.

805. Bumgarner, Marlene Anne. Rev. of *Bank Street Music Writer*, from Mindscape. *Family Computing* May 1985: 80-81. Music composition software for the C-64 and Atari designed to allow the user, with little or no musical background, to create original music.

806. Burger, Jeff. "Inside the MIDI Studio: A Sea of Equipment That Grows with Your Needs." *Computer Shopper* Mar. 1988: 10+ Overview of music equipment available for use with personal computers. Focus is primarily on synthesizers.

807. ---. "MIDI and Computers: Electronic Music for the Masses." *Computer Shopper* Mar. 1988: 9+ General discussion of personal computers and their music capabilities.

808. ---. "MIDI Column." *Computer Shopper* Jan. 1989: 295+ Clear explanation of MIDI synchronization using MIDI clock. Excerpt from *The Murphy's Law MIDI Handbook* by the same author (See #1306). Includes excellent illustrations.

809. ---. "MIDI Column." *Computer Shopper* Sep. 1988: 281+ The author discusses how programs can be changed remotely via MIDI commands on most programmable MIDI devices, and explains MIDI system exclusive codes. Excerpt from *The Murphy's Law MIDI Handbook* by the same author (See #1306).

810. ---. "Surviving a SYNCing Ship." *Music Technology* Oct. 1988: 50-53. Comprehensive survey of SMPTE-to-MIDI converters including Southworth's *Jambox/4+* (Macintosh), Dr. T's *Phantom* (Atari ST), Passport's *MIDI Transport* (IBM and Mac), Steinberg's *Time-Lock* (Atari ST), and many others.

811. Butler, Chris. "DataGlove." *Music, Computers & Software* June 1988: 29. Introduction of a lightweight computer input device (a glove) that senses hand gesture, position, and orientation. DataGlove is the result of a search by Tom Zimmermann for a method of turning pantomime gestures into sound.

812. Campbell, Alan Gary. "Sources." *Electronic Musician* Feb. 1988: 107+ Bibliography of sources for information on musical electronics. Includes a section on microcomputers.

813. "Can Your Computer Make Music?" *Changing Times* June 1985: 72. Brief discussion of the personal computer and music. Includes a list of music software.

814. Cano, Howard. "SAM: A Simple Sound Sampler." *Electronic Musician* Nov. 1987: 80+ Instructions on how to build SAM, a sampling device dedicated to converting rapidly changing voltages into a series of numbers and storing them in memory. Numbers can then be transmitted to a personal computer via an RS-232 link. Includes a parts list and a detailed schematic.

815. Chandler, James. "Additive Programming: The Secret Life of the Kawai K5." *Electronic Musician* Feb. 1989: 24+ Program listing and description of *Sample Converter*, a Fast Fourier Transform that converts sampled sounds to K5 files. It is written in MS BASIC and MIDIBASIC for the Macintosh. A version for the C-64 is also available.

816. Charbeneau, Travis. "Music's Electronic Future." *The Futurist* Sep.-Oct. 1987: 35-37. General overview of MIDI and the personal computer. The author states that the "discomfort originally felt by traditional musicians upon first encountering synthesizers" has now shifted to "outright fear and loathing."

817. Colosimo, Frank. "*VIC Music Maker*." *Compute!* Dec. 1984: 130-34. Music composition program for the VIC-20. Features include play, record, sound effects, and save.

818. Combs, Jim. "Computer Music Basics: MIDI Music for Beginners." *Music, Computers & Software* June 1988: 40+ General introduction to MIDI and personal computers containing information on current software, synthesizers, MIDI interfaces, and a glossary of MIDI/computer terminology.

819. Comer, Brooke. "Computers in the Studio: How Hard Drives Changed Four Engineers' Lives." *Music, Computers & Software* Oct. 1987: 50+ Examination of equipment used in four different recording studios.

820. "Computer Music Systems." *Keyboards, Computers & Software* Feb. 1987: 35+ Descriptions of five computer-based studios ranging in price from $1,000.00 to $7,000.00.

821. Cooper, J. "Modifications and Maintenance: Got the Down in the Memory Dump Blues?" *Keyboard Magazine* Aug. 1985: 70.

822. ---. "Modifications and Maintenance: Radio MIDI, Disk Care and Feeding, and Techno Miscellany." *Keyboard Magazine* Oct. 1985: 91+

823. ---. "Technology: Mind over MIDI: LANs and MIDI." *Keyboard Magazine* Dec. 1987: 126+ Interesting discussion of the potential of local area networks in the MIDI recording studio.

824. Cope, David. "Music LISP." *AI Expert* Mar. 1988: 26-34. Description of how composers might overcome a creative block by using LISP and artificial intelligence techniques to create a "composer's assistant." The code required for implementation is described in detail.

825. Cummings, S. "Desktop Music Scores." *Publish!* Jan.-Feb. 1987: 66-69. Provides useful information on music publishing software. Includes a sidebar entitled "Traditional Ways of Transcribing Music."

826. ---. "Keyboard Report: Notation/Sequencing Software for IBM PC, Apple IIe, and Macintosh Computers." *Keyboard Magazine* Aug. 1985: 82+

827. ---. "Keyboard Report: Voice Editors, Librarians, and System-Exclusive Miscellany." *Keyboard Magazine* Oct. 1986: 126+ Description of *FM Drawing Board*, *Bacchus Voice Manager*, *CZ-Rider*, *CZ-Patch Librarian*, and others.

828. ---. "MIDI: Computers -- Brain Power of an Intelligent System: The Top Computers for Music." *Keyboard Magazine* Jan. 1986: 40-42.

829. Cummings, S., and D. Milano. "MIDI: Computer-To-MIDI Interfaces; How Do I Byte Thee? Let Me Count the Ways." *Keyboard Magazine* Jan. 1986: 41+

830. Damiano, Bob. "The Plucked String Revisited." *Electronic Musician* Dec. 1987: 24+ Algorithm for the Apple II or C-64 that

generates new sounds for the Ensoniq Mirage synthesizer. Based on the Karplus-Strong Algorithm, the program is presented in BASIC and Assembler.

831. Daniel, Walter. "Dr. T's *CZ-Patch Librarian.*" *Electronic Musician* July 1986: 74-75. Commodore 64/128 and Atari ST.

832. Davies, Rick. "Just Another Day in MIDI Hell." *Music Technology* Aug. 1987: 16-21. Interview with Danny Elfman (Oingo Boingo) that exposes some of the negative and positive aspects of the personal computer in music production.

833. De Furia, Steve. "Software for Musicians." *Keyboard Magazine* Nov. 1988: 138. Presents a program written in Lightspeed Pascal and routines from Altech's MIDIPascal code library that allows a computer's MIDI out to serve as a MIDI thru.

834. ---. "Software for Musicians: Getting Your Program Structures under Control." *Keyboard Magazine* July 1986: 128-29. Discussion of sequence and repetition structures. Subtopics of repetition structures include the FOR loop, REPEAT loop, and the WHILE loop.

835. ---. "Software for Musicians: Language and Software Design." *Keyboard Magazine* Apr. 1986: 106+ Programming tips for designing music software. Considers all aspects of software development, language basics, and required features of a programming language for music.

836. ---. "Software for Musicians: Program Your Own." *Keyboard Magazine* Feb. 1986: 92. Introduction to a series of articles devoted to the fundamentals of music software design. The author gives an overview of what will be covered in future articles i.e., general programming concepts, MIDI, translation of structured programs, and music software design incorporating MIDI interfaces.

837. ---. "Software for Musicians: References & Resources for C & Pascal Programmers." *Keyboard Magazine* Sep. 1987: 131. Annotated bibliography of books dealing with C and Pascal that could be helpful in music programming.

838. ---. "Software for Musicians: Relational and Logic Operators." *Keyboard Magazine* June 1986: 128-29.

839. ---. "Software for Musicians: The Treacherous Trail of the MIDI Programmer." *Keyboard Magazine* Nov. 1986: 127-29. Tips on preparation and education for programming projects in music.

840. Deckard, J. "Plucked String Oscillator Using the 6502 Microprocessor." *Polyphony* 10.1 (1984): 30-34. Karplus and Strong

plucked string algorithm technique of simulating plucked string and drum sounds.

841. Dery, Mark, and Bob Doerschuk. "The Nitti Gritti on Scritti Politti: David Gramson Talks." *Keyboard Magazine* Mar. 1988: 42+ Gramson offers his thoughts on the music applications of the IBM PC and the Macintosh.

842. Dewdney, A. K. "Computer Recreations: The Sound of Computing Is Music to the Ears of Some." *Scientific American* Apr. 1987: 14+ Descriptions of two programs that deal with melody and two-part harmony.

843. Di Perma, A. "MIDI Protocol: The Diplomacy of Digital -- How Musical Nations of Many Languages Do Business Together." *Musician* Feb. 1986: 76-78.

844. Di Silvestro, Laile L. "*Music Synthesizer*: Is This the Program That Will Finally Reveal the Wonders of the TI Music Chip?" Rev. of *Music Synthesizer*, from Asgard Software. *Home Computer Magazine* Aug. 1985: 37. Music composition software for the TI-99/4A.

845. Dodge, Charles, and Curtis R. Bahn. "Musical Fractals." *Byte* June 1986: 185-96. Overview of applications for fractal geometry in music and graphics.

846. Drake, A., and J. Grant. "Music Gives Disability a Byte." *New Scientist* 22 Jan. 1987: 37-39. Interesting overview of how disabled children at the Charlton Park School in Southeast London are using a BBC Micro and a Casio synthesizer to make music.

847. Dupler, S. "Music Maker Scores at Age 17: *Music Construction Set*." *Billboard* 9 June 1984: 36. Music composition/notation software for the Apple II and C-64 from Electronic Arts.

848. Eltgroth, Marlene. "*Music Studio*." Rev. of *Music Studio*, from Activision. *Family Computing* Oct. 1986: 96. Music composition software for the Atari ST, Amiga, and Apple IIGS. Features include editing, sound programming, notation, and playback. Includes more than 15 built-in instrumental sounds.

849. Emmett, Arielle. "The New Sound of Computerized Music." *Personal Computing* July 1983: 72+ General discussion of personal computers and music. Includes a guide to music software and hardware.

850. Favaro, Peter, Sarah Kortum, and Steven C. M. Chen. "A Musical Departure: Turn Your Computer into a Piano; Then

Discover the Secret." *Family Computing* Feb. 1985: 72-84. A musical puzzle with a program to solve it. Apple II, C-64, IBM PC, Atari, TRS-80, and others.

851. Frederick, D. "Art in the Computer Age: A View from Silicon Valley (Don Buchla)" *Keyboard Magazine* May 1986: 18. Summary of the Silicon Valley Festival of Electronic Arts (Feb 86) presented by the Institute of San Jose State University (Computers in Art and Design -- Research and Education, CADRE). The festival is designed to show, through a variety of disciplines, the creative potential of computers.

852. ---. "Keyboard Report: Dump Your Sound Storage Problems on System-Exclusive Software." *Keyboard Magazine* Mar. 1986: 98+ Description of *SYS/EX* from Key Clique Inc., a system-exclusive data storage and transmission program for the Apple II series, C-64/128, and IBM PC. Features include custom dump command strings and the ability to store patch, sequencer, and drum machine data.

853. Freff. "The Well-Tempered Computer Family: How the Hell Did All These Computers Get in My Studio?" *Musician* Aug. 1985: 78+

854. Freiberger, Paul. "The *Music Construction Set*." *InfoWorld* 14 Nov. 1983: 73. Music composition/notation software for the Apple II and C-64 from Electronic Arts. Product announcement.

855. Fryer, T. "Digital Sampling: The Roots of Keyboard Sampling." *Keyboard Magazine* Jan. 1986: 114. Includes bibliography and discography.

856. Garvin, Mark. "Designing a Music Recorder." *Dr. Dobb's Journal of Software Tools* May 1987: 22-48. Discussion on how to write MIDI software. Includes references to three user groups and three periodicals.

857. Goldstein, Dan, Rick Davies, and Paul White. "Biggest Is Best." *Music Technology* Mar. 1987: 12-21. Overview of the 1987 National Association of Music Merchants Exposition. Topics include music software for the IBM PC, Atari ST, and Macintosh.

858. Goldstein, Shelby. "Making Music with Your VIC." Rev. of *Piper*, *Vic Music Composer*, and *Synthesound*. *Creative Computing* July 1983: 43-47.

245518

859. Gotcher, Peter. "Computers for Keyboardists: Choosing a Computer for Music, Pt. II." *Keyboard Magazine* July 1987: 131+ A brief look at popular microcomputers and their music potential. Models discussed include the Macintosh, Amiga, Atari ST, C-64, Apple II, and IBM PC.

860. ---. "Computers for Keyboardists: Choosing a Computer for Musical Applications, Pt. I." *Keyboard Magazine* May 1987: 103. The author stresses the importance of selecting software first, then purchasing a computer that will run it. Other considerations include operating systems, portability, color or black and white monitors, and MIDI interfaces.

861. ---. "Computers for Keyboardists: Mass Storage Media." *Keyboard Magazine* Feb. 1987: 126-28. The pros and cons of hard disk systems.

862. ---. "Computers for Keyboardists: Now You See It, Now You Don't: Optical Storage." *Keyboard Magazine* Mar. 1987: 106-08. A look at several different optical disk systems currently available for mass storage of sampled sounds.

863. ---. "Making Waves, Pt. I: Visual Editing Basics." *Electronic Musician* July 1986: 32+ Discussion of how computers can be used to display sound waveforms and edit sampled sounds.

864. ---. "Making Waves, Pt. II: Digital Signal Processing." *Electronic Musician* Aug. 1986: 36-38. Interesting overview of personal computers and digital sound processing. Topics include digital equalization, Fast Fourier Transform, and signal analysis/resynthesis. Includes illustrations and a bibliography.

865. ---. "Technology: Digital Sampling: Hard Disks for Samplers." *Keyboard Magazine* June 1988: 136+ In-depth discussion of the advantages and disadvantages of hard disk systems and an informative comparison of internal and external drives.

866. Gray, David Julian, and James Stockford. "No More Violins: Jamming on Home Computers." *Whole Earth Review* Winter 1985: 110. Brief discussion of how home computers can be used to produce music.

867. Greenwald, T. "MIDI Sequencer Software: Ten Leading Programmers Tell Why Computer Magic Won't Solve all Your Musical Problems (Yet)." *Keyboard Magazine* May 1986: 34-45. Interview with significant developers of sequencing software including Tim Ryan, Jim Miller, Roger Powell, Dave Oppenheim, and Doug Fisher. Topics include important features of sequencers, Macintosh, Atari, Commodore, and the future potential of sequencing software.

868. ---. "NAMM: But Wait -- There's More! MIDI Controllers, Signal Processors, Memory Expansions, Mixers, Amps, Samplers, Patches, Upgrades, Cases..., Pt. II." *Keyboard Magazine* May 1987:

38+   National Association of Music Merchants Expo. Includes descriptions of music software.

869.   ---.   "NAMM: Several Tons of Music Hardware and Several Gigabytes of Software All Crammed Together in One Enormous Building and Surrounded by Crowds of People Wearing Three-Piece Suits and Purple Hair, Pt. I." *Keyboard Magazine* Apr. 1987: 52+ National Association of Music Merchants Expo. Includes descriptions of music software.

870.   ---.   "Technological Vision: Tangerine Dream: 15 Years on the Cutting Edge." *Keyboard Magazine* Nov. 1988: 98+ Interview with the members of Tangerine Dream. Topics include the various microcomputers used in their musical activities (Atari ST, IBM PC, and Macintosh).

871.   ---.   "NAMM Music Expo '87: They're Showing What You'll Be Playing." *Keyboard Magazine* Oct. 1987: 38+ National Association of Music Merchants. Includes a section on music software and computers, and cites Atari as the first computer company to display at a NAMM show.

872.   Grehan, Richard. "Computers and Music." *Byte* June 1986: 143. Introduction to six articles in this issue of *Byte* dealing with computers and music. All six articles are cited in this bibliography.

873.   Gualtieri, D. M.   "MIDI Output Interface to a Parallel Printer Port." *Computer Music Journal* 10.3 (1986): 79-82. Presents a simple computer-to-instrument MIDI interface that converts the parallel printer output of various computers to a MIDI output port. It allows information to be transmitted from a computer to a MIDI instrument but it will not allow musical keyboard information to be read by the computer. Includes a detailed schematic.

874.   Hagerty, Roger. "Random Music." *Compute!* Mar. 1984: 176-78. Program that plays random combinations of pitch, duration, and volume. For the VIC, C-64, and Atari 800.

875.   Halfhill, Tom.   "Sound Synthesis: Telharmoniums, Theremins, and Rhythmicons." *Compute!* Jan. 1983: 26-34. General discussion of the history of synthesized music and the potential for personal computers in musical applications. Includes an overview of the C-64 SID chip.

876.   Hall, I. K.   "Music and the Personal Computer." *Guitar Review* Spring 1984: 10-13. General overview of music applications of personal computers. Includes bibliography.

877. Hanlon, Caroline D. "Buyer's Guide to Music Composition and Programming Software." *Compute!'s Gazette* Aug. 1988: 45+ Descriptive list of current music software. Includes a directory of publishers.

878. Hospers, Al. "The Transcontinental MIDI Songwriting Shuffle." *Electronic Musician* Dec. 1988: 36+   Discussion and tips on long-distance, computerized, MIDI songwriting collaborations.

879. Hunkins, Arthur. "*Player ZX81*: A Tune-Playing Program for the Sinclair/Timex." Rev. of *Player ZX81*. *Compute!* Jan. 1983: 142.

880. ---. "Sound on the Sinclair/Timex." *Compute!* Jan. 1983: 68-70. Four programs that produce simple melodies.

881. ---. "Update on Sinclair/Timex Sound." *Compute!* Apr. 1983: 164. Presents a method of extending the sound range of the Sinclair to almost middle c.

882. Hussey, Leigh Ann. "Music Notation in ASCII." *Electronic Musician* Nov. 1987: 76-78. Discusses the possibility of placing compositions on electronic bulletin boards by using a standard file format that will work with any notation program.

883. Jimenez, Maria. "MIDI Studio." *Music, Computers & Software* Aug. 1988: 72-73. Discussion of automated mixing. Mentions *MegaMix* from Musically Intelligent Devices for the IBM, Macintosh, and Atari ST. Features include moving fader graphics, fader volume, mute/solo, copy/paste functions, and real/step time editing.

884. Johnson, Jim. "Computing." *Music, Computers & Software* Aug. 1988: 18+ Overview of general computer terminology e.g., CPU (Central Processing Unit), ALU (Arithmetic Logic Unit), data bus, address bus, control line, clock speeds, instruction set, etc.

885. ---. "Computing." *Music, Computers & Software* Dec. 1988: 18+ Interesting overview of the similarities between computer disks and analog tape. The author states that although they appear to be very different, both use a combination of metallic particles, adhesive, and lubricant to store data.

886. ---. "Computing." *Music, Computers & Software* June 1988: 18+ In-depth discussion of the many different types of monitors currently available e.g., RGB, CGA, EGA, etc. Topics include resolution, color capabilities, screen size, and other factors one should consider when purchasing a monitor for music applications.

887. ---. "Computing." *Music, Computers & Software* Nov. 1988: 18+ Descriptive comparison of high and low level programming languages; compilation and interpretation; and source code and object code. Languages discussed include Assembler, FORTRAN, BASIC, and C.

888. ---. "Computing." *Music, Computers & Software* Oct. 1988: 18+ Informative discussion of the different types of standards in the computer industry. The author stresses the importance of connectivity and the various ports found on most popular microcomputers e.g., RS-232, SCSI, mouse, DMA (Direct Memory Access), etc.

889. ---. "KCS Applications." *Keyboards, Computers & Software* Feb. 1987: 8+ Discussion of algorithmic composition and available programs.

890. ---. "Sequencing for Live Performance." *Electronic Musician* Mar. 1988: 72-76. General overview of some of the problems encountered in live performance with MIDI equipment and how they can be minimized.

891. ---. "MCS Applications: You Can Do Plenty of MIDI Programming with the BASIC That Comes with Your Computer." *Music, Computers & Software* May 1987: 8+ Discussion of how one can design simple programs that may augment the usefulness of commercial software. Applications discussed include file processing and MIDI data processing.

892. Jungleib, Stanley. "Stanford's Computer Music Lab, Where Today's Research Becomes Tomorrow's Pushbutton Magic." *Keyboard Magazine* Dec. 1987: 58+ In-depth discussion of what is taking place at CCRMA (Center for Computer Research in Music and Acoustics, Stanford University) in the areas of digital synthesis, signal processing, and computer-assisted composition. Includes bibliography.

893. Kaczynski, Richard. "MIDI Applications." *Music, Computers & Software* Oct. 1988: 24-25. Discusses the differences between using MIDI technology in performance and at home. Topics include cables, program changes, and the importance of backups. The author states that a multitasking operating system is best for live performance.

894. Kaplan, Gary M. "On Screen: Many People Have Been Put Off..." *Home Computer Magazine* Aug. 1985: 7. Debut of a new column devoted to electronic music.

895. Kauffman, Jim. "Coping with Information Overload: How to Survive the Data Deluge and Keep Your Mind on Making Music."

Music, Computers & Software June 1988: 49-51. The author discusses how the time involved in learning the various aspects of MIDI and personal computing can be discouraging to many musicians. Factors to consider when looking for a system include frequency of use, time available, ease-of-use, and personal finances.

896. "Keyboard Report: Updates and Short Takes: *Akai S900* 2.0, Aphex Type E, *Akai S700*, Voyetra *Sequencer Plus*, & Hybrid Arts *ADAP*." *Keyboard Magazine* Dec. 1987: 148+ Includes an overview of *Sequencer Plus* for the IBM PC and *ADAP* for the Atari ST.

897. Koberstein, Wayne. "The Music of Sound." *Home Computer Magazine* Mar. 1985: 32-37. Reviews of 17 music producing items including hardware e.g., keyboard overlay and touchpad.

898. Krauss, Bill. "*Steamshuffle & Winterbreath*: Notes from the Underground." *Music, Computers & Software* Apr. 1988: 36." Description of *Steamshuffle*, an outdoor interactive sculpture powered by an Apple IIe, and *Winterbreath*, "the first permanent winter participatory steam/sound fountain." The latter utilizes a Macintosh SE. The artists responsible are Christopher Janney and Joan Brigham.

899. Lansky, Paul. "The Sound of Software-Computer-Made Music." *Perspectives in Computing* Fall-Winter 1985: 34-42. Excellent overview of electronic music and personal computers from historical and practical perspectives. Contains a recording and a bibliography.

900. Latimer, Joey. "1986 Buyer's Guide to Music Hardware and Software: Regardless of Musical Talent, Your Family Can Make Beautiful Music." *Family Computing* Aug. 1986: 36-40. Evaluation of 17 programs for composing and sound-editing, several add-on keyboards, and MIDI interfaces. Includes an interview with Barry Manilow.

901. ---. "Buyer's Guide to Music Hardware and Software." *Family Computing* Aug. 1985: 33-38. Includes vendor guides to music software and hardware, and a discussion of MIDI.

902. ---. "Compose a Tune Or a Symphony." *Family Computing* July 1985: 31. Brief descriptions of seven music programs.

903. ---. "Making Money Making Music." *Family & Home Office Computing* July 1988: 46-48. Kate and Jack Goga describe how they use an Atari 1040 ST and sequencing software to compose music for *Cagney and Lacey* and the *CBS Movie of the Week*. In addition, Mark Freedman discusses his use of the Macintosh in his New York recording studio. Includes a MIDI equipment directory and a glossary of MIDI terminology.

904. ---. "Making Music." *Family Computing* July 1987: 35-39. Includes a guide to music software and briefly explains the built-in music capabilities of most popular microcomputers.

905. ---. "Microtones." *Family Computing* Feb. 1985: 90-91. Presents four music programs that make use of multivoice sound and white noise. Atari, C-64, VIC-20, and TI 99/4A.

906. ---. "Microtones." *Family Computing* Jan. 1985: 106-07. Presents a program called *Tune Generator* that creates music by randomly selecting chords and notes. Adam, Atari, C-64, and VIC-20.

907. ---. "Microtones: Three-Voice Sound Effect." *Family Computing* Aug. 1987: 17. Program listings for Atari 800, C-64, IBM PCjr., Macintosh, and TI-99.

908. ---. "Music by the Numbers." *Compute!* Dec. 1988: 40+ General overview of products available for music applications. Also gives some possible configurations from inexpensive to very expensive systems. Covers all popular microcomputers and includes a directory of manufacturers and a glossary of computer music terms.

909. ---. "*The Twelve Days of Christmas.*" *Family Computing* Dec. 1986: 92-105. A computer program for the Apple II series, 8-bit Ataris, C-64/128, IBM PC, and Tandy Color Computer that plays *The Twelve Days of Christmas* and displays the lyrics.

910. Lawler, Brian. "Musical Scales on the VIC." *Compute!* Mar. 1983: 147. Presents a program for the VIC-20 that plays musical scales.

911. Lehrman, Paul D. "Noteworthy Publishing: Personal Computers Have Been Far More Successful at Making Music Than Transcribing It. Until Now." *Personal Publishing* Feb. 1989: 24+ Detailed coverage of the most popular programs for desktop music publishing. Programs discussed include *Personal Composer System/2*, *HB Music Engraver*, *Finale*, *NoteWriter*, *Deluxe Music Construction Set*, and *ConcertWare* +. Includes an interesting account of how Christopher Yavelow created the opera *Countdown* entirely from the desktop, excellent illustrations, and addresses for further information.

912. ---. "So You Want to Be a Music Software Company." *Electronic Musician* Nov. 1986: 66+ Suggestions and tips for success in the business of music software.

913. ---. "Software Fact & Fiction--What You Need to Know to Sell Computer Music." *Music Trades* Nov. 1986: 44+

914. Leibs, Albert S. "Music & the Microchip: Instruments Get User Friendly." *InformationWEEK* 3 Aug. 1987: 18-21. Discussion of the growing use of electronics and personal computers in the musical instruments industry. Includes a brief overview of MIDI.

915. Leonard, S. "Computers for Keyboardists: Back It up Or Pack It Up." *Keyboard Magazine* Jan. 1986: 117.

916. ---. "Computers for Keyboardists: Choosing a Computer, MIDI Interface Card, and Software Sequencer and Librarian." *Keyboard Magazine* Aug. 1985: 74-75.

917. ---. "Computers for Keyboardists: Data Transmission, Data Storage, and Input/Output Devices." *Keyboard Magazine* Oct. 1985: 95.

918. ---. "Computers for Keyboardists: Getting Your Soft Wares to Market." *Keyboard Magazine* June 1986: 141.

919. ---. "Computers for Keyboardists: Glossary of Computer Terms for Keyboardists." *Keyboard Magazine* Nov. 1985: 88-89.

920. ---. "Computers for Keyboardists: How They Do What They Do for Keyboard Players." *Keyboard Magazine* Feb. 1986: 98. Covers the basic operating functions and terminology of personal computers. Topics discussed include ROM, DOS, input/output data, program disks, and elementary programming concepts.

921. ---. "Computers for Keyboardists: Setting Things Straight with Your Interface Card." *Keyboard Magazine* July 1986: 124.

922. ---. "Computers for Keyboardists: Some Computer Basics: Bits, Bytes, Buses, and Turning Little Numbers into Big Ones." *Keyboard Magazine* Sep. 1985: 78+

923. Levitt, David. "Pushing the Sound Envelope." *Dr. Dobb's Journal of Software Tools* May 1987: 16-19. Includes a brief history of computer music and discusses recent developments in music software and MIDI.

924. Levy, S. "Bliss, Microchips, and Rock & Roll: The Inside Data on the U. S. Festival." *Rolling Stone* 14 Oct. 1982: 14-16. Interesting article covering a music festival sponsored by Steve Wozniak. Reflects a growing interest in computers by popular musicians e.g., "Computers used to be seen as cold, emotionless. Now people are realizing there's flesh and blood in computers..." Jerry Garcia (Grateful Dead).

925. Lewis, Bill. "Alone in the Spotlight: A Workingman's Guide to MIDI." *Music, Computers & Software* Oct. 1987: 62+ Discussion of the advantages of MIDI-based equipment in live performance. Topics considered include portability, sound quality, and the financial rewards of solo performance.

926. ---. "Hard Disks: Mega-Storage of Mega-Bytes." *Keyboards, Computers & Software* Dec. 1986: 42-44. Description and evaluation of hard disk systems. Includes a list of manufacturers of hard disks for many popular microcomputers.

927. ---. "MCS Computing." *Music, Computers & Software* Feb.-Mar. 1988: 89-90. General overview and discussion of computer terminology e.g., binary, decimal, bit, byte, parallel, gigabytes, etc.

928. ---. "MCS Computing: DOS Is a Generic Term Which Describes the Software Used by Any Computer to Interact with Its Disk Drive." *Music, Computers & Software* Apr. 1988: 73-74. Brief but informative description of the various operating systems used by most personal computers.

929. ---. "Starting Up." *Music, Computers & Software* Dec. 1987: 45+ Basic introduction to MIDI and personal computers, and the equipment needed to implement a working system i.e., computers, MIDI interfaces, software, etc. Includes bibliography.

930. ---. "Telecommunicating: The Next Wave of Musical Interaction." *Music, Computers & Software* Feb. 1989: 40+ Excellent introduction to online communications and related terminology e.g., modem, data bit, stop bit, parity, Xmodem, Ymodem, etc. Also includes informative sidebars entitled "Starting Your Own BBS" and "The *MCS* MIDI Forum on CompuServe."

931. Lewis, Bill, and Steve Friedman. "Choosing a Computer: There Are Special Needs a Musician Must Consider before Turning to the Computer for Musical Assistance." *The 1987 KCS MIDI Buyer's Guide* 1987: 14+ General overview of personal computers and their musical potential. (*Keyboards, Computers & Software*)

932. Lipson, Stefan B. "Legal Issues & the High-Tech Musician, Pt. I: Copy Protection." *Music Technology* Aug. 1988: 66-67. Brief but informative article on how copy protection works and why software companies may or may not use it.

933. ---. "Massive Memory." *Music Technology* Feb. 1988: 64-65. Overview of how hard disks can be of help to computer musicians.

934. ---. Rev. of MIDIPascal and MIDIBASIC, from Altech Systems. *Music Technology* July 1988: 79. Programming language utilities for the Macintosh and IBM PC.

935. ---. "The *Music Studio* for Amiga and Atari ST." Rev. of *Music Studio*, from Activision. *Compute!* Nov. 1986: 70. Music composition software. Features include a sound editor, more than 15 built-in instrumental sounds, and MIDI compatibility.

936. ---. "User Groups." *Music Technology* Apr. 1988: 76-77. Discussion of user groups, how they operate and how they can help musicians obtain helpful information and public domain software. Includes numbers for several user groups for Atari, Apple, Commodore, and IBM.

937. Loy, G. "Musicians Make a Standard: The MIDI Phenomenon." *Computer Music Journal* 9.4 (1985): 8-26. An excellent introduction and survey of the MIDI standard 1.0. Includes the physical specification and many helpful illustrations.

938. Mace, Scott. "Electronic Arts' Music Program Scores a Hit." *InfoWorld* 10 Oct. 1983: 1+ Preview of *Music Construction Set*, music composition/notation software for the Apple II and C-64.

939. ---. "Electronic Orchestras in Your Living Room: MIDI Could Make 1985 the Biggest Year Yet for Computer Musicians." *InfoWorld* 25 Mar. 1985: 29-33. Brief overview of MIDI including an annotated guide to vendors of MIDI hardware and software. Also explores computers in music education.

940. Mahin, Bruce. "Digital Composition." *The Instrumentalist* Dec. 1986: 15-18. A look at recent developments in electronic music. Emphasis is on MIDI, the personal computer, digital synthesizers (Yamaha DX7), and music software (*Performer* and *Professional Composer* from Mark of the Unicorn).

941. "Making Music." *Family Computing* July 1987: 35-39. Description of the basic concepts of producing music on a computer. Includes a list of 10 pieces of hardware that boost a computer's music making potential and 13 music programs. Also includes a buyer's guide that discusses the musical ability of 22 popular computers.

942. Mancini, Joseph. "Computer-Music Pioneer Turns His Attention to Micros." *InfoWorld* 27 June 1983: 29-30. Description of UPIC, an 8086-based CAD/CAM system for music.

943. Mancini, Joseph, and Paul Freiberger. "European Computer Music Research Challenges American Efforts." *Popular Computing* Apr. 1985: 22. Overview of the 10th Annual International Computer

Music Conference in Paris. The author states that IRCAM (Institute for Research in Acoustics and Music, France) is becoming a world leader in electronic music technology.

944. Mann, M. "Music: Creation of Swine Lake, Computerized Music Based on Hog Sounds." *Omni* Dec. 1986: 38. A professor at Virginia Commonwealth University uses a synthesizer, a sampler, and a computer to capture and alter various sounds made by his pigs.

945. Mansfield, Richard. "Different Kinds of Programs / Graphics / Music." *Compute!* Apr. 1983: 18. Brief introduction to music software.

946. ---. "Dr. T's Sequencer for C-64 and Apple." *Compute!* Jan. 1986: 86-87. Features include real time and step time input. In step time the user can specify and control the MIDI channel, pitchbend, and after-touch.

947. ---. "Music in the Computer Age." *Compute!* Jan. 1985: 30-39. Discussion focusing on the impact of music synthesizers in the music industry. Topics include the Kurzweil and the Ensoniq Mirage.

948. ---. "Now-Silent Beethovens." *Compute!* Jan. 1985: 51. Commentary voicing the author's fears that music synthesizers may one day replace musicians.

949. Many, Chris. "Dr. T *Copyist*: Software for IBM PC and Atari ST." *Music Technology* June 1987: 60-62. Score editing/printing program. Features include music entry by keyboard, mouse, or a sequencer; music keyboard simulation mode (on-screen note entry); and many editing features e.g., copy, move, insert, etc.

950. ---. "*MegaMix* MR16/IPC: Software for IBM PC and Apple Mac." *Music Technology* Mar. 1987: 42-43. MIDI-based automation software that interfaces with a mixing console to assist in multitrack recording.

951. ---. "*Texture* Version 2.5: Software for IBM PC and Commodore Amiga." *Music Technology* May 1987: 56-58. MIDI sequencer for the IBM PC. Features include auto-punch and note editing with accuracy of up to 1/192 of a beat.

952. Mathews, Max V., and John R. Pierce. "The Computer as a Musical Instrument." *Scientific American* Feb. 1987: 126-33. Good general explanation of sound sampling and sound synthesis. Includes bibliography.

953. Maxwell, J. T. III, and S. M. Ornstein. "*Mockingbird*: A Composer's Amanuensis." *Byte* Jan. 1984: 384+ Music scoring program from Xerox. *Mockingbird* runs on a microcomputer developed at PARC (Palo Alto Research Center) called the Xerox 1132 which features high resolution graphics and 2-8 Megs of RAM. Includes bibliography.

954. McConkey, Jim. "Report on the Fourth Annual Symposium on Small Computers in the Arts." *Computer Music Journal* 9.2 (1985): 53-59. Chronological summary of events. Topics include music education and MIDI applications.

955. ---. "Report on the Third Annual Symposium on Small Computers in the Arts." *Computer Music Journal* 8.2 (1984): 41-47. Chronological summary of events. Topics include musical uses of small computers, computers in music education, and legal and commercial issues.

956. ---. "The Second Annual Symposium on Small Computers in the Arts." *Computer Music Journal* 7.3 (1983): 25-30. Chronological summary of events.

957. McConkey, Jim, and R. Dreier. "Report on the Fifth Annual Symposium on Small Computers in the Arts." *Computer Music Journal* 10.2 (1986): 69-74. Chronological summary of events. Topics include new music tools (music software for the Macintosh and the IBM PC) and MIDI applications. Includes a guide to manufacturers of products mentioned.

958. Means, Ben, and Jean Means. "Desktop Music Video: From Music to Visuals -- a Users Guide." *Music, Computers & Software* Feb.-Mar. 1988: 55-59. Discussion of how high quality video camcorders, color microcomputers, and accessories can be used to make impressive music videos. Emphasis is placed on the Atari ST, the Amiga, and the Macintosh II.

959. "MIDI Manufacturers." *Keyboard Magazine* Jan. 1986: 108. List of manufacturers.

960. Milano, D. "Keyboard Report: Digidesign *Sound Designer Emulator II* Software." *Keyboard Magazine* Oct. 1985: 112-14.

961. ---. "Keyboard Report: *DX-Pro*, *DX-Heaven*, and *Data/7* DX7 Voicing Software." *Keyboard Magazine* Oct. 1985: 118+

962. ---. "The Pros Tell How Sequencers Changed Their Lives (Or Didn't)" *Keyboard Magazine* June 1987: 50+ Interviews with Jan Hammer, Mark Isham, Jeff Lorber, Wendy Carlos, and others focusing on various hardware- and software-based sequencers.

963. Miller, Erik. Rev. of *The Fantastic Music Machine*. *InfoWorld* 19 Dec. 1983: 63-66. Music composition software for the Timex/Sinclair.

964. Minor, David. "Music: A Buyer's Guide to Software." *Popular Computing* Dec. 1984: 244. Overview of music software and hardware available for various personal computers. Software discussed includes *Synthy 64* (C-64), *Music Construction Set* (Apple II & C-64), and *Orchestra 90* (TRS 80 Model III).

965. Mocsny, Daniel. "Synaptic Systems: Creating the Ultimate Mind to MIDI Connection." *Music, Computers & Software* Oct. 1988: 44+ General overview of new ideas and technologies being developed for music and computers. Topics include new computer systems, artificial intelligence, and advanced user interfaces.

966. Moody, Glyn. "*The Music System*: Making the Most of the BBC." Rev. of *The Music System*, from Island Logic Ltd. *Practical Computing* (U.K.) Sep. 1985: 60-62. A music processor, synthesizer, and sequencer with Macintosh-like features. States that a version for the C-64 is forthcoming.

967. Moog, Robert. "Digital Music Synthesis: The Many Different Shapes of the Waveform of the Present." *Byte* June 1986: 155-68. General overview of the physics of sound and how to produce it with the help of a personal computer.

968. Moore, F. Richard. "The Disfunctions of MIDI." *Computer Music Journal* 12.1 (1988): 19-28. In-depth look at the various disfunctions of MIDI from a purely musical perspective. Topics discussed include performance capture, the digital representation of musical control processes, and synthesizer control. Includes bibliography.

969. Nelson, Steve, and Andy Widders-Ellis. Rev. of *Music Construction Set*, from Electronic Arts. *Home Computer Magazine* Aug. 1985: 38-39. Music composition/notation software for the Apple II and C-64.

970. Netsel, Tom. "Computers: The Powerful New Music Machines." *Compute!* Mar. 1988: 6+ General discussion of music, MIDI, and the personal computer. Jon Appleton, professor of music at Dartmouth College, conveys his thoughts on new technology in music production and education.

971. ---. "MIDI Made Simple." *Compute!'s Gazette* Aug. 1988: 14+ General overview of MIDI and personal computers. Includes information on several bulletin board services in a sidebar entitled "MIDI By Modem."

972. Newquist, Harvey. "Multitasking." *Music Technology* May 1988: 72+ Discusses the potential music applications of a multitasking environment e.g., sequencing a piece of music while another is being printed. The Amiga, IBM PS/2 and Macintosh II (*Multifinder*) are covered in detail.

973. ---. "Sing a Song of Software, a PC Full of RAM." *Computerworld* 15 Dec. 1986: 17. Introduction to MIDI and a brief discussion of music software being developed by Roland Corp. for the IBM PC and Apple computers.

974. O'Brien, Walter. "KCS Telecom." *Keyboards, Computers & Software* Dec. 1986: 12+ General discussion of telecommunications software for various microcomputers and how one can use online services in music. Topics include downloading and uploading MIDI files.

975. O'Donnell, Bob. "Interactive Music." *Music Technology* Oct. 1988: 56-58. Interesting discussion of how new forms of media e.g., CD-I (Compact Disk-Interactive) and CD + MIDI (compact disks encoded with MIDI) are offering new ways of presenting music.

976. ---. "Taking Control: The Summer NAMM Report." *Music Technology* Sep. 1988: 58-65. Highlights from the National Association of Music Merchants Expo. Includes brief descriptions of *Finale*, a professional music publishing and composition program for the Macintosh from Coda Music Software (a version for the IBM is forthcoming), *Encore*, a notation program for the Macintosh from Passport, and the IBM compatible C1 laptop from Yamaha.

977. O'Donnell, Craig. "MIDI Standard Proposed." *Macworld* Nov. 1987: 95+ Brief discussion of a new file-transfer format being developed by Dave Oppenheim. The format would make file exchanges between different systems possible regardless of the manufacturer.

978. Oppenheimer, Larry. "The Arrival of Intelligent Instruments." *Electronic Musician* Aug. 1987: 37+ An overview of algorithmic composition. Includes "mini-reviews" of *M* and *Jam Factory* (Intelligent Music) for the Macintosh, *Music Mouse* (Opcode) for the Macintosh and Amiga, and *Algorithmic Composer* (Dr. T.) for the Commodore 64/128.

979. Parisi, Deborah. "The Big Score." *Music Technology* Nov. 1988: 90-94. Overview of the activities at Robert Redford's Sundance Institute in Utah, a summer camp for film composers. Composers Alan Silvestri, Ralph Grierson, and Don Walker discuss how they use MIDI, electronic musical instruments, and personal computers in scoring for film.

980. ---. "From Zen to Vice." *Music Technology* June 1988: 52-57. Interview with Jan Hammer who uses a Vic 20, IBM PC, and a Macintosh for music applications. Hammer states that no matter how sophisticated computers get they will never be able to do all of the work for any composer.

981. Peters, Constantine. "Computer Speed: Upgrades to Faster Computing." *Music, Computers & Software* Jan. 1989: 43+ Part two of a two-part series dealing with ways to increase the speed of most personal computers. This article focuses primarily on operating systems and microprocessors.

982. ---. "Speeding up Your Computer, Pt. I." *Music, Computers & Software* Dec. 1988: 41-43. Discussion of the various ways one can upgrade an existing system. Covers hard disks, disk CACHE, and virtual memory.

983. Petersen, George. "Portable Power: Computers for the Road." *Electronic Musician* July 1988: 123-26. Discussion of the options available to musicians who need a computer for performance situations. Computers discussed include the Rackmount Personal Computer from Advanced Digital Systems of Tarzana, California, and the Music Package from Computer Music Supply of Walnut, California.

984. Pickering, Roly. "Virus!" *Music Technology* Jan. 1989: 58-61. General overview of viruses and the effects they can have on computer hardware and software. Includes a sidebar containing a descriptive list of available vaccines for various computers.

985. Pierson-Perry, Jim. "Panning for Gold: The PAN BBS for Professional Musicians." *STart: The ST Monthly* Mar. 1989: 71-72. Excellent overview of PAN, the Performing Artist's Network. Includes logon procedures via direct access, Telenet, and Tymnet; address and phone number; features and available services; and general information applicable to all users.

986. Powell, Roger. "The Challenge of Music Software: An Overview of the Current State of Computers in Music." *Byte* June 1986: 145-50. In-depth discussion of the present and future potential of MIDI and personal computers

987. Powell, Roger, and Richard Grehan. "Four MIDI Interfaces: MIDI Interfaces for the Commodore 64, IBM PC, Macintosh, and Apple II Family." *Byte* June 1986: 265-72. TDS-AP for the Apple II and TDSC-64 for the C-64 (Syntech Corp.), MPU-401 for the IBM PC or Apple II (Roland), and MIDIMac for the Macintosh (Opcode).

988. Regena, C. "Making Music with BASIC." *Compute!* Mar. 1988: 55-56. Review of some of the more common BASIC sound commands. Computers discussed include the Amiga, Atari ST, C-128, and the IBM PC.

989. ---. "Mixing Graphics and Music." *Compute!* Jan. 1985: 141-44. Summary of the methods used to design a program incorporating sound and graphics. SOUND statements are used for the music in a program entitled *Jolly Old St. Nick* for the TI.

990. ---. "Playing Music on the TI." *Compute!* Oct. 1983: 224-28. Presents a program called *Ludwig* which illustrates a unique use of the CALL SOUND command for the TI-99/4A.

991. ---. "The Singing Computer." *Compute!* Aug. 1984: 115-18. Overview of music programming techniques for the TI. The author begins by demonstrating the speech capabilites of the TI (TI Speech Synthesizer required). Later, code is introduced that alters the pitch and slope of the voice making it sound more like a song. A program called *Alphabet Song* is included that demonstrates simple singing on the TI.

992. Reifsnider, Randal J. "*Musical TI Keyboard.*" *Compute!* Sep. 1984: 148-49. Program for the TI-99/4A that demonstrates the capabilities of its sound chip.

993. Riger, Norman L. "*QuickBASIC Music Editor.*" *Computer Shopper* Nov. 1987: 199+ Music editing software that allows the user to input, store, and playback music from the computer keyboard.

994. Roberts, Jeremy. "MCS Applications." *Music, Computers & Software* Feb.-Mar. 1988: 8+ Brief overview of several standard MACRO commands that can streamline computer applications e.g., Command-X, Command-C, Command-Q, etc.

995. Rona, Jeff. "Computer Concepts." *Keyboard Magazine* June 1988: 82+ Discussion and explanation of basic computer terminology. Terms covered include MIDI, operating system, microprocessor, CPU, memory, and peripherals. The author also discusses various things to consider when purchasing a system.

996. ---. "Taming the Wild Algorithm." *Electronic Musician* Feb. 1989: 86+ *Jam Factory* from Intelligent Music is used to demonstrate the basic concepts of algorithmic composition.

997. ---. "Technology: Computers On-Line: It's a Hard Life, Pt. I: Survival with Floppies." *Keyboard Magazine* Oct. 1988: 131. Topics include management of system files, desk accessories, utilities, etc.;

the importance of backup copies; and disk quality. Jeff Rona is the current president of the MIDI Manufacturers Association.

998. ---. "Technology: Computers On-Line: It's a Hard Life, Pt. II: The Crash of '88." *Keyboard Magazine* Dec. 1988: 125. Brief discussion of the importance of backups.

999. ---. "Technology: Computers On-Line: Safe Sectors: Living With Viruses." *Keyboard Magazine* Mar. 1989: 104+ General overview of viruses. The author states that the Computer Virus Industry Association recorded about 300 "events" regarding some type of computer virus in 1988. However, only 4% of those reported were actually verified as true viruses. The author also suggests ways in which users can become susceptible to viruses and how to avoid them. Includes the address for the Computer Virus Industry Association.

1000. ---. "Technology: Computers On-Line: Twelve Well-Known Computer Lies Exposed." *Keyboard Magazine* May 1988: 127+ Summary of 12 common sales-pitches the first-time computer shopper is likely to encounter e.g., "You can learn to use it in just one afternoon."

1001. "Running Bytes." *Music, Computers & Software* Feb.-Mar. 1988: 20. Richard Einhorn describes how he created a motion picture score for a 90-piece orchestra using *Texture* and an IBM PC. *Performer* was then used to sync the music with the film.

1002. Scholz, Carter. "Algorithmic Composition." *Music Technology* Oct. 1988: 74-78. Historical overview of algorithmic composition and a survey of the products currently available. Mentions *M* and *Jam Factory* (Macintosh), *MusicBox* (IBM), and *Ludwig* (Atari ST). Includes a glossary of terms and a bibliography.

1003. ---. "Do-It-Yourself Software: Any MIDI Keyboard Can Play in Just Intonation with Computerized Pitch-Bending." *Keyboard Magazine* Feb. 1986: 49+ Describes a program in Pascal that "detunes" MIDI data to Just Intonation. The program discussed is for the Yamaha DX7 and an IBM PC but can be adapted to any equipment.

1004. ---. Rev. of HMSL, from Frog Peak Music. *Music Technology* Sep. 1988: 82-83. Programming language developed at the Mills College Center for Contemporary Music specifically for music. HMSL (Hierarchical Music Specification Language) runs on the Macintosh or Amiga and is, technically, an "object-oriented extension of the Forth programming language."

1005. ---. "MIDI Resources: Programming Languages for Do-It-Yourself Software." *Keyboard Magazine* Nov. 1988: 74+ Discussion of how musicians can work outside the limits of mass market software by writing their own MIDI programs. The author presents the basics of programming and briefly discusses various programming languages for popular microcomputers e.g., MIDIBASIC and MIDIPascal (Macintosh), Formula (Atari ST), and CMU MIDI Toolkit (IBM PC).

1006. ---. "Mind over MIDI: A MIDI Data Analyzer Program." *Keyboard Magazine* Aug. 1986: 110-12. Presents a program in Turbo Pascal that monitors MIDI output, translates the data into a readable form, and displays it on the screen. The program is called *Peek* and is designed to be used with the Roland MPU-401 MIDI interface and any computer that supports the Turbo Pascal compiler.

1007. "Scoring a Hit in Music Publishing: Reading [And Writing] between the Lines." *Music, Computers & Software* Oct. 1988: 51+ In-depth discussion of music publishing with personal computers. Topics include computer hardware, software, and printing devices. The author states that the best computers for music scoring are the Macintosh and IBM PC. Includes a sidebar listing the features of popular programs.

1008. Scott, Jordan. "MIDI Applications." *Music, Computers & Software* Aug. 1988: 24-25. Brief overview of software synthesis. The author states that software synthesis can offer more features than traditional synthesizers if used with a computer such as the Macintosh or Atari ST. The basic features of *SoftSynth* from Digidesign are also discussed.

1009. Selman, Tom, and David Lourik. "Technology: Computers On-Line: Computer Viruses -- Nemesis of the Public Domain." *Keyboard Magazine* June 1988: 133. Brief discussion of the potential hazards of downloading untried and untested public domain shareware from networks and bulletin boards.

1010. ---. "Technology: Computers On-Line: Mac II & MIDI, IBM Emulation, & Developments." *Keyboard Magazine* Dec. 1987: 131. Topics of discussion include some of the problems associated with IBM emulation devices on non-IBM computers. The authors mention that compatibility between timing devices and MIDI interfaces is essential in MIDI applications.

1011. ---. "Technology: Computers On-Line: Mega Ataris, Apple Meets MIDI, PS/2 Noise, & Vapor Trails." *Keyboard Magazine* Apr. 1988: 128+ Brief discussion of the new Mega STs from Atari, the new Apple MIDI interface, and compatibility problems with the new PS/2 Model 30 from IBM.

1012. ---. "Technology: Computers On-Line: Multitasking & Other News from the Front Lines." *Keyboard Magazine* Nov. 1987: 122. General discussion of the potential and advantages of multitasking operating systems.

1013. ---. "Technology: Computers On-Line: The NeXT Computer & Music." *Keyboard Magazine* Jan. 1989: 105. Brief overview of the NeXT computer from NeXT, Inc. (Steve Jobs). The authors state that a MIDI interface is not built into the machine but it should be able to use the new Apple interface. It does, however, include a Motorola 56001 digital signal processor that has tremendous potential for music applications.

1014. ---. "Technology: Computers Online: The Yamaha C1 & Apple System Blues." *Keyboard Magazine* Nov. 1988: 140. Brief overview of the new Yamaha C1 IBM AT compatible featuring a 10 MHz 80286 processor, 1 Meg of RAM, optional 20 Meg hard drive, 2 MIDI ins, 1 MIDI thru, and 8 MIDI outs. Additional topics include System 6.0 for the Macintosh and the lack of MIDI software for the Apple IIGS.

1015. "Sequencers: Further Reading and Listening." *Keyboard Magazine* June 1987: 126. Bibliography of sources.

1016. Serafine, F., and R. Schwartz. "Passport's *MIDI/8 Plus*." Rev. of *MIDI/8 Plus*, from Passport Designs. *Electronic Musician* Jan. 1986: 66+ MIDI sequencer for the Apple II and C-64. Features unlimited overdubbing on up to 8 separate channels, auto-correct to 32nd note triplets, and sync to tape.

1017. Shannon, W., and D. Frederick. "Tired of Imitation Rhodes Patches? Generate and Graph Exotic New DX7 Sounds with This Random Program in BASIC." *Keyboard Magazine* July 1986: 72+ Discussion of how computers can be used to generate new patches for the Yamaha DX7 synthesizer. A program listing in BASIC is included.

1018. Sherman, S. P. "Musical Software: Take a Personal Computer, a Couple of Synthesizers, and 'Voila'--Studio-Quality Sound." *Fortune* 14 Oct. 1985: 145+ General overview of personal computers and music. Topics include *Total Music* from Southworth.

1019. Sillery, Bob. "The Computer Composer." Rev. of *Bank Street Music Writer*, from Mindscape and *The Music Shop*, from Broderbund Software. *Personal Computing* June 1985: 189-90. *BSMW* is for the Atari and C-64; *MS* is for the C-64.

1020. Silverman, L. A. "Music-Synthesis Software: A Beginner's Guide." *High Fidelity* Dec. 1983: 66-67. Brief introduction to music software.

1021.   Slepian, Don.   "What Can Be Done with a *Music Mouse?*" *Electronic Musician* Aug. 1987: 52-54. Description of *Music Mouse* from Opcode for the Macintosh and Amiga. Requires no keyboard skills or knowledge of music notation.

1022.   Smith, David G.   "Beyond Notes: Percussion/Sequence Calls." *Electronic Musician* Aug. 1988: 36+   Discusses the concept of triggering sound events to construct percussive patterns. Topics include *Total Music, Texture,* and *MIDIPaint.*

1023.   Smith, Steve.   "Toe Tappin' Data Storage." *CD-ROM Review* Oct. 1988: 27-29. Discussion of the *Universe of Sounds* from Optical Media International. Two compact disks that contain a broad range of sampled sounds including period acoustical and orchestral instruments. Compatible with the Apple CD drive.

1024.   "Software." *Musicians' Equipment Guide* Summer 1987: 64-70. Excellent overview of music software e.g., sequencers, patch editors and librarians, music notation, etc. From the publishers of *Musician* magazine.

1025.   Sonneborn, Henry.   "The Well-Tempered Computer." *Popular Computing* Dec. 1983: 218-24. Two programs in BASIC that explore modifications of the 12-tone chromatic scale. For the TI 99/4A.

1026.   Spangler, Clark.   "Song Construction." *Music, Computers & Software* Oct. 1988: 80-82. General discussion of some of the problems encountered when trying to compose a piece of music with the help of a personal computer. Focuses primarily on tempo and transposition.

1027.   "Special Report: Winter '88 NAMM Show." *Electronic Musician* Apr. 1988: 13+ Description of products exhibited at the National Association of Music Merchants trade show. Items include music software for all popular microcomputers.

1028.   Stewart, Michael.   "The Feel Factor: Music with Soul." *Electronic Musician* Oct. 1987: 56-62. Discussion of the "cold and inhuman" sound of computer music and how composers can program "feeling" into their compositions.

1029.   Stockford, James.   "*Data/7* and *Performance/7.*" Rev. of *Data/7* and *Performance/7. Whole Earth Review* Winter 1985: 111. Both provide high speed storage and retrieval of individual voices and banks of 32 voices. For the Yamaha DX7, Apple II series, and Commodore 64/128. From Mimetics.

1030.   Stockford, James, and Joe West.   "MIDI Interface, *MIDI/8 Plus, Leadsheeter.*" Rev. of *MIDI/8 Plus* and *Leadsheeter,* from Passport Designs. *Whole Earth Review* Winter 1985: 110-11. *MIDI/8*

Plus is available for the Apple IIe and C-64/128. *Leadsheeter* is a music transcription program for the Apple IIe.

1031. Strange, Allen. "Building Blocks for Computer-Generated Music: Do-It-Yourself C-64 and Apple II Software." *Keyboard Magazine* June 1987: 106+ Overview of a high-level computer language for music composition and performance called *MASC* (Meta-Language for Adaptive Synthesis and Control). Developed at the San Jose State University Electro-Acoustic Studios, *MASC* allows the user to build specialized "software modules" capable of producing user-specified MIDI data.

1032. Strom, P. A. "Programming -- Listening to the Language of Sound." *Electronic Musician* May 1986: 50.

1033. Styles, Bob, and Bill Lewis. "Software Overview." *The 1987 KCS MIDI Buyer's Guide* 1987: 22+ An analysis and overview of music application programs for personal computers. The *Buyer's Guide* is published annually by *Keyboards, Computers & Software*.

1034. Summers, Tan. Rev. of *Rock 'n' Rhythm*, from Spinnaker. *Family Computing* Apr. 1985: 89. For the C-64 and Atari.

1035. The´, Lee. "The Music Connection: Even If You Can't Read Or Write Music, Your Computer Can." *Personal Computing* Jan. 1986: 89-95. General overview of music hardware, software, MIDI, and various computer applications in music. The author states that many microcomputers can generate the basic sounds for music production without peripheral devices.

1036. Tolinski, Brad. "Stewart Copeland: Computers Liberate the Rhythmatist." *Keyboards, Computers & Software* Feb. 1987: 22+ Stewart Copeland, drummer for The Police, describes how he uses computers in his musical activities.

1037. Tucker, J. B. "Making Music with Micros." *High Technology* July 1984: 53+

1038. Tully, Tim. "Good Vibrations: The PC Joins the Band." *PC Computing* Feb. 1989: 172-85. Excellent article covering the present state of music and personal computers. Includes a sidebar by Paul D. Lehrman entitled "PC Chartbusters" that gives a descriptive overview of popular programs for the IBM PC and Apple Macintosh.

1039. Vail, Mark. "NAMM." *Keyboard Magazine* Apr. 1988: 34+ National Association of Music Merchants trade show report. Many interesting products are described including *JamBox/2* and *Video JamBox* from Southworth for the Macintosh and *Prelude* from Dynaware for the IBM PC.

1040.   ---.   "Sounds and Editor/Librarian Software: A *Keyboard* Survey." *Keyboard Magazine* Jan. 1989: 78+ Descriptive overview of editor/librarian software available for all popular microcomputers. Includes a directory of publishers.

1041.   ---.   "Summer NAMM 88." *Keyboard Magazine* Oct. 1988: 74+ Overview of the National Association of Music Merchants trade show. Products discussed include the Yamaha C1 IBM-PC compatible, *HB Music Engraver* and *Music Publisher* (sophisticated music transcription programs for the Macintosh), and various programs for the Atari ST.

1042.   Van Gelder, Lindsy.   "Enjoying the Brave New World of Computer Music." *Ms.* Oct. 1987: 42+ General introduction to MIDI and descriptions of popular music software. Products discussed include *Performer*, *Master Tracks Pro*, *Professional Composer*, and *Deluxe Music Construction Set*.

1043.   Visco, Christopher.   "*Guitar Tuner.*" *Compute!* Jan. 1985: 99-101. A program that helps the user tune a 6- or 12-string guitar. For the C-64, IBM PC, and Atari (8-bit).

1044.   Walsh, Kevin.   "Taking Aim at the Music Colossus: The Companies Behind the Software." *Music, Computers, & Software* Dec. 1987: 53+ General overview of significant music software developers and their products.

1045.   Watts, Susan.   "The Jury Is Still Out on the Day the Music Died." *Computerweekly* 8 May 1986: 40+ Eric Radcliffe and Martin Rushent, music producers, comment on the use of computers in music production.

1046.   Wells, Richard, et al.   "Studios of the (Not Yet) Rich and (Almost) Famous." *Electronic Musician* Feb. 1989: 68+ Five *EM* readers ranging from amateurs to professionals discuss ways musicians, with limited funds and time, can build a highly functional MIDI studio.

1047.   West, Joe.   "Breathe in Sound, Breathe Out Music... The Decillionic DX-1/the Interpolator." Rev. of Decillionic DX-1 and the Interpolator (Utility for the DX-1) *Whole Earth Review* Mar. 1985: 99. Sound generator for the Apple II series and Franklin.

1048.   Westfall, Lachlan.   "I Want My MTC!" *Electronic Musician* Nov. 1988: 63+ Discussion of the MIDI Time Code, an interface designed to link MIDI and the film and video industry's synchronization standard (SMPTE/EBU Time Code).

1049. ---. "MCS MIDI: The STANDARD File Format Is One of the Oldest 'If Only's' in the World of MIDI." *Music, Computers & Software* June 1987: 14+ Discussion of ANSI X3V1.8M and MIDI Files (D. Oppenheim/Opcode).

1050. ---. "Technology: Mind over MIDI: Birth of a Standard for MIDI Files." *Keyboard Magazine* Oct. 1988: 120. The author states that the MMA (MIDI Manufacturers Association) has officially adopted MIDI Files 1.0 as part of the MIDI specification. Theoretically, this should allow a MIDI file created on one system to be transferred to another, regardless of manufacturer.

1051. ---. "Technology: Mind over MIDI: MIDI Files in Action." *Keyboard Magazine* Nov. 1988: 139+ Discussion of the MIDI file standard and the problems involved in distributing sequencer data to different types of applications.

1052. Whelchel, Greg. "Computers Live." *Music Technology* Sep. 1988: 76-78. Discussion of factors to consider when using computers in live performance. Topics covered include hardware, software, and operating systems (*Multifinder* for the Macintosh and *HybriSwitch* for the Atari ST).

1053. Whitten, Terry. "The Tapeless Home Studio: Turning Your PC into a Digital Audio Workstation." *Music, Computers & Software* Feb.-Mar. 1988: 38+ Interesting discussion of how inexpensive sampling equipment may one day replace the tape deck in the recording studio. Includes a general introduction to digital recording.

1054. Widders-Ellis, Andy. "The New Age of Music Making." *Home Computer Magazine* Aug. 1985: 62. Presents a brief overview of music and the personal computer. Topics include MIDI, computers and synthesizers, sound sampling, and other significant developments in music technology.

1055. Widoff, Antony. "MIDI Files." *Music Technology* Nov. 1988: 74-77. In-depth discussion of the standardization of MIDI data files. Topics include the MIDI file specification, MIDI file formats, capturing and exporting data, and transferring data between computers from different manufacturers.

1056. Williams, Joseph. "Mixing Music and Micros." *Family Computing* Apr. 1985: 74.

1057. Williams, Wheat III. "Computer Notation." *Music Technology* July 1988: 80-84. In-depth discussion of music notation software and its effect on the music publishing business. Considers system requirements and available tools i.e., software and hardware.

1058.   Williamson, C.   "Dr. T's *Keyboard Controlled Sequencer* (Version 2)" *Electronic Musician* Feb. 1986: 60-61. Enhanced version of the *KCS* introduced in 1984. Features include full editing of all MIDI parameters, step time mode, 48 tracks in track mode, live edit, and automatic punch-in/out. For the Amiga, Apple II, Atari ST, and C-64/128.

1059.   Wilson, Blake. "VIC Musician." *Compute!* July 1983: 212-14. Describes how to take music from a printed score and enter it into the VIC for playback. The program included, however, is limited to 61 notes due to the size of the cassette buffer.

1060.   Yakal, Kathy.   "The Computerized Musician: *Compute!* Interviews Wendy Carlos and Frank Zappa." *Compute!* Jan. 1986: 36-46. General discussion of MIDI and its potential applications with personal computers.

1061.   Yavelow, C.   "Artificial Intelligence: Communicating with Intelligent Instruments." *Music, Computers & Software* June 1987: 47-50. General discussion of the musical applications of artificial intelligence. Brief descriptions of *Music Mouse, Nightingale, Jam Factory*, and *M*.

1062.   ---. "Direct to Hard Disk Recording." *Music Technology* June 1988: 78+ Overview of equipment currently available for computer assisted recording. Systems discussed include *ADAP*, *WaveFrame*, *Dyaxis*, *MaxAudio*, and 13 others. Includes a comparative list of features.

1063.   ---. "The Musical Future of Computers and Software: MIDI 5.0 to Be Scrapped in 1992?" *Music, Computers & Software* May 1987: 43+ Fifteen music software and hardware developers express their views on the future of music in the next five to ten years.

1064.   Youngblood, J. "Plot It Yourself: Display FM Waveforms on Your Apple or IBM with These BASIC Programs." *Keyboard Magazine* Nov. 1985: 41-42.

1065.   Zientara, Marguerite.   "Breakthrough Promises to Give Musicians Total Control." *InfoWorld* 30 Apr. 1984: 23.   Brief introduction to MIDI.

1066.   Zuckerman, A. J. "Recording Music on Floppy Disks." *High Technology* May 1986: 68-69.

Part III
Music Education

1067. Anshell, Pearl. "Music and Micros." Rev. of *Practical Music Theory*, from Alfred Pub. Co. *The Instrumentalist* Nov. 1984: 90-92. For the Apple II series and C-64. Complete music curriculum software with accompanying workbooks. Includes a summary of each lesson containing drill-and-practice and tutorial-style presentations.

1068. Arenson, Michael A., and Fred T. Hofstetter. "The *GUIDO* System and the *PLATO* Project." *Music Educators Journal* Jan. 1983: 46-51. Educational systems for programming lessons in all areas of music theory and ear training e.g., intervals, melodic dictation, chord quality, transposition, etc.

1069. Baker, G. W. "Personal Computers -- to Buy Or not to Buy." *The Instrumentalist* Mar. 1984: 10-11. Brief discussion of things one should consider when purchasing a personal computer. The article is very general in nature and is not restricted to musical considerations.

1070. Bakich, Michael E. "*Guitar Chord Tutor*: This Applesoft Program Uses Lo-Res Graphics to Help You Learn to Play Guitar Chords Correctly." *Nibble* Mar. 1986: 86-88.

1071. Bales, W. K., and R. E. Foltz. "More for Less with Computers." *Clavier* 22.5 (1983): 46-47. Discussion of how computers can supplement instruction in areas like music theory and music history. The author states that this can leave more time for the instructor to work with the student on applied instruction.

1072. Baugh, Ivan W. "Using Logo to Teach the Elements of Music." *Music Educators Journal* Dec. 1986: 37. Description of Terrapin Logo for the Apple IIe. Includes ideas for using it in music instruction and compares it to other versions of Logo.

1073. Bernstein, Jeremy, and Gary S. Roos. "Breakdancing with the Turtle." *Classroom Computer Learning* May 1986: 65. Interesting overview of a project in which students choreograph dance and music for the Logo Turtle.

1074. Blackman, Jaimie M. "The MIDI Potential." *Music Educators Journal* Dec. 1986: 29. Brief discussion of the potential for sequencers, drum machines, and MIDI instruments in music education.

1075. Boody, Charles G. "Floppy Discography." Rev. of *Magic Piano*, from EduSoft. *Music Educators Journal* Feb. 1988: 104-07. Ear training and creative drills for the Apple II series.

1076. ---. "Floppy Discography: *Deluxe Music Construction Set* and *ConcertWare* +." Rev. of *Deluxe Music Construction Set*, from Electronic Arts and *ConcertWare* +, from Great Wave. *Music Educators Journal* May 1988: 55-57. Excellent comparison exposing the weaknesses and strengths of each program. *ConcertWare* + is for the Macintosh and *DMCS* is for the Macintosh and Commodore Amiga. Includes a sample printout from each program.

1077. Brawer, Jennifer. "Teacher's Toolbox: An Exemplary High School Electronic-Music Lab Uses Apple IIe Computers as MIDI Workstations." *A*+ June 1988: 90-93. Description of how San Jose High Academy is using MIDI-equipped computers and peripherals to teach music fundamentals, keyboard techniques, notation, composition, voice, theory, and history.

1078. Breen, Christopher. "Music for Minors." *MacUser* Dec. 1988: 40. Brief overview of *Kids Time*, a package of five educational programs. The music section is called *Kids Notes*. From Great Wave Software for the Macintosh.

1079. Brown, James. *"Music Flash Cards."* *Antic: The Atari Resource* Feb. 1985: 66+ Educational program for teaching the position of notes on the staff.

1080. Burch, F. "Bach by Computer: Making Music on the Atari 800." *Classroom Computer Learning* Apr.-May 1984: 62-63. Introduction to music programming in PILOT and BASIC.

1081. Camp, J. "The College Computing Lab: MACing Music: Powerful Programs for under $500.00." *Electronic Learning* Feb. 1987: 39-40. Discussion of four college-level music training programs i.e., *ConcertWare* +, *Performer*, *Professional Composer*, and *Listen*.

1082. Carey, D., and R. Morse. "Readers Comment: Select Software Carefully." *Music Educators Journal* Nov. 1984: 7+ Overview of criteria for evaluation and selection of music software. The author states that music educators responsible for software selection should be well acquainted with the music capabilities of the microcomputers they operate.

1083. Carpenter, Robert A. "MIDI Goes to (Public) School: Integrating Technology into Existing Ensembles." *Music, Computers & Software* Nov. 1988: 47+ Interesting overview of how the Crestview Middle School in Columbus Ohio has integrated MIDI technology (including a Macintosh, an Apple IIe, and a C-64) into its instrumental music program.

1084. Chang, D. "Programming the Blues." *Jazz Educators Journal* 16.3 (1984): 18-20. Presents a program in Applesoft BASIC that generates blues melodies by making random selections from a set of specific pitches and rhythms defined by the user. The author states that the procedure is analogous to improvisation where the performer draws upon a vocabulary of motives, scales, and harmonic patterns.

1085. Chopp, Joseph M. "The Computer: Integrating Technology with Education." *Music Educators Journal* Dec. 1986: 22. Considers the pressure on students, teachers, and school boards to get involved in the new technology available for music instruction.

1086. Coale, Kristi. "Scale Models." *MacUser* Dec. 1988: 42. Brief overview of *Guitar Wizard*, a guitar tutorial for the Macintosh from Baudville.

1087. Coffman, Don D., and Duane Smallwood. "Some Software Cures for the Rhythm Blues." *Music Educators Journal* Dec. 1986: 40. Overview of software for teaching rhythm.

1088. Cohen, Danny. "ShorTakes." Rev. of *Music Shapes*, from Music Systems for Learning. *Music, Computers & Software* Dec. 1987: 64. Music education software for the Apple II series, a Passport compatible MIDI card, and a Casio CZ synthesizer.

1089. Dames, Jean, and Douglas Susu-Mago. Rev. of *Magic Piano*. *Computing Teacher* Nov. 1985: 52-54. Three games that introduce kids to the basics of music composition. For the Apple II from Edusoft.

1090. ---. "Music and Micros." Rev. of *Music Readiness*, from Sterling Swift Pub. Co. *The Instrumentalist* July 1985: 59. Set of pitch and rhythm exercises designed for children between the ages of 3 and 8. For the Apple II series.

1091. ---. "Music and Micros." Rev. of *Songwriter*, from Scarborough System. *The Instrumentalist* June 1985: 44. Designed to give students the ability to experiment with musical concepts beyond the reach of their technical skill. Suggested for ages 5 through adult. Features include notation and playback. For the Apple II series, Atari, C-64, and IBM PC.

1092. ---. "On Line." Rev. of *Alfred's Basic Piano Theory Software*. *Clavier* Mar. 1987: 42. Game-oriented piano instruction software for the Apple II and C-64. Each game can be used in conjunction with the *Lesson Books* in *Alfred's Basic Piano Library*.

1093. ---. "On Line." Rev. of the *Bare Facts Series*, from Waterloo. *Clavier* Apr. 1986: 24-25. Elementary drill programs covering music history, notes, rhythms, music terminology, and chords for the Apple II series.

1094. ---. "On Line." Rev. of *Concert Master*, from Melodian. *Clavier* Oct. 1985: 30. Expands the musical possibilities of the C-64 and comes with an attachable keyboard.

1095. ---. "On Line." Rev. of *Croakoff*, from MuSoft. *Clavier* Jan. 1986: 40-41. Game-like drill program for pitch recognition for the C-64.

1096. ---. "On Line." Rev. of *Crossword Magic*, from Mindscape and *Music FUNdamentals*, from Silver Burdett. *Clavier* Oct. 1986: 34-35. For the Apple II, C-64, IBM PC, and Atari 800 or 1200XL.

1097. ---. "On Line." Rev. of *DiscCovering Rudiments*, from MusicWare. *Clavier* Feb. 1987: 30-31. Four volume series of drill and practice sessions in music theory for the IBM PC.

1098. ---. "On Line." Rev. of *Kids Time*, from Great Wave Software. *Clavier* Sep. 1987: 28-30. Introductory music program for the Apple IIGS. Also includes a brief discussion of the new Apple IIGS.

1099. ---. "On Line." Rev. of *MIDI/4*, from Passport Designs. *Clavier* Feb. 1985: 28-29. Sequencer for the Apple II or C-64. Features include 4 tracks, punch-in/out, and single-step playback.

1100. ---. "On Line." Rev. of *Maestroscope Music Theory, Level I*, from Maestro Music. *Clavier* Feb. 1986: 34-35. Introduction to music theory designed for independent teachers. For the Apple II series.

1101. ---. "On Line." Rev. of *Maestroscope Music Theory, Level II*, from Maestro Music. *Clavier* May-June 1987: 28. Intended to teach music theory to students in all music disciplines as the program requires no piano skills. For the Apple II series.

1102. ---. "On Line." Rev. of *Mr. Metro Gnome* and *Rhythm I*, from Wenger. *Clavier* Nov. 1986: 34-35. Rhythmic instruction software for the Apple II series and C-64.

1103. ---. "On Line." Rev. of *Music Games*, from Howard Sams and Co. *Clavier* Nov. 1984: 46-47. Basic music skills for the Apple II.

1104. ---. "On Line." Rev. of *Music Made Easy*, from Alfred Pub. Co. *Clavier* May-June 1985: 30-31. Music theory for the Apple II and C-64.

1105. ---. "On Line." Rev. of *Music Readiness*, from Sterling Swift. *Clavier* Jan. 1985: 27. Educational software designed to help students master pitch and rhythm. For the Apple II.

1106. ---. "On Line." Rev. of *Polywriter*, from Passport Designs. *Clavier* July-Aug. 1986: 34-35. Program that enables the user to play a piece of music through a MIDI-equipped synthesizer and print it out in traditional notation. For the Apple II.

1107. ---. "On Line." Rev. of *Practical Music Theory*, Vol.I, from Alfred Pub. Co. *Clavier* Apr. 1985: 24-25. Educational software designed to teach music theory at the keyboard. For the Apple II and C-64/128.

1108. ---. "On Line." Rev. of *Rhythmmaster*, from Melodian. *Clavier* Dec. 1985: 25. Rhythmic instruction for kids using bass and treble clefs in a video game format. For the C-64.

1109. ---. "On Line." Rev. of *Songwriter*, from the Scarborough System. *Clavier* Dec. 1984: 33. Music composition software for the Apple II, Atari, C-64, and IBM PC.

1110. ---. "On Line." Rev. of *Teaching Assistant* and *Study Guide*, from the Minnesota Educational Computing Consortium. *Clavier* Sep. 1985: 28. Both programs enable instructors to generate tests or quizzes. *TA* (IBM PC), *SG* (Apple II).

1111. ---. "On Line." *Clavier* Nov. 1987: 38. Description of the *ATMI Courseware Directory*. The *Directory* contains music software reviews and offers brief descriptive listings of music hardware. Includes information regarding membership in the ATMI organization. (See #1298)

1112. ---. "On Line: So, You're a Novice." *Clavier* July-Aug. 1985: 27. Bibliography of music software reviewed in previous issues of *Clavier*.

1113. ---. "On Line: The Apple IIGS and *Kids Time II*." Rev. of *Kids Time II*, from Great Wave Software. *The Instrumentalist* Sep. 1987: 86-89. Elementary music education software.

1114. ---. Rev. of *MIDI/4*, from Passport Designs. *The Instrumentalist* Aug. 1985: 88-89. Sequencer for the Apple II and C-64.

1115. Danielowski, Dan. Rev. of *Listen*, from Resonate. *Booklist* 1 Feb. 1988: 949-50. Ear training software for the Macintosh.

1116. "Databank: Experts on Educational Uses of Computers." *Music Educators Journal* Jan. 1983: 71-73. A directory of over 40 organizations and sources.

1117. Davis, W. D., Susan Pierce, and Dwight D. Satterwhite. "Pros and Cons of Computer Application to Music Education." *Georgia Music News* Fall 1986: 44.

1118. Deal, J. J. "Computer-Assisted Instruction in Pitch and Rhythm Error Detection." *Journal of Research in Music Education* Fall 1985: 159-66. Addresses some of the problems and limitations of several programs designed for pitch and rhythm error detection. Includes a description of a program developed to overcome some of these limitations.

1119. DeLoughry, Thomas J. "Computers Are Giving Music Educators New Sounds and New Ways to Teach: Although Many Universities Have High-Tech Studios, Some Professors Are Less Than Enthusiastic." *Chronicle of Higher Education* 21 Oct. 1987: A14-A16. Interesting discussion of the many viewpoints held by music instructors in regard to computer-aided music instruction.

1120. Deutsch, Herbert A. "Music Education: Pondering the Future." *Music, Computers & Software* Nov. 1988: 40-44. General overview of how computers are being used, and could be used, in all levels of music education. Topics covered include music composition, performance, and basic theory.

1121. Dods, Stuart C. "Preventing Dis-Chord." *The Rainbow* June 1988: 140-43. Presents an educational program called *Chord Producer* that displays piano fingering positions for 6 different chord types in root position.

1122. Ehle, Robert C. "Musicians and Computers." *American Music Teacher* Apr.-May 1986: 30. General overview of personal computers and how they can be used in music instruction. The author also discusses the different types of music software available e.g., composition, scoring, and music theory.

1123. ---. "Some Applications of Computers in Music Theory and Composition." *American Music Teacher* June-July 1986: 21+ Informative discussion of the Apple IIe and the features that make it an ideal tool for music instruction.

1124. Embry, D. "Music Computer-Assisted Instruction." *American Music Teacher* June-July 1985: 27. General discussion of the positive aspects of CAI. The author states that the computer is an excellent tool for ear training drills and, with the right software, can spark creativity.

1125. Evans, Jeffrey. "Behind *Practica Musica*: Computers in the Arts." *Academic Computing* Nov. 1987: 12+ In-depth discussion of *Practica Musica*, ear training software for the Macintosh. Includes many helpful illustrations.

1126. Feldstein, Sandy. "Focus: The Music Industry, Technology for Teaching." *Music Educators Journal* Mar. 1988: 35-37. General discussion of technology (synthesizers and computers) and music education. The author urges educators to become involved with electronic keyboards and computers.

1127. Flagg, Helen S. "A Computer Concert That Showcases Student Compositions." *Music Educators Journal* Dec. 1986: 30-32. Description of an activity that allows students to explore and utilize programs such as *Bank Street Music Writer* and *The Music Shop*.

1128. "Floppy Discography: *Clef Notes*." Rev. of *Clef Notes*, from Electronic Courseware Systems. *Music Educators Journal* Sep. 1985: 54+ Note reading drill for the Apple II, C-64, IBM PC, and Tandy 1000.

1129. Franklin, J. L. "What's a Computer Doing in My Music Room?" *Music Educators Journal* Jan. 1983: 29-32. Considers the computer revolution and its effect on society, how a computer processes information, and the advantages and disadvantages of instruction by computer.

1130. Frick, T. W. "Micro's, Mini's, and Mainframes: Which Computer Is Best for You?" *Jazz Educators Journal* 18.3 (1986): 42-47. The author discusses the advantages and disadvantages of different types of computers for music instruction. He states that mainframes and minis are attractive because the user does not have to worry about maintenance and regular backups. These operations are usually taken care of by the computer operations center. However, a primary disadvantage of these larger systems is the high cost.

1131. Froelich, John P. "Floppy Discography: *Music Publisher* Version 2.0." Rev. of *Music Publisher* 2.0, from Graphic Notes.

Music Educators Journal Mar. 1989: 55-57. Professional-level music printing software for the Macintosh. Features include a "Presto" keyboard that facilitates note input. The author includes an interesting comparison of printed scores from Peters Edition and *Music Publisher*.

1132. Gilkes, Lolita Walker. Rev. of *Magic Piano*, from Edusoft. *Educational Technology* Apr. 1985: 49-50. Three games for kids that teach the basics of music composition. For the Apple II series.

1133. "Glossary of Computer Terms." *Music Educators Journal* Jan. 1983: 79-81. Basic terminology e.g., boot, compiler, flow chart, ROM, RAM, DOS, etc.

1134. Greenwald, T. "An Apple for the Teacher: Computer Music in Universities." *Keyboard Magazine* Jan. 1987: 40+ General discussion of computer applications in music education.

1135. Grove, D., and T. Griffey. "Music and Computers." *Jazz Educators Journal* 18.2 (1986): 24-25. Dick Grove (President, Grove School of Music) discusses the potential of computers for creating and presenting music in the classroom. Topics include the music capabilities of the IBM PC, Macintosh, and Commodore.

1136. Grushcow, B. "Computers in the Private Studio." *Music Educators Journal* Jan. 1985: 25-29. Considers the advantages and disadvantages of computer assisted instruction. Other areas discussed include hardware, software, and finances. Includes bibliography.

1137. Haerle, D. "Computer for Jazzers: An Overview of Applications." *Jazz Educators Journal* 16.3 (1984): 6-8. The primary focus is on software. Areas discussed include data management, accounting, word processing, instructional programs, music generating programs, and game programs. The author offers suggestions as to how each of these applications can be used by music instructors.

1138. Hall, W. Vann. "Conquering the MIDI Muddle." *Music Educators Journal* Dec. 1986: 26. General overview of MIDI and how it can be used as a teaching tool.

1139. Hayworth, Bill. "Music and Micros." Rev. of *Marching Band Computer Show Design Software*, from Music Education Incentives. *The Instrumentalist* Oct. 1984: 92+ For the TRS-80 or IBM PC.

1140. Hofstetter, Fred T. "Computers in the Curriculum: Art and Music." *Electronic Learning* May-June 1985: 45-47.

1141. Holsinger, Erik. "The Musical Tutor." Rev. of *Listen* 2.0, from Imaja. *Macworld* Dec. 1987: 148-49. Ear training drills that include 15 different exercises grouped into 3 main areas: melody, intervals, and chords.

1142. Hopper, Dale. "On Line." Rev. of *Multi-Dimensional (Corps Style) Show Design Software*, from Music Education Incentives. *The Instrumentalist* July 1986: 46. For the IBM PC.

1143. Horan, Catherine. "Music and Micros." Rev. of *Elements of Music*, from Electronic Courseware Systems. *The Instrumentalist* Dec. 1984: 91-92. Designed to teach music notation. For the Apple II series, IBM PC, and C-64.

1144. ---. "On Line." Rev. of *Elements of Music*, from Electronic Courseware Systems. *Clavier* Mar. 1985: 24+ Designed to teach music notation. For the Apple II series, IBM PC, and C-64.

1145. Hudson, J. "The Influence of Computers on Music Educators." *Jazz Educators Journal* 16.3 (1984): 21. The author states that since computers can handle repetitive and time consuming aspects of music instruction efficiently, many schools are eager to implement computer-based instruction. Also, with computers becoming such an important part of everyday life, several schools have instituted college-wide computer literacy requirements.

1146. Hunkins, Arthur. Rev. of *Guitar Wizard*, from Baudville. *Compute!* Feb. 1988: 52-53. Educational program designed to teach guitar chords and scales. For the Atari 800 XL/XE and Macintosh.

1147. Imburgio, Frank. "*Guitar Tutor*: Learn to Play Guitar Chords on Your Atari." *Antic: The Atari Resource* June 1985: 35+ Program written in BASIC that diagrams and plays guitar chords.

1148. "Industry Resources Directory." *Music Educators Journal* Jan. 1983: 75-77. Directory of 40 manufacturers of software, computers, synthesizers, and other electronic musical equipment. Includes addresses and product information.

1149. Ingber, P. "The Apple District: The Apple as Musician: New Software Packages Are Music to the Ear." *Electronic Learning* Nov.-Dec. 1986: 42-43. Evaluation of *Hear Today...Play Tomorrow*, an ear training program from Electronic Courseware Systems.

1150. Jackson, H. "Computers for Piano Teachers." *American Music Teacher* 33.4 (1984): 32-33.

1151. Jainschigg, John. "*AtariMusic I & II*: State-Of-The-Art CAI for Music Theory... No MIDI Required." Rev. of *AtariMusic I & II*.

Atari Explorer: The Official Atari Journal Nov.-Dec. 1987: 66-68. Beginning music theory for the Atari 8-bit.

1152. Jarvis, David T. *"Ear Trainer,* Your Personal Music Teacher." *STart: The ST Quarterly* Feb. 1988: 103-06.   Software package consisting of a series of exercises and practice sessions that teach the recognition of four different musical elements: intervals, chords, scales, and melodies.

1153. Jones, David L., and Robert W. Placek. "Getting Started: Designing and Programming a CAI Music Lesson." *Music Educators Journal* Dec. 1986: 33-36. Instructions on programming a music lesson using *SuperPILOT.*

1154. Kahn, Robert A. Rev. of *Bank Street Music Writer,* from Mindscape. *Classroom Computer Learning* Jan. 1986: 24-25. Music composition software for the Atari 800 and C-64.

1155. Kassner, Kirk. "Rx for Technophobia." *Music Educators Journal* Nov. 1988: 18-21. Overview of the reservations many teachers have toward computers, synthesizers, and other electronic instruments. Topics include the high cost of equipment, the fear of being replaced by automation, and the fear of limited learning.

1156. Kerr, Charles W. *"Ear Trainer* for the Commodore 128." *Commodore Magazine* Mar. 1988: 97-99. Ear training software in a game format.

1157. Kevorkian, Kyle. "Teaching & Learning Music: The Experts Debate Bold New Approaches." *Keyboard Magazine* June 1988: 58+ A discussion of how new technology can be integrated with music instruction in traditional settings i.e., private studios, universities, conservatories, etc.

1158. Kunitz, Jim. "Business of Teaching: Does Your Studio Need a Computer?" *Clavier* Sep. 1985: 42-44. Tips on acquiring a computer for instructional purposes.

1159. ---. "On Line." *Clavier* Jan. 1988: 30-31. Tips on purchasing music software.

1160. Kunitz, S. L. "I like My Computer Because." *Clavier* 23.10 (1984): 42. Four teachers in Albuquerque, New Mexico discuss their presentation on the use of computers in the independent studio in preparation for the New Mexico Music Teacher's Association Convention.

1161. Kuzmich, J. "Computers for Music Teachers: Consider the Software." *The Instrumentalist* Apr. 1984: 10-14. General overview of available software. Includes bibliography.

1162. ---. "Computers Today: An Economical Way to Start." *The Instrumentalist* Nov. 1984: 36+ Helpful tips on how to shop for music hardware and software.

1163. ---. "Computers Today: How to Choose What's Right for Your Program, Pt. I." *The Instrumentalist* Sep. 1984: 15-18. Includes a directory of selected computer hardware and music software.

1164. ---. "Computers Today: Looking at a Real Time System, Pt. II." *The Instrumentalist* Oct. 1984: 26+ Evaluation of *Soundchaser* products from Passport Designs. Available in three configurations i.e., the Home System, the Educator's System, and the Pro System. All three programs are educational in nature and designed to show that computers can be fun and easy to use. For the Apple II series.

1165. ---. "Instrumental Music Technique Software -- Check It Out." *The School Musician* Mar. 1986: 10-13. Annotated list of instructional software for strings, winds, double reeds, brass, guitar, etc.

1166. ---. "Marching Band Computer Show Designs: Getting Involved -- Step-By-Step." *The School Musician* June-July 1986: 8-11. Overview of marching band show design software.

1167. ---. "Tuning Software: Applied Ear Training." *The School Musician* Nov. 1986: 4+

1168. Lancaster, E. L. "A Computer for Every Studio." *Clavier* Sep. 1984: 44-46. The author states that piano instructors should acquire "computer literacy and computer wisdom" as soon as possible. Various applications are discussed i.e., word processing, record keeping, and piano instruction.

1169. ---. "On Line." Rev. of *Practical Music Theory*, from Alfred Pub. Co.; *Magic Musical Balloon Game*, from Temporal Acuity; and *Musiquiz*, from Barton/Griswold. *Clavier* Oct. 1984: 46-47. Six other programs for the Apple II series are also reviewed.

1170. Lawn, Rick. "Scoring with Computers, Pt. I" *Jazz Educators Journal* 21.1 (1988): 22+ Introduction to a three-part series of articles exploring the pros and cons of music notation software. Includes many useful suggestions of things to consider when purchasing hardware and software.

1171. ---. "Scoring with Computers, Pt. II." *Jazz Educators Journal* 21.2 (1989): 33+ In-depth analysis of three programs for music notation i.e., *Music Publisher* 1.02 from Graphic Notes (Macintosh), *Deluxe Music Construction Set* from Electronic Arts (Macintosh and Amiga), and *Music Printer Plus* 2.0 from Temporal Acuity (IBM). Includes illustrations.

1172. ---. "Sequencers and Software: A Descriptive Guide for Music Educators." *Jazz Educators Journal* 20.3 (1988): 27+ Excellent introduction to all functional aspects of sequencers. Three popular sequencers are discussed in detail i.e., *Performer* 2.0 from Mark of the Unicorn, *Master Tracks Pro* from Passport Designs (Macintosh), and *Texture* from Magnetic Music (IBM PC).

1173. Linzmayer, Owen. Rev. of *Kids Time II*, from Great Wave. *Nibble* Oct. 1987: 46-48. Two music education programs for the Apple IIGS covering keyboard skills and note recognition.

1174. Litterst, George F. "An Introduction to Computer Technology for the Classical Pianist." *The Piano Quarterly* 36.140 (1987): 28+ Overview of basic terminology and concepts.

1175. ---. "The Well-Tempered Mac." *MACazine* Aug. 1987: 83-86. Brief descriptions of 11 music education programs for the Macintosh including *MacVoice* 2.0, *Appletones* 2.0, *Mozart* 2.0 (Kinkos), *Practica Musica* 1.1 (Periscope Press), *Listen* 2.02 (Imaja), and *Guitar Wizard* (Baudville). Includes illustrations.

1176. Littlefield, Patti. "*Basic Guitar I*, Tutorial Software Package for Apple." Rev. of *Basic Guitar I*. *InfoWorld* 24 Jan. 1983: 46-48.

1177. Lowe, Donald R. "Floppy Discography." Rev. of *Orchestral String Teacher's Assistant*, from Swan Software for the Arts Education. *Music Educators Journal* Jan. 1988: 65-67. Drill-and-practice program for note identification, string positions, and fingerings for violin, viola, cello, and bass. For Apple II series, C-64/128, and IBM PC.

1178. Mahin, Bruce. "Choosing a Computer." *The Instrumentalist* June 1987: 23+ Comparative overview of popular computers for education i.e., the Macintosh Plus, Apple IIGS, Amiga, and Atari ST. Includes a bibliography and a list of user groups.

1179. ---. "Digital Composition." *The Instrumentalist* Dec. 1986: 15-18. General discussion of MIDI, music software, and music synthesizers. Topics include the Macintosh and Yamaha DX7.

1180. ---. Rev. of *HyperCard*, from Apple Computer Co. *The Instrumentalist* Aug. 1988: 58. Brief discussion of *HyperCard*, a hypertext application that allows the user to link text, graphics (*MacPaint* compatible), and sound. For the Macintosh.

1181. ---. "On Line." Rev. of *Sound Designer*, from Digidesign. *The Instrumentalist* Dec. 1987: 6. Sound editing software for the Macintosh. Allows one to view and edit different waveforms.

1182. ---. "On Line: Opcode *MIDIMac* Music Sequencer." Rev. of *MIDIMac* 2.5, from Opcode. *The Instrumentalist* Aug. 1987: 72. MIDI sequencer for the Macintosh. Features include track looping, recordable tempo changes, song pointer with SMPTE synchronization, and up to 26 sequences per file.

1183. ---. "Programming Pascal." *The Instrumentalist* May 1988: 56+ First in a series of articles that teach basic computer programming skills using Pascal. The author includes an elementary program that asks the user his age and prints a message on the screen.

1184. ---. Rev. of *Sideman DXT*, from Voyetra. *The Instrumentalist* Dec. 1988: 9. A voice editor/librarian for the Yamaha DX/TX/DX7-II synthesizers and IBM PC. Requires the MPU-401 or compatible MIDI interface and DOS 2.0 or higher.

1185. Makas, George. "On Line." Rev. of *Sebastian II*, from Temporal Acuity Products. *The Instrumentalist* May 1986: 76-79. Visual and aural error detection program for the Apple II series.

1186. Manoliu, Mihai. Rev. of *The Ear*, from Steinberg/Jones. *Music Technology* Aug. 1988: 68-69. Ear training software for the Atari ST. Features exercises in intervals, scales, chords, and melody. For all levels.

1187. Many, Chris. Rev. of *Basic Composer*, from Education Software Consultants. *Music Technology* Dec. 1988: 60. Brief description of a notation program for the IBM PC and compatibles. Includes illustrations.

1188. Matt, Fred. "'Must Have' Programs for the Color Computer." *Electronic Learning* May-June 1985: 40. Contains a brief review of *Musica 2*.

1189. McDowell, Linwood. "The Laptop Music Teacher." *PCM: The Personal Computer Magazine for Tandy Users* June 1987: 12-17. Presents a program in BASIC that teaches music notation. The user can play up to 38 notes and display staff and keyboard position.

1190. Medsker, Larry. "A Course in Computers and Music." *Collegiate Microcomputer* May 1983: 133-40. Description of an undergraduate course on computers and music. Topics covered include computer-assisted music analysis, computer music, and computer-assisted composition. Includes bibliography.

1191. Milak, J. J. "Programming Music for the Non-Programmer." *Jazz Educators Journal* 16.3 (1984): 9+ A somewhat misleading title as this article is not about programming. The primary focus is on selecting a computer system for music education. Other topics include various electronic music systems, music peripherals, and music education software.

1192. Moore, Herb. "The Anatomy of a Note." *Classroom Computer Learning* Jan. 1986: 70-72. Brief discussion of waveforms and sound envelopes. Includes a program that explores attack, decay, sustain, and release for the C-64.

1193. ---. Rev. of *Music Shapes*, from Music Systems for Learning, Inc. *Classroom Computer Learning* Mar. 1988: 54-56. Elementary music composition program in which boxes on the screen are used to represent musical shapes or musical "building blocks." Each block contains a single sound or patterns of sound that can be combined with others. For Apple II series.

1194. ---. "What Shape Does Music Have?" *Classroom Computer Learning* Mar. 1985: 38-41. General discussion of waveforms. Several programs in BASIC for the Atari are included for illustration.

1195. Moore, Herb, and Holly Brady. "Kids Can Write Music!: Have You Taken a Close Look at Music Software Now Available?" *Classroom Computer Learning* May 1986: 12-14. Brief overview of several elementary music programs i.e., *Magic Piano*, *Rock 'n' Rhythm*, *Music Studio*, and *The Music Shop*.

1196. Moorhead, Jan. "Computers and Your Brain: Musical Aerobics." *Electronic Musician* Oct. 1987: 26+ Discussion of music education with personal computers. Includes a list of current music education software.

1197. Moran, Karen M. Rev. of *Music Logo*, from Terrapin, Inc. *Classroom Computer Learning* Mar. 1987: 16. Teaches students how to program and allows them to hear their compositions. Requires 64K, an ALF music card, a stereo amplifier, and speakers. For the Apple II series.

1198. Morgenstern, Steve. Rev. of *The Notable Phantom*, from Designware. *Family Computing* Apr. 1986: 83. Software for teaching the names and sounds of notes on the staff and piano keyboard. Recommended for ages 5-10. For the Apple II.

1199. Morse, R. Rev. of *MusicWorks*, from Hayden Software. *Computing Teacher* May 1985: 38-40. Music composition software for the Macintosh. Allows one to compose using either a grid and symbols or conventional music notation.

1200. "Music, MIDI and Manufacturers." *The Instrumentalist* June 1987: 67-71. General overview of MIDI technology and related products. Includes a comprehensive list of computers, software, and accessories.

1201. Neiman, Marcus L. "On Line." Rev. of *Tuner Intonation Drill* and *Interval Drillmaster*, from CONDUIT and *Double Reed Fingering*, from Electronic Courseware Systems. *The Instrumentalist* Aug. 1986: 49-50. For the Apple II series.

1202. ---. Rev. of the *Music Editor, Scorer and Arranger*, from Roland Corp. *The Instrumentalist* May 1988: 67. Software for the IBM PC that functions in three modes i.e., Song Mode (recording), Score Mode (transcribing), and Print Mode. The Print Mode displays up to eight staves at a time in high resolution graphics. College-level.

1203. ---. Rev. of *MUSICOM J1 Jazz Course*, from Roland. *The Instrumentalist* Apr. 1988: 78. Programmed instruction in jazz harmony and rhythm, suited for most college music classes. For the IBM PC and Apple II series.

1204. ---. "On Line." Rev. of Swan Software (Music Education Series) *The Instrumentalist* Nov. 1986: 93. Consists of 11 programs in the Music Education Series and 17 programs in the Fingers Series (instrumental fingering). The Music Education Series is designed for students in elementary general music through high school performance and theory. Programs in the Fingers Series are geared more toward beginning instrumentalists. For the Apple II series and C-64/128.

1205. ---. "On Line." Rev. of *Aural Skills Trainer*, from Electronic Courseware Systems. *The Instrumentalist* May 1987: 88. Aural and visual identification of intervals and chords. For the Apple II series, C-64, and IBM PC.

1206. ---. "On Line." Rev. of *CAMUS: Melodic Dictations*, from CONDUIT. *The Instrumentalist* Jan. 1987: 77. Ear training software for the Apple II series and the IBM PC.

1207. ---. "On Line." Rev. of *Clef Notes*, from Electronic Courseware Systems. *The Instrumentalist* Dec. 1986: 92-93. Instructional software for note identification using different clefs. For the Apple II series, C-64, Victor 900, and IBM PC.

1208. ---. "On Line." Rev. of *Early Music Skills*, from Electronic Courseware Systems. *The Instrumentalist* Feb. 1987: 12. Flash card drill program for the Apple II series, IBM PC, and C-64.

1209. ---. "On Line." Rev. of *Music Education Series*, from Richmond Educational Series. *The Instrumentalist* Nov. 1987: 8+ Set of 11 computer-assisted instructional programs in note reading, rhythm reading and dictation, rhythm identification, interval construction, ear training, and key signature identification.

1210. ---. "On Line." Rev. of *The Copyist*, from Dr. T. *The Instrumentalist* Feb. 1988: 12. High quality score editing and printing program for the IBM PC and Atari ST.

1211. ---. "On Line." Rev. of *The Percussion Rudiment Tester*, from Etude Software. *The Instrumentalist* Jan. 1988: 74. Program for teaching the sticking patterns of all 26 drum rudiments. For the Apple II series.

1212. ---. "On Line." Rev. of *The Rhythm Machine*, from Temporal Acuity Products. *The Instrumentalist* Sep. 1986: 95. Rhythmic instruction software for the Apple II series.

1213. Newcomb, Steven R. "Computer-Based Arts Instruction: How Are We Doing?" *Design for Arts in Education* May-June 1988: 46-49. Discussion of the advances that have been made in the implementation of drill-and-practice algorithms for ear training and recently released systems for music appreciation. The author also discusses the various aspects and potential of the Integrated Services Digital Network (ISDN).

1214. Newquist, Harvey. "Real Music Through Artificial Intelligence." *Music Technology* Feb. 1988: 60-62. Description of *THE MUSES* (*THEory of MUSic Expert Systems*) software for music theory instruction. Intended for college-level students, *THE MUSES* currently runs on an IBM mainframe linked to micros and synthesizers.

1215. Pembrook, Randall G. "Some Implications of Students' Attitudes Toward a Computer-Based Melodic Dictation Program." *Journal of Research in Music Education* Summer 1986: 121.

1216. Perelman, Charles. "*B$ Sharp* (Music-Note Recognition)" *80 Micro* Mar. 1983: 236-43. A BASIC program for the TRS-80 Model II for teaching note recognition to children.

1217. Peters, G. D. "Computer Technology in Instrumental Music Instruction." *The Instrumentalist* Feb. 1983: 35-37. Discussion of the minimum hardware components necessary for computer-assisted instruction in music. Topics include computer-generated sound, recording, and display of music notation.

1218. Peterson, Dennis. "An MECC Education." Rev. of *Music*, from the Minnesota Educational Computer Consortium. *Hot CoCo* Oct. 1985: 20-23. For the Color Computer.

1219. "Piano Teachers Are Joining the Computer Age." *Changing Times* June 1985: 70-73. Discussion focusing on piano teachers in private schools and ways they are beginning to use music software for instructional purposes.

1220. Pierson-Perry, Jim. Rev. of the *ECS MIDI Musicware Series*. *STart: The ST Monthly* Oct. 1988: 71-72. Evaluation of 16 programs for music education from Electronic Courseware Systems. Programs cover a wide variety of topics from note recognition to jazz harmony.

1221. ---. Rev. of *Guitar Wizard*, from Baudville. *Antic: The Atari Resource* Oct. 1987: 12. Guitar instruction software. Features include chord fingerings, scale guides, and improvisation instruction.

1222. Placek, Robert W. "Choosing the Best Software for Your Class." *Music Educators Journal* Sept 1985: 49. A brief look at software currently available for music education.

1223. ---. "Floppy Discography: *AtariMusic I -- Notes and Steps*." Rev. of *AtariMusic I -- Notes and Steps*, from Atari. *Music Educators Journal* Apr. 1986: 21-22. Elementary music education software for Atari computers (8-bit).

1224. ---. "Floppy Discography: *Basic Musicianship* -- an Introduction to Music Fundamentals with Computer Assistance." Rev. of *Basic Musicianship*, from Wadsworth Pub. Co. *Music Educators Journal* Nov. 1985: 14-17. For the Apple II.

1225. ---. "Floppy Discography: *Foundations of Music: A Computer Assisted Introduction*." Rev. of *Foundations of Music: A Computer Assisted Introduction*, from Wadsworth Pub. Co. *Music Educators Journal* Mar. 1987: 56-58. Music fundamentals course for the Apple II.

1226. ---. "Floppy Discography: *GUIDO* Music Learning System: Ear Training Lessons." Rev. of *GUIDO*. *Music Educators Journal* Oct. 1987: 76-79. Comprehensive ear training program for the IBM PC, XT, AT, and PS/2.

1227. ---. "Floppy Discography: *Keyboard Fingerings*." Rev. of *Keyboard Fingerings*, from Electronic Courseware Systems. *Music Educators Journal* Mar. 1986: 18-20. For the Apple II and C-64.

1228. ---. "Floppy Discography: *Keyboard Jazz Harmonies.*" Rev. of *Keyboard Jazz Harmonies*, from Electronic Courseware Systems. *Music Educators Journal* Dec. 1987: 68-71. MIDI compatible drill and quiz program for teaching selected seventh chords. For the Apple II, IBM PC, Tandy, and C-64/128.

1229. ---. "Floppy Discography: *Listen.*" Rev. of *Listen*, from Imaja. *Music Educators Journal* Jan. 1987: 18+ Ear training drill program for the Macintosh. MIDI compatible.

1230. ---. "Floppy Discography: *Micro-Trumpet.*" Rev. of *Micro-Trumpet*, from Temporal Acuity. *Music Educators Journal* Oct. 1985: 20+ Trumpet-fingering drill and game for the Apple II.

1231. ---. "Floppy Discography: *Mr. Metro Gnome/Rhythm II.*" Rev. of *Mr. Metro Gnome/Rhythm II*, from Wenger. *Music Educators Journal* Jan. 1986: 17-19. Rhythm perception program for the Apple II and C-64.

1232. ---. "Floppy Discography: *Music FUNdamentals -- Beginning Music III*: Extending Rhythm and Melody Skills." Rev. of *Music FUNdamentals -- Beginning Music III*, from Silver Burdett. *Music Educators Journal* May 1986: 67-70. For the Apple II and Atari XL.

1233. ---. "Floppy Discography: *Music Shapes.*" Rev. of *Music Shapes*, from Music Systems for Learning. *Music Educators Journal* Apr. 1988: 57-60. Graphic music construction program with the ability to alter waveform, pitch, rhythm, timbre, and sequence. Excellent tool for teaching and experimenting with acoustics. For the Apple II series.

1234. ---. "Floppy Discography: *Practical Music Theory.*" Rev. of *Practical Music Theory*, from Alfred Pub. Co. *Music Educators Journal* Dec. 1985: 8-11. For the Apple II and C-64.

1235. ---. "Floppy Discography: *Rhythmaticity.*" Rev. of *Rhythmaticity*, from The Note Factory. *Music Educators Journal* Oct. 1986: 72+ For the C-64.

1236. ---. "Floppy Discography: *Trumpet Fingerings.*" Rev. of *Trumpet Fingerings*, from Wenger. *Music Educators Journal* Apr. 1987: 58-61. For the C-64/128.

1237. ---. "Floppy Discography: *Tuner Intonation Drill.*" Rev. of *Tuner Intonation Drill*, from CONDUIT. *Music Educators Journal* Feb. 1986: 18-21. For the Apple II.

1238. Placek, Robert W., and Leonard V. Ball Jr. "Floppy Discography: *Performer*: The MIDI Sequencer Software." Rev. of

Performer, from Mark of the Unicorn. *Music Educators Journal* Dec. 1988: 65-68. Professional-level sequencer for the Macintosh. Illustrated.

1239. ---. Rev. of *Texture II*, from Magnetic Music. *Music Educators Journal* Jan. 1989: 59-62. Sequencer for the IBM and Amiga. Comes in two versions i.e., 3.11R for use with the Roland MIDI interface and 3.11K for use with the IBM Music Feature.

1240. Pogue, David. Rev. of *Practica Musica* 2.0, from Ars Nova Software. *Macworld* Dec. 1988: 164+ MIDI compatible ear training software for the Macintosh.

1241. "Quick Clicks." Rev. of *Practica Musica*, from Periscope Press. *MacUser* Nov. 1987: 76+ Interactive program for ear training and music theory for the Macintosh.

1242. Rae, Richard. "AmigaNotes." Rev. of *Music Student I* and *Quiz Master*, from Associated Computer Services. *Amazing Computing* 2.9 (1987): 43-45. Music education software for the Amiga.

1243. Regena, C. "*Music Steps and Triads.*" *ST-Log: The Atari ST Monthly Magazine* May 1987: 23-28. Educational program in ST BASIC.

1244. Riggs, R. L. "Computers: A Music Teacher's Asset." *The Instrumentalist* Oct. 1985: 40+

1245. ---. "On Line." Rev. of *Personal Composer*, from Standard Productions. *The Instrumentalist* June 1987: 72-73. Music composition/MIDI sequencer software for the IBM PC. Features include score playing and editing, printing, automatic transcription, and 32 track MIDI recording.

1246. Robinson, Phillip. "The Music Class Software." *A+* Feb. 1988: 70+ In-depth discussion of *The Music Class* from Wenger. Designed for teaching music fundamentals, *The Music Class* is divided into 5 volumes i.e., Fundamentals, Rhythm, Ear Training, Music Symbols, and Note Reading. For ages 8 and up.

1247. Rosch, Winn L. "Musical Interludes with the PC." *PC Magazine* 14 Oct. 1986: 265+ Description of *MUSICOM*, computerized music courses for the IBM PC from Roland and the Tecmar Music Synthesis system board that can create up to 16 independent voices. The Tecmar synthesizer also contains a sequencer for digital recording.

1248.   Rumery, Kenneth R.   "Bringing Your Classroom On-Line."
Music Educators Journal Jan. 1985: 20-24.   Discussion of products
available for computer-assisted music instruction.

1249.   ---.   "Computer Applications in Music Education."   *T.H.E.
Journal* Sep. 1986: 97-99.   Results of a survey conducted in the spring
of 1985 that identified postsecondary schools using computers in
music instruction. The results showed that "a significant number" of
schools have computer facilities, most of which are based on the
Apple II.

1250.   Schultz, R.   "Bibliography: An Annotated List of Available
Computer Programs."   *National Association of Schools of Music,
Proceedings* 71 (1983): 121-27.

1251.   Sherbon, J. W.   "Chips and Diodes of Microcomputers."   *Music
Educators Journal* Jan. 1983: 32-38.   Discussion of common computer
terminology, computer systems, and peripherals. The author also
discusses factors to consider when purchasing a computer system
e.g., objectives and needs, software availability, and hardware
configurations that fit a given budget.

1252.   Sherouse, Vicki.   Rev. of *Coco-Notes*, from CBS Software.
Booklist 1 Oct. 1985: 283.   Music instruction tool for ages 8-12 for the
C-64 and Atari.

1253.   Sisk, Lawrence.   "On Line."   Rev. of *Professional Composer*,
from Mark of the Unicorn. *The Instrumentalist* Feb. 1988: 14.   Music
notation and transcription software for the Macintosh.

1254.   Smith, Gary E., and Joseph R. Scagnoli.   "Music and Micros."
Rev. of *Halftime*, from Wenger Corp. and *Pyware Charting Aid
System*, from Pygraphics.   *The Instrumentalist* Sep. 1984: 19+
Software for designing marching band formations and routines. For
the Apple II and TRS-80 Model IV.

1255.   "Software: Side by Side."   *Electronic Learning* May-June 1985:
48-51.   Comparative buyer's guide to eight music programs.

1256.   Steinhaus, Kurt A.   "Putting the Music Composition Tool to
Work."   *Computing Teacher* Dec.-Jan. 1986/87: 16-18.   General
discussion of music composition software and its use in the
classroom. Includes a list of programs for the Apple II.

1257.   ---.   "Software That's Music to Your Ears."   *Computing
Teacher* Feb. 1987: 23-26.   Includes a descriptive list of 7 CAI
packages for music instruction for the Apple II.

1258. Sternberg, K. "Making Music on Micros." *Electronic Learning* Feb. 1986: 52. Discussion of music software from Random House for the IBM PC and the Apple II.

1259. Stradler, Neal. "Exploring Music with Logo." *Computing Teacher* Mar. 1985: 16-18.

1260. Swan, P. D. "Running a Computer in the Bandroom." *The Instrumentalist* Aug. 1986: 46-48. Timpview High School in Provo Utah has based their computer lab in the band room so all students have the opportunity to receive individual tutoring and study drill and practice routines. The system is described in detail.

1261. Taylor, Jack. "Computers as Music Teachers." *Music Educators Journal* Jan. 1983: 43-45. General discussion of the potential of computers in music education e.g., sight singing, dictation, applied instruction, and composition.

1262. ---. "Computers in Music and Music Instruction: The Joys of Hardware and the Woes of Software." *Design for Arts in Education* May-June 1988: 50-55. The author examines how computers are being used in music and music instruction today. Topics covered include performance, composition and instruction, and software. The author also discusses *MEDICI*, a melodic dictation program developed on the *PLATO* computer system at the Center for Music Research (Florida State University). Includes bibliography.

1263. Thornburg, David D. "Computer-Assisted Explorations with Music." *Compute!* Aug. 1984: 24-26. Discussion of *Musicland*, a program from Syntauri for the Apple II. *Musicland* is an educational tool that allows the user to learn music in the same discovery-based learning environment one learns math with Logo. For children and adults. Requires the MusicSystem cards from Mountain Hardware.

1264. ---. "Computers and Society: Creativity with Constraints." *Compute!* Apr. 1988: 46-47. Discussion of how music software such as *Dancin' Feats* (Atari 800) and *Jam Session* (Macintosh) can help develop skills necessary for more serious study of music.

1265. Tutaj, D. Rev. of *Master Tracks Pro* 2.0, from Passport Designs. *The Instrumentalist* Oct. 1988: 70. MIDI sequencer for the Apple II, IBM PC, Macintosh, and Atari ST. Features include 64 tracks; real and step time note entry; a song editor; and graphic display of pitch, key pressure, modulation, and program change.

1266. ---. "Music and Micros." Rev. of *M.E.C.C. Music Theory. The Instrumentalist* Feb. 1985: 95-97. A group of 17 lessons from the Minnesota Educational Computer Consortium that defines a workable curriculum for the study of music. Designed for the Apple II, Commodore, Acorn, and Tandy. However, software evaluated in this article is for the Apple II exclusively.

1267. ---. "On Line." Rev. of *Music Printer*, from Temporal Acuity Products. *The Instrumentalist* Oct. 1986: 70-71. Music notation/printing software for the Apple II.

1268. ---. "On Line: Wenger's Akron Series Music Software." *The Instrumentalist* Apr. 1986: 94. Overview of Rhythm Tutors and Ear Training Tutors included in the Akron series.

1269. ---. "On Line: Wenger's Akron Series Music Software." *The Instrumentalist* Mar. 1986: 63+ Series of 16 programs covering all areas of music instruction e.g., rhythm, basic music reading, and ear training (melodic and harmonic).

1270. Upitis, R. "Milestones in Computer Music Instruction." *Music Educators Journal* Jan. 1983: 40-42. Discussion of how CAI in music is being applied to theory, the study of musical instruments, and composition.

1271. Vail, Mark. "MIDI with Class: Leading College Educators on Their Electronic Music Programs." *Keyboard Magazine* Sep. 1988: 74+ In-depth discussion of electronics and computers in music education. Topics include the future job outlook (generally optimistic), performance, and composition. Schools represented include Eastman, Northwestern Univ., Univ. of N. Texas, Univ. of Illinois, and the Univ. of Miami (Fla.).

1272. Voorhees, Jerry L. "Music in a New Age: The Challenge of Electronics." *Music Educators Journal* Oct. 1986: 32-36. The author expresses his views as to what extent computers should be used in music education and composition. He suggests that they be used as a creative medium (musical instrument) and not as a compositional aid because they do not possess judgment or emotion.

1273. Wagner, Michael J. "Technology: A Musical Explosion." *Music Educators Journal* Oct. 1988: 30-33. Very general discussion covering digital recording, compact disk technology, electronic instruments (synthesizers), and computers. Includes brief definitions of various terms e.g., analog-to-digital converter (ADC), digital-to-analog converter (DAC), digital audiotape (DAT), and MIDI.

1274. Walnum, Clayton. Rev. of *Guitar Wizard*, from Baudville. *Analog Computing* Apr. 1988: 76-77. Instructional software designed to teach guitar chords and scales. For the Atari 800 XL/XE and Macintosh.

1275. Walsh, Kevin. "Reading, 'Riting and Algorithmatic: An Overview of Music Education Software." *Music, Computers & Software* Oct. 1987: 45-48. Discussion of CAI software (*Music Flash Cards* and *Super Challenger*), performance assistance software (*MIDI Jazz Improvisation I*), MIDI, and artificial intelligence software (*M*, *Jam Factory*, and *UpBeat*).

1276. ---. "ShorTakes." Rev. of *Listen*, from Imaja. *Music, Computers & Software* Aug. 1987: 76. Interactive ear training software for the Macintosh. Includes a variety of melodic and harmonic exercises ranging from intervals and triads to four-part harmony. MIDI compatible.

1277. ---. "ShorTakes." Rev. of *Practica Musica*, from Periscope Press. *Music, Computers & Software* Apr. 1988: 69+ Ear training software for the Macintosh. Contains exercises for intervals, harmonies, and melodies with various levels of difficulty. Includes digitized organ, piano, and harpsichord sounds. MIDI compatible.

1278. Watt, Dan. "Musical Microworlds: New Software Could Lead to a Breakthrough in Music Learning and Creativity." *Popular Computing* Aug. 1984: 91-94.

1279. Weiss, Lane. Rev. of *Rock 'n' Rhythm*, from Spinnaker Software. *Computing Teacher* May 1985: 37-38. Elementary music education software that allows students to compose music with different instruments on each track then mix the tracks into a finished composition. Knowledge of traditional notation is not required. For the Atari and C-64.

1280. Wesley, Michael D. "Playing It by Ear." *MacUser* July 1987: 55-56. Evaluation of *Practica Musica*, MIDI compatible ear training software for the Macintosh. Intended for college-level students.

1281. "What's New in the Music Industry?" *The Instrumentalist* Feb. 1988: 38+ Includes a section on computer hardware and software. Products described include the IBM Music Feature, *Versatracs* (music processing program for the Apple IIGS), and *Performer* 2.0 (MIDI sequencer for the Macintosh).

1282. Williams, D. B. "Microcomputers Interface with the Arts." *Music Educators Journal* Jan. 1983: 39. A brief discussion of how Illinois State University is using microcomputers to support administrative, creative, and teaching research activities in art, music, and theater.

1283. Winter, M. J. "*Major & Minor*: VIC Music Theory." *Compute!* Apr. 1983: 252-54. Software for the VIC-20 that teaches basic musicianship.

1284. Wittlich, Gary E. "Computers and Music." Rev. of *Clef Notes*, *Spell and Define*, *Early Music Skills*, and *Music Flash Cards*, from Electronic Courseware Systems. *The School Musician* May 1985: 24+

1285. ---. "Computers and Music." Rev. of *Drum-Key*, from Peripheral Visions. *The School Musician* Aug.-Sep. 1984: 38-39. Real time percussion instrument software for the Apple II.

1286. ---. "Computers and Music." Rev. of *Maestroscope: Music Theory: Level I and II*, from Maestro Music. *The School Musician* Mar. 1985: 28-29.

1287. ---. "Computers and Music." Rev. of *Marching Band Show Design*, from Music Education Incentives. *The School Musician* Jan. 1985: 22-23. Computer-assisted marching band show design software for the Tandy Color Computer and IBM PC/compatibles.

1288. Wolfe, G. "CAI in Jazz Education." *Jazz Educators Journal* 16.3 (1984): 12-13. The author urges jazz educators to become involved in the educational applications of new technology. Includes a summary of instructional uses of computers e.g., information drill, drill-and-practice, simulation, tutorial, educational games, and utilities.

1289. ---. "CAI in Jazz Education: Choosing Music Peripherals." *Jazz Educators Journal* 17.1 (1984): 27-28. Products discussed include DAC boards (digital-to-analog converters), keyboards, and printers. The author states practical guidelines for purchasing each type of equipment.

1290. ---. "CAI in Jazz Education: What to Look for in Educational Software." *Jazz Educators Journal* 16.4 (1984): 23+ Excellent article in which the author suggests specific questions one might ask when purchasing music software.

1291. ---. "Computer Systems for Disabled Musicians." *Jazz Educators Journal* 19.2 (1987): 70-74. Significant article that focuses primarily on computer hardware adapted to serve disabled persons. Areas considered include alternative keyboard interfaces e.g., light pens, input using eye movement, and scanning devices. Includes a list of sources for electronic aids for the handicapped.

1292. ---. "Creative Computers -- Do They Think?" *Music Educators Journal* Jan. 1983: 59-62. The author presents a computerized simulation of creativity in order to draw conclusions about the human creative process. Music composition serves as the medium for research.

1293. ---. "MIDI-Tutor Laboratory: Keyboard Instruction with Computers." *Jazz Educators Journal* 19.1 (1986): 29+ Discussion of factors to consider when developing a keyboard instruction laboratory via MIDI e.g., cost and required equipment. Other considerations include software, method of presentation, and sources of new teaching materials. Includes a list of companies that can provide useful information on instructional music software and related equipment.

1294. Zientara, Marguerite. "Hitting the High Notes." *InfoWorld* 30 Apr. 1984: 22-23. General discussion of microcomputer software designed to teach music. Includes a guide to vendors.

Part IV
Books

1295. Abad, Jerry, and Valerie Abad. *Sound and Graphics for the Apple II+, IIe, and Franklin Computers*. Chatsworth, CA: Datamost, 1984. ISBN 0881903515. Pub. address: 20660 Nordhoff St., Chatsworth, CA. Cost: $9.95.

1296. Adams, Robert Train. *Electronic Music Composition for Beginners*. Dubuque, IA: Wm. C. Brown, 1986. ISBN 0697004570. Pub. address: 2460 Kerper Blvd., Dubuque, IA, 52001. Includes information on personal computers and music composition.

1297. Anderton, Craig. *MIDI for Musicians*. Amsco Publications, 1986. Reviewed in the *Computer Music Journal*, V.11, No.3 (Fall 1987). Available from Music Sales Corp.: 24 E. 22nd St., New York, NY, 10010. Ph: 800 431-7187. Order #AM61219. Cost: $14.95.

1298. *Association for Technology in Music Instruction: Courseware Directory*. Hopkins, MN: Association for Technology in Music Instruction (See #1367). In-depth descriptions and prices of music software and hardware for music education. Cost: $10.00 including the ATMI Newsletter.

1299. Bartle, Barton K. *Computer Software in Music and Music Education: A Guide*. Metuchen, NJ: Scarecrow Press, 1987. ISBN 0810820560. Reviewed in *Choice*, Feb. 1988. Pub. address: 52 Liberty St., Box 4167, Metuchen, NJ, 08840. Cost $22.50. Focuses primarily on music education software and does not include many programs available for the Macintosh, Amiga, or Atari computers. Most software considered is for the C-64, Apple II, or IBM PC.

1300. Behrendt, Bill L. *Music and Sound for the Commodore 64*. Englewood Cliffs, NJ: Prentice Hall, 1983. ISBN 0136070949. Pub. address: Rte. 9W, Englewood Cliffs, NJ, 07632. Available with disk, ISBN 0136071023.

1301. ---. *Music and Sound for the Macintosh*. Englewood Cliffs, NJ: Prentice Hall. Pub. address: Rte. 9W, Englewood Cliffs, NJ, 07632.

1302. ---. *Music and Sound for the PCjr*. Englewood Cliffs, NJ: Prentice Hall, 1985. ISBN 0136071104. Pub. address: Rte. 9W, Englewood Cliffs, NJ, 07632. Cost: $14.95. Available with disk, ISBN 0136071287. ($29.95).

1303. Bigelow, Steven. *Making Music with Personal Computers*. San Diego, CA: Park Row Press, 1987. ISBN 0935749217. Pub. address: 4640 Jewell St., No. 101, San Diego, CA, 92109. Cost: $16.95.

1304. Boom, Michael. *Amiga: Image, Sound, & Animation on the Commodore Amiga*. Redmond, WA: Microsoft Press, 1986. ISBN 0914845624. Pub. address: 16011 N.E. 36th Way, Box 97017, Redmond, WA, 98073-9717. Cost: $19.95.

1305. ---. *Music Through MIDI: Using MIDI to Create Your Own Electronic Music System*. Redmond, WA: Microsoft Press, 1987. ISBN 1556150261. Reviewed in *The Instrumentalist*, Feb. 1988. Pub. address: 16011 N.E. 36th Way, Box 97017, Redmond, WA, 98073-9717. Cost: $19.95. Excellent coverage of MIDI and the personal computer. Topics include synthesizing sound, MIDI connections, MIDI messages, MIDI equipment, and how MIDI and the personal computer can be used in live performance, education, and recording. Includes a bibliography and a glossary of related terms.

1306. Burger, Jeff. *The Murphy's Law MIDI Handbook*. Newbury Park, CA: Alexander, Pub., 1987. ISBN 0939067560. Pub. address: 3537 Old Conejo Rd., Suite 101, Newbury Park, CA, 91320. Cost: $19.95.

1307. Casabona, Helen, and D. Frederick. *Using MIDI*. Sherman Oaks: Alfred Pub. Co., 1987. ISBN 0882843540. Pub. address: 15335 Morrison St., Sherman Oaks, CA, 91413. Ph: 800 821-6083. Cost: $14.95.

1308. Cassel, Don. *Graphics, Sound, & Music for the Commodore 64*. Dubuque, IA: Wm. C. Brown, 1984. ISBN 0697004236. Pub. address: 2460 Kerper Blvd., Dubuque, IA, 52001. Cost: $15.95.

1309. Cathcart, Glee. *Apple Music for Apple II Plus, IIe & IIc*. San Jose, CA: Enrich, 1984. ISBN 0865821674. Pub. address: 2325 Paragon Dr., San Jose, CA, 95131. Ph: 800 ENRICH-1. Cost: $3.95.

1310. Chamberlin, Hal. *Musical Applications of Microprocessors*. 2nd ed. Hasbrouck Heights: Hayden Book Co., 1985. ISBN 0317003623. Reviewed in *Byte*, June 1986. Pub address: 10 Mulholland Dr., Hasbrouck Heights, NJ, 07604. Cost: $39.95.

1311. Clark, Ron. *The Color Computer Songbook*. Woodsboro, MD: ARCSoft, 1983. ISBN 086668011X. Pub. address: P.O. Box 132, Woodsboro, MD, 21798. Cost: $7.95.

1312. *Coda*. Owatonna, MN: Wenger Corp., 1987. Pub. address: 555 Park Drive, Owatonna, MN, 55060. Ph: 800 843-1337. Cost: $4.00, free to educators. A comprehensive listing and description of music software available for microcomputers.

1313. *Compute!'s Music System for the Commodore 64 and 128*. New York: *Compute!* Publications, 1987. ISBN 0874550742. Pub. address: 825 Seventh Ave., 9th floor, New York, NY, 10019. Cost: $24.95.

1314. *Computer Musicians Source Book*. Peoria, IL: Computer Musicians Cooperative (See #1371). Contains information on new products, test reports, a consultant directory, a dealer directory, a user group directory, and a manufacturer directory. Updated regularly. (Binder format). Cost: $75.00/year.

1315. Conger, Jim. *C Programming for MIDI*. Redwood City, CA: M & T Books, 1988. Pub. address: 501 Galveston., Redwood City, CA, 94063. Ph: 800 533-4372. Cost: $22.95 ($37.95 with disk). Techniques covered include the development of a patch librarian program, sequencing applications for the MPU-401 interface, how to create screen displays, low-level assembly routines for MIDI, and diagnostic tools for reviewing data.

1316. Davis, Deta S. *Computer Applications in Music: A Bibliography*. Madison, WI: A-R Editions, 1988. ISBN 0895792257. Reviewed in *Choice*, Feb. 1989. Pub. address: 315 W. Gorham St., Madison, WI, 53703. Broad coverage of computers in music. Will be useful to researchers as it includes many sources of historical importance. Includes sources on electronic organs, synthesizers, sound generation, and acoustics.

1317. De Furia, Steve, and Joe Scacciaferro. *The MIDI Book: Using MIDI and Related Interfaces*. Third Earth Productions, 1987. ISBN 0881885142. Distributed by Hal Leonard: 8112 W. Bluemound Rd., P.O. Box 13819, Milwaukee, WI, 53213. Ph: 800 558-4774. Cost: $14.95.

1318. ---. *The MIDI Implementation Book*. Belleville, NJ: Ferro Technologies, 1987. ISBN 0881885584. Pub. address: 228 Washington Ave., Belleville, NJ, 07109. Also available from Hal Leonard. Cost: $19.95.

1319. ---. *MIDI Programming for the Macintosh*. Redwood City, CA: M & T Books, 1988. ISBN 1558510214. Pub. address: 501 Galveston Dr., Redwood City, CA, 94063. Ph: 800 533-4372. Cost: $22.95 ($37.95 with disk). Covers most every aspect of program design, MIDI code resources, and programming basics for the Mac's toolbox. Includes example programs in Pascal and BASIC.

1320. ---. *The MIDI Resource Book*. Belleville, NJ: Ferro Technologies, 1987. ISBN 0881885878. Pub. address: 228 Washington, Ave., Belleville, NJ, 07109. Cost: $17.95. Also available from Hal Leonard. Contains the official MIDI specification as released by the MIDI Manufacturers Association.

1321. ---. *The MIDI System Exclusive Book*. Belleville, NJ: Ferro Technologies, 1987. ISBN 088188586X. Pub. address: 228 Washington Ave., Belleville, NJ, 07109. Also available from Hal Leonard. Cost: $24.95.

1322. *Directory of Computer Assisted Research in Musicology*. Menlo Park, CA: Center for Computer Assisted Research in the Humanities. (See #1368). Contains information on music printing, conferences, a resource list, address lists, an overview of current applications, and facilities and programs of study. Published annually. Cost: $12.00/year.

1323. Dodge, Charles, and Thomas A. Jerse. *Computer Music: Synthesis, Composition, and Performance*. New York: Schirmer Bks., 1985. ISBN 002873100X. Reviewed in *Byte*, June 1986. Pub. address: 866 Third Ave., New York, NY, 10022. Cost: $29.95.

1324. Dorfman, L., and D. Young. *Atari ST Introduction to MIDI Programming*. Grand Rapids, MI: Abacus Software, Inc., 1986. ISBN 0916439771. Pub. address: P.O. Box 7219, Grand Rapids, MI, 49510. Cost: $19.95.

1325. Gilkes, Lolita Walker. *Commodore 64 & 128 Music Software Guide*. Champaign, IL: Electronic Courseware Systems. Pub. address: 1210 Lancaster Dr., Champaign, IL, 61821. Order #DO 1183. Cost: $12.95.

1326. Glickman, Hal. *The Musical Atari*. Chatsworth, CA: Datamost, 1984. ISBN 0881903450. Pub. address not available. Cost: $14.95. For Atari 8-bit computers.

1327. ---. *The Musical Commodore 64*. Chatsworth, CA: Datamost, 1984. ISBN 0881904252. Pub. address not available. Cost: $14.95.

1328. Hofstetter, Fred T. *Computer Literacy for Musicians*. Englewood Cliffs, NJ: Prentice Hall, 1988. ISBN 0131644777. Pub. address: Rte. 9W, Englewood Cliffs, NJ, 07632. Cost: $26.67. Excellent source of information for musicians wishing to become computer literate. Coverage includes components of computer music systems, musical capabilities of popular microcomputers, MIDI, computer music terminology, how to purchase a computer music system, and informative reviews of music software. Also includes a bibliography and many helpful illustrations.

1329. ---. *Making Music on Micros: A Musical Approach to Computer Programming*. New York: Random House, 1985. ISBN 0676324436 (disk & text). Pub. address: 201 E. 50th St., NY, 10022. Ph: 800 638-6460. Cost: $69.95. Available for the Apple II (ISBN 0676321402). Tutorial in BASIC programming and music theory consisting of 53 program files for the IBM PC.

1330. Holland, Penny. *Looking at Computer Sounds and Music*. New York, NY: Watts, Franklin, Inc., 1986. ISBN 0531100979. Pub. address: 387 Park Ave. S., New York, NY, 10016. Ph: 800 672-6672. Cost: $10.40. Part of the "Easy-Read Computer Activity Books Series." For grades K-6.

1331. *Introduction to MIDI Programming*. Alexandria, MN: E. Arthur Brown Co. Order #440-525. Pub. address: 1702 Oak Knoll Dr., Alexandria, MN, 56308. Cost: $12.95.

1332. Jaxitron. *Cybernetic Music*. Blue Ridge Summit: Tab Bks., 1985. ISBN 0830608567. Reviewed in *Electronic Musician*, December 1987. Pub. address: P.O. Box 40, Blue Ridge Summit, PA, 17214. Cost: $18.95. Music programming in APL.

1333. Jefimenko, Oleg D. *Thirty Music Programs for Timex-Sinclair 2068*. Morgantown, WV: Electret Scientific, 1984. ISBN 0917406206. Pub. address: P.O. Box 4132, Morgantown, WV, 26505. Cost: $13.00.

1334. Kater, David. *Macintosh Graphics & Sound: Programming in Microsoft Basic*. Berkeley, CA: Osborne/McGraw-Hill, 1985. ISBN 0078811775. Pub. address: 2600 10th St., Berkeley, CA, 94710. Ph: 800 227-0900. Cost: $17.95.

1335. Krepack, Benjamin, and Rod Firestone. *Start Me Up: The Music Biz Meets the Personal Computer*. Redmond, WA: Mediac Press, 1986. ISBN 0961644605. Pub. address: P.O. Box 89, Redmond, WA, 98073. Cost: $12.95.

1336. Krute, Stan. *Commodore 64 Graphics & Sound Programming*. Blue Ridge Summit, PA: Tab Bks., 1983. ISBN 0830601406. Pub. address: P.O. Box 40, Blue Ridge Summit, PA, 17214. Cost: $15.50.

1337. Lister, Craig. *The Musical Microcomputer: A Resource Guide*. New York, NY: Garland Publishing, Inc., 1988. ISBN 082408442X. Reviewed in *Choice*, Jan. 1989. Pub. address: 136 Madison Ave., New York, NY, 10016. Cost: $26.00. Annotated bibliography of 336 entries covering journal articles, dissertations, books, and software titles.

1338. Manning, Peter. *Electronic and Computer Music*. New York: Oxford University Press, 1987. ISBN 0193119234. 1985 edition reviewed in *Byte*, June 1986. Pub. address: 200 Madison Ave., New York, NY, 10016. Cost: $18.95. Historical study.

1339. Massey, Howard, et al. *The Complete Guide to MIDI Software*. New York: Amsco Publications, 1986. Order #AM65715. Available from Music Sales: 24 E. 22nd St., New York, NY, 10010. Ph: 800 431-7187. Cost: $19.95. Updated in 1988 and divided into four computer-specific *Compact Guides to MIDI Software* (Atari, C-64/128, IBM PC/PS, and Macintosh) $3.95. each. Available through the *Mix Bookshelf*.

1340. *MIDI Primer*. Port Chester, NY: Cherry Lane Technologies. Pub. address: 110 Midland Ave., Port Chester, NY, 10573. Cost: $15.00.

1341. Milano, D., ed. *Mind over MIDI: A Basic Reference Guide on How MIDI Works and How to Use It*. GPI Publications, 1987. ISBN 0881885517. Available from Hal Leonard: 8112 W. Bluemound Rd., P.O. Box 13819, Milwaukee, WI, 53213. Ph: 800 558-4774. Cost: $12.95.

1342. Moore, Herb, Judy Lower, and Bob Albrecht. *Atari Sound and Graphics*. New York, NY: John Wiley & Sons, Inc., 1982. ISBN 0471095931. Pub. address: 605 3rd Ave., New York, NY, 10158. Cost: $9.95. For Atari 400/800 computers.

1343. Moore, Janet. *Understanding Music Through Sound Exploration & Experiments*. Lanham, MD: University Press of America, 1986. ISBN 0819152315. Pub. address: 4720 Boston Way, Lanham, MD, 20706. Cost: $8.50.

1344. *The Musician's Music Software Catalog from Scherzando Music*. Milford, CT: Scherzando Music, 1987. Pub. address: P.O. Box 3438, Milford, CT, 06460. Cost: $2.00. Discount catalog with in-depth descriptions of popular music software. Published annually.

1345. *The Musician's Music Software Catalog!* Milford, CT: Digital Arts & Technologies, 1988. Pub. address: P.O. Box 11, Milford CT, 06460. Cost: $3.00. Formerly published by Scherzando Music.

1346. Paturzo, Bonaventura. *Making Music with Microprocessors*. Blue Ridge Summit, PA: Tab Bks., 1984. ISBN 0830607293. Pub. address: P.O. Box 40, Blue Ridge Summit, PA, 17214. Cost: $16.95.

1347. Roads, Curtis, ed. *The Music Machine: Selected Readings from Computer Music Journal*. Cambridge, MA: MIT Press, 1989. Pub. address: 55 Hayward St., Cambridge, MA, 02142. Ph: 800

356-0343. Cost: $45.00. Contains significant articles published in the *Computer Music Journal* from 1980-85.

1348. ---, ed. *Composers and the Computer*. Los Altos, CA: W. Kaufmann, 1985. ISBN 0865760853,0853. Pub. address: 95 First St., Los Altos, CA 94022. Cost: $24.95.

1349. Roads, Curtis, and John Strawn, eds. *Foundations of Computer Music*. Cambridge, MA: MIT Press, 1985. ISBN 0262181142. Reviewed in *Byte*, June 1986. Pub. address: 55 Hayward St., Cambridge, MA, 02142. Ph: 800 356-0343. Cost: $50.00.

1350. Rona, Jeff. *MIDI, The Ins, Outs, & Thrus*. Milwaukee, WI: Hal Leonard Bks., 1987. ISBN 0881885606. Reviewed in the *Computer Music Journal*, V. 12, No. 4. (Winter 1988). Pub. address: 8112 W. Bluemound Rd., P.O. Box 13819, Milwaukee, WI, 53213. Ph: 800 558-4774. Cost: $12.95.

1351. Rudolph, Thomas E. *Music and the Apple II: Applications for Music Education, Composition, and Performance*. Drexel Hill, PA: Unsinn, 1984. ISBN 0961538600. Pub. address: P.O. Box 672, Drexel Hill, PA, 19026. Also available from Electronic Courseware Systems, Order #DO 1178. Cost: $17.95.

1352. Sanders, William B. *Compute!'s Guide to Sound and Graphics on the Apple IIGS*. New York, NY: *Compute!* Publications Inc., 1987. ISBN 0874550963. Pub. address: 825 7th Ave., 9th floor, New York, NY, 10019. Ph: 800 638-3822. Cost: $16.95.

1353. Simpson, Henry. *Atari ST: Graphics and Sound Programming*. Blue Ridge Summit, PA: Tab Bks., 1986. ISBN 0830627618. Pub. address: P.O. Box 40, Blue Ridge Summit, PA, 17214. Cost: $14.95.

1354. *ST Graphics and Sound*. Alexandria, MN: E. Arthur Brown Co. Order #440-524. Pub. address: 1702 Oak Knoll Dr., Alexandria, MN, 56308. Cost: $12.95.

1355. Strawn, John, ed. *Digital Audio Engineering: An Anthology*. Los Altos, CA: W. Kaufmann, 1985. ISBN 086576087X. Pub. address: 95 First St., Los Altos, CA, 94022. Cost: $29.95.

1356. ---, ed. *Digital Audio Signal Processing: An Anthology*. Los Altos, CA: W. Kaufmann, 1985. ISBN 0865760829. Pub. address: 95 First St., Los Altos, CA, 94022. Cost: $34.95.

1357. *Synthesizers and Computers*. GPI Publications, 1987. ISBN 0881887161. Available from Hal Leonard: 8112 W. Bluemound Rd., P.O. Box 13819, Milwaukee, WI, 53213. Ph: 800 558-4774. Cost: $12.95.

1358. Traister, Robert J. *Music and Speech Programs for the IBM PC*. Blue Ridge Summit, PA: Tab Bks., 1983. ISBN 0830605967. Pub. address: P.O. Box 40, Blue Ridge Summit, PA, 17214. Cost: $11.50.

1359. *Understanding MIDI*. New York: Music Sales Corp., 1986. Order #AM63462. Pub. address: 24 E. 22nd St., New York, NY, 10010. Ph: 800 431-7187. Cost: $8.95.

1360. Van Buren, Christopher. *Making Music with Microcomputers*. San Diego: Park Row Press, 1986. ISBN 0935749217. Pub. address: 1418 Park Row, San Diego, CA, 92037. Cost: $16.95.

1361. Wadhams, Wayne. *Dictionary of Music Production and Engineering Terminology*. New York, NY: Schirmer Books, 1988. ISBN 002872691X. Reviewed in the *Computer Music Journal*, V. 12, No. 4 (Winter 1988). Pub. address: 866 Third Ave., New York, NY, 10022. Ph: 800 257-5755. Includes many terms associated with music and personal computers, excellent illustrations, and a bibliography.

1362. Walkowiak, J. *Atari: Graphics & Sound*. Grand Rapids, MI: Abacus Software, Inc., 1986. ISBN 0916439496. Pub. address: P.O. Box 7219, Grand Rapids, MI, 49510. Cost: $19.95.

1363. Winsor, Phil. *Computer-Assisted Music Composition: A Primer in BASIC*. Princeton, NJ: Petrocelli Books, 1986. ISBN 0894332627. Pub. address: Research Park, 251 Wall St., Princeton, NJ, 08540. Cost: $29.95. BASIC programming for musicians.

1364. Wittlich, Gary E., John W. Schaffer, and Larry R. Babb. *Microcomputers and Music*. Englewood Cliffs, NJ: Prentice Hall, 1986. ISBN 0135805155. Pub. address: Rte. 9W, Englewood Cliffs, NJ, 07632. Cost: $25.95.

1365. Wolfe, G., ed. *Guide to Instructional Computing for Music Educators*. Manhattan, KS: National Association of Jazz Educators, 1988. Pub. address: Box 724, Manhattan, KS, 66502. Cost: $14.50. Collection of articles and information on various topics including electronic music aids for the handicapped, sources for music software, and a glossary of computer music terms.

Appendix: Associations and Online Services

1366. Association for Computers and the Humanities.
Small organization of scholars interested in computer applications in most areas of the humanities including music. Publishes *Computers and the Humanities* (journal). Address: 2009 Lind Hall, Univ. of Minnesota, Minneapolis, MN 55455 (612) 625-2888.

1367. Association for Technology in Music Instruction (Division of the Association for the Development of Computer-based Instruction Systems).
Excellent source for information regarding all aspects of computers in music instruction. Publishes a newsletter and an annual Courseware Directory. (See #1298.) Address: Hopkins School District, Administrative Offices, 1001 Highway 7, Hopkins, MN 55343 (612) 933-9270.

1368. Center for Computer Assisted Research in the Humanities.
Very small, non-profit organization in operation since 1985. At the present time, the Center is involved in a computerized cataloging project for unpublished works of various composers of the Baroque period e.g., Bach, Corelli, etc. Publishes the *Directory of Computer Assisted Research in Musicology* annually. (See #1322.) Address: 525 Middlefield Rd., Suite 120, Menlo Park, CA 94025 (415) 322-7050.

1369. Center for Electronic Music.
Non-profit organization offering various educational services in all areas of music technology particularly the musical applications of microcomputers. CEM sponsors numerous workshops, seminars, private instruction, and outreach programs; publishes a quarterly newsletter; and is currently planning to establish an international online bulletin board service in 1990. Address: 432 Park Ave. S., New York, NY 10016 (212) 686-1755.

1370. The Computer Music Association.
Excellent source for information on all aspects of computer music.
The CMA consists of about 500 members and offers various services
e.g., a quarterly newsletter, discount programs, concerts, and
proceedings from computer music conferences. Presently active in
many areas of research and development. Address: The Computer
Music Association, P.O. Box 1634, San Francisco, CA 94101.

1371. Computer Musicians Cooperative (Division of the Association
of Independent Microdealers, Inc.).
Provides useful information for computer musicians, consultants,
publishers, dealers, and manufacturers. Publishes the *Computer
Musicians Source Book*. (See #1314.) Address: Microdealers, Inc.,
3010 N. Sterling Ave., Peoria, IL 61604 (309) 685-4843.

1372. East Coast MIDI Bulletin Board System.
Online MIDI resource for music professionals. Includes information
on MIDI and all popular microcomputers, MIDI data, and support
for MIDI software. Address unavailable: (516) 928-4986 (modem)
(516) 474-2450 (modem).

1373. International MIDI Association.
Provides technical support for MIDI related activities. Maintains a
MIDI database and electronic library containing sounds, rhythms,
and sequences. Publishes the *IMA Bulletin* monthly and the *MIDI
Technical Specifications*. Also serves as the central headquarters for
the MIDI Manufacturers Association. Address: 11857 Hartsook St.,
N. Hollywood, CA 91607 (213) 649-6434.

1374. *MCS* MIDI Forum.
MIDI information service that serves as an online extension of
Music, Computers & Software. Covers all aspects of MIDI technology
and can be accessed through CompuServe. CompuServe offers many
other databases and bulletin board services dedicated to musical
applications of microcomputers and MIDI. Address: CompuServe,
5000 Arlington Centre Blvd., P.O. Box 20212, Columbus, OH 43220
(800) 848-8199 (voice) (614) 457-8650 (voice).

1375. MIDI-Net.
Network of bulletin boards containing information on MIDI related
topics and MIDI data. Also useful as a source for industry news. A
popular member of the MIDI-Net group is the American MIDI Users
Group (AMUG) bulletin board service in Dallas Texas (214) 276-8902.
A list of names and phone numbers to MIDI-Net BBS members can
be found in *A+* June 1988. (See #98.) The central headquarters for
MIDI-Net is the MidWest MIDI BBS in Oklahoma City. Complete
address unavailable: (405) 733-3102 (modem).

1376. MIDI/WorldMusic Roundtable.
Part of the General Electric Network for Information Exchange
(GEnie). Provides bulletin board services, conferences, and an
extensive software library. Also contains many sources for machine
specific files e.g., Apple II Roundtable, Apple Macintosh Roundtable,
etc. Address: GEnie, 401 N. Washington St., Rockville, MD 20850
(800) 638-9636 (voice) (301) 340-4000 (voice).

1377. The Music Conference.
The Music Conference is part of the *Byte* Information Exchange
(BIX) and offers information on MIDI related topics as well as MIDI
files. The author of *Cakewalk*, a popular MIDI sequencer for the IBM
PC, is on this system for technical assistance. Address: BIX, 1
Phoenix Mill Lane, Peterborough, NH 03458 (603) 924-9281 (voice)
(800) 227-2983 (voice).

1378. The PAN Network.
Performing Artist's Network. Probably the oldest and largest online
service dedicated to music professionals. PAN is international in
scope consisting of about 2,000 professionals throughout the music
industry. Allows the user to download MIDI data such as patches,
samples, programs, etc. at speeds of up to 9,600 baud. Other services
include international teleconferencing, private networks, e-mail,
network-wide discussion forums, and synth and MIDI support
hotlines. Address: The PAN Network, P.O. Box 162, Skippack, PA
19474 (215) 584-0300 (voice).

Author Index

[Note: References are to entry numbers.]

Subject Index

[Note: References are to entry numbers.]

About the Compiler

WILLIAM J. WATERS is a Reference Librarian at Pensacola Junior College and an Adjunct Professor of Music Theory at the University of West Florida.